Where Keynes Went Wrong

Where Keynes Went Wrong

And Why World Governments Keep Creating Inflation, Bubbles, and Busts

Hunter Lewis

AXIOS

John Maynard Keynes, *The General Theory of Employment, Interest, and Money*, published 1973, reproduced with permission of Palgrave Macmillan.

John Maynard Keynes, *Essays in Persuasion*, published 1972, reproduced with permission of Palgrave Macmillan.

Axios Press
P.O. Box 118
Mount Jackson, VA 22842
888.542.9467   info@axiospress.com

Library of Congress Cataloging-in-Publication Data

Lewis, Hunter.
     Where Keynes went wrong : and why world governments keep creating inflation, bubbles, and busts / Hunter Lewis.
     p. cm.
     Includes bibliographical references and index.
     ISBN 978-1-60419-017-5
     1. Keynes, John Maynard, 1883–1946. 2. Keynesian economics. 3. Economic policy. 4. Monetary policy. 5. Financial crises. I. Title.

HB99.7.L49 2009

330.15'6—dc22

                                                                2009022820

Contents

Part Four

More on Keynes

Part Five

Conclusion

Part Six

Envoi

This book is dedicated to the memory of Henry Hazlitt, an individual whose life, character, and economics are worthy of emulation. All of his books are highly recommended, but especially *The Failure of the "New Economics"* and *Economics in One Lesson*.

Part One

Introduction

1

Commonsense Economics

W**HAT WOULD A** commonsense economics look like? What would it have to say about the Crash of 2008, the ensuing economic slump, or the best policy response for a crisis of this kind?

We might begin by addressing this question to Timothy J. Kehoe, distinguished professor of economics at the University of Minnesota. He is a self-described "lifelong Democrat and Obama voter." He tells us that "if you postpone short-term pain, you end up with long-term pain."

He is thinking in particular of the Bush administration's bailout of banks, a giant insurer, and two auto companies: "[The] money disappeared; it was scandalous. . . . Unproductive firms need to die."[1]

This is hard advice, but it does sound commonsensical. Is it not better for sound companies to buy cheap assets from failed companies and put them to productive use?

We might next turn to Kenneth Rogoff, professor of public policy at Harvard and former chief economist of the International

Monetary Fund. He says, in regard to the 2008 economic crisis and its aftereffects, "we borrowed too much, we screwed up, so we're going to fix it by borrowing more."[2] Rogoff is, of course, being ironical. He may also be trying to inject an element of commonsense into the economic policy discussion.

Consider this background. During the 1980s, the 1990s, and the 2000s, the US economy grew, but the amount of new debt grew much faster, especially during the housing bubble. Economist Marc Faber drew the commonsense conclusion: "When debt growth vastly exceeds nominal GDP [gross domestic product] growth, sooner or later something will have to give."[3]

Given this background, is it not defiant of commonsense for the US government to start up another and even bigger round of printing money, lending, and borrowing? This does sound suspiciously like trying to cure a hangover with more alcohol.

Wait a moment. We need to address an important question. Does commonsense actually have any relevance for national or global economic policy?[A][*] If an individual, family, or business has been living for the day without regard for the morrow, spending more than it makes, buying what it does not need, saving nothing, making foolish and reckless investments, and borrowing more than it can repay, we do not prescribe more of the same. We counsel abstinence. But societies and governments are different, are they not? Has economics not taught us that the rules applying to an individual do not apply to society as a whole?

The general principle here is labeled by logicians the fallacy of composition. In this particular economic application, it is commonly referred to as the Keynesian paradox of thrift. The argument runs approximately as follows. If one spendthrift gets religion and

---

[*] Uppercase superscripted letters refer to Endnotes, which begin on p. 307.

starts saving, that is good. But if we all stop spending at the same time, that is bad, because the economy needs the spending.

If the spending stops, an economy does not just collapse. It keeps on collapsing, because a market economy is not self-correcting. Everything gets worse until the government steps in and starts spending on our behalf. Once this happens, the free fall stops, we all shake off our panic and start borrowing and spending again.

This kind of thinking takes some getting used to. Can the act of saving, so virtuous for the individual, really be so destructive for society at large? Veteran Keynesian economist Peter L. Bernstein says that it is so. He warned in July of 2008, a few months before the Crash, that "a mass effort by American consumers to save [as little as] 3.9% of their after-tax incomes would be a disaster for the world economy."[4]

President Bush seemed to agree. In December 2006, with air leaking out of the housing bubble, he advised the American people to "go shopping more."[5] He also knew that additional spending would have to come from the consumer, because new Democratic majorities in Congress were critical of his government budget deficit spending. At that time, they would not let him run up a bigger budget deficit to stimulate the economy.

When the crisis hit in late 2008, a Congressional majority comprised of both Democrats and Republicans finally agreed on the need for more government borrowing and spending, for bailouts and stimulus. President Bush explained his actions to conservative critics in the following way:

> I've abandoned free market principles to save the free market system. . . . You can sit there and say to yourself, "Well, I'm going to stick to principle and hope for the best, or I'm going to take the actions necessary to prevent the worst."[6]

One wonders. How exactly did Bush know that his actions were necessary, or that they would prevent the worst? How could he be sure that his actions would not make matters worse, either immediately or over time?

Bush said that he was relying on advice from Henry Paulson, secretary of the Treasury, and Ben Bernanke, chairman of the Federal Reserve Board. Paulson and Bernanke were in turn relying on and reflecting the ideas of John Maynard Keynes. Gregory Mankiw, Harvard economist, former chair of Bush's Council of Economic Advisors, and author of a best-selling economics textbook, agrees that

> If you [are] going to turn to only one economist to understand the problems facing the economy, there is little doubt that the economist would be John Maynard Keynes. Although Keynes died more than a half-century ago, his diagnosis of recessions and depressions remains the foundation of modern macroeconomics.

Mankiw then summarizes Keynes's view of recessions and depressions: "According to Keynes, the root cause of economic downturns is insufficient aggregate demand." He touches on the Keynesian "paradox of thrift": "For the overall economy . . . a recession is not the best time for households to try to save more." And he concludes by noting that "policymakers at the Fed and Treasury [whether appointed by Bush or by Obama] will be looking at [policy responses] through a Keynesian lens."[7]

Keynes's influence has had its ups and down. During World War II and its immediate aftermath, Keynes was immensely influential. In 1947, a year after his death, the leading French economist Jacques Rueff said that "the Keynesian philosophy is unquestionably the basis of world policy today,"[8] and this remained true for another quarter century.

By the 1970s, a Great Inflation was unfolding and it created something of a backlash. Some thought that Keynesian ideas had been responsible. But even Keynes's chief critics, such as economists Milton Friedman or Robert Mundell, still retained many Keynesian assumptions. Keynes was in the air that everyone breathed, and with the crisis of 2008 Keynesian policies came back with a bang and reoccupied center stage.

In essence, Keynesianism is the opposite of commonsense economics. It offers not only "the paradox of thrift," but, as we shall see, numerous other paradoxes. It is complicated and technical. Some of it is presented in mathematical terms. Most people do not, therefore, try to understand Keynes themselves. They rely on others. Like President Bush, and perhaps President Obama, they essentially take Keynes on faith.

Following the Crash of 2008, this is no longer satisfactory, if it ever was. If the entire global economy is to follow Keynesian prescriptions, which require more money printing, spending, borrowing, and bailing out, on top of all the money printing, spending, and borrowing that preceded the crisis, then we need to understand more of the thinking behind the prescriptions. We need to look at them with fresh and critical eyes.

The place to begin is with what Keynes actually said. Because few people read Keynes, it is easy to be confused about what he said. Because his name has acquired such immense authority, it is tempting to take one's own ideas and falsely attribute them to him. An example of this is the attempt by some Republicans to describe tax cuts as Keynesian.[9] Keynes clearly wanted to create government budget deficits by spending, not by cutting taxes.[B]

When we do read Keynes, we find much that is puzzling. In his *General Theory*, he said that, as a rule, people save too much. He proposed to deal with this alleged problem by having government print a lot of new money, which he said we should regard as "genuine savings."[10] Printing new money does not sound like saving. But even if we accept this premise, why will more of the new "savings" help alleviate an alleged problem of people saving too much?

We will not try to disentangle this particular paradox just yet, but will mention that part of the solution involved bringing interest rates lower and lower until they eventually reached zero. Think about that for a moment. Interest rates at zero. Definitely not a commonsense idea.[c]

What is perhaps most startling when we actually read Keynes is the complete lack of support for his ideas. He exhibits a brilliant and fertile mind, full of intuited hunches, but it is intuitive hunches by and large that we are getting, not closely reasoned chains of logic or empirical evidence.

When the world responded to the Crash of 2008 by launching an immense economic experiment on Keynesian lines, most people just assumed that the rationale was clearly spelled out in Keynes's own writings. It is not. Keynesian policies are still mostly based on intuitions, no more, even if some of the intuitions have been dressed up in mathematical form. It is unsettling to discover how unsupported these anticommonsense intuitions really are.

A Harvard University course from the 1970s was named "The Failure to Be Factual." It covered Marx and Freud, but might have included Keynes as well. In each case, these important thinkers present us with a "science" that is really the opposite of science. Indeed, to accept it as science requires the complete suspension of our rational faculties of disbelief.

This is in no way meant to denigrate intuition. Keynes said of the great scientist Isaac Newton, "I fancy his preeminence is due to his muscles of intuition being the strongest and most enduring with which a man has ever been gifted."[11] Keynes is right about this. Intuition will always be the leading trait of a truly creative thinker. But it is not enough. Conclusions must eventually be presented in the language of logic and evidence, just as Newton eventually presented them, or they remain mere speculation.

It is sometimes argued that Keynes's prescriptions for economic crashes and depression may not be fully supported in his books, but that they were tested during the Great Depression of the 1930s and proved themselves then. After all, did not President Roosevelt rely on Keynes's ideas, and did not President Roosevelt pull us out of the Great Depression? We will discuss the Depression further in the body of the book, but the short answer is no on both counts. President Roosevelt did not rely much on Keynes, although his policies were broadly Keynesian.□ Roosevelt's policies did not pull us out of the Great Depression, which continued for a decade until World War II.

There are many books that present Keynes's ideas in a positive light. Some of them are quite good; they have the initial advantage of being much better organized than Keynes himself. There is, however, a shortage of good books on the other side, the critical side.

Friedrich Hayek, Keynes's chief critic in England during his lifetime, should have written a full-scale rebuttal of *The General Theory*. He said he regretted not doing so, but thought that Keynes would soon change his mind, so that it would be a waste of time. Since Keynes frequently changed his mind, the mistake was understandable. Hayek did write a shorter critique, as did many other economists.

By far the best book criticizing Keynes's *General Theory* is Henry Hazlitt's *The Failure of the "New Economics,"* published in 1959. Hazlitt was a genius and a polymath: journalist, literary critic, philosopher, and self-schooled economist who wrote about economics for *The New York Times* and *Newsweek*. One of his books, *Economics in One Lesson*, published in 1946, sold over a million copies and remains popular today.

Hazlitt's book on Keynes directly inspired this one. Why, it might be asked, is another book even needed? Why not just rely on Hazlitt?

The answer is that Hazlitt, like a hunting dog in pursuit of prey, follows Keynes through every briar and thicket of *The General Theory*. Keynes was especially good at creating briars and thickets, so Hazlitt must follow him wherever he leads, disentangling and refuting hundreds of logical fallacies, large and small, as he goes.

It is truly a tour de force, and it is hard to imagine anyone other than Hazlitt having the knowledge, skill, and, above all, patience to accomplish the task. But it necessarily takes the reader over technical, repetitive, and often barren ground. The reader too must have much patience.

In his introduction, Hazlitt wrote that

> my first thought was that I might do a short work, an-
> alyzing Keynes's chief doctrines so that the reader who
> wished a critical analysis would be able to find one in a
> brief and readable form. But when I actually embarked
> on a line-by-line analysis, . . . [of *The*] *General Theory* . . .
> I . . . found . . . [such] an incredible number of fallacies, in-
> consistencies, vaguenesses, shifting definitions, and usages
> of words, and plain errors of fact [that the book grew].[12]

Where Keynes Went Wrong may be thought of as the book that Hazlitt initially planned to write, or at least something along similar lines. It does not follow Keynes page by page, but rather concentrates on a few key topics. It is meant to be understandable by almost anyone, whether or not a student of economics.

Keynes's *General Theory* does not begin with economic policy prescriptions. It begins with economic theory and slowly twists and turns, wanders and meanders toward the policy prescriptions, a majority of which are at the back of the book. *Where Keynes*

Went Wrong takes a different tack and focuses on the policy pre-scriptions. The *Theory* is discussed, but within the policy context.

This is clearer and more relevant for the contemporary reader. It is also the way that Keynes himself thought. Economist John H. Williams, who knew Keynes, said that "it was policy, in [his] case, that led to *Theory*,"[13] and most of Keynes's contemporaries agreed. Keynes's most authoritative biographer, Robert Skidelsky, also agrees: "He invented *Theory* to justify what he wanted to do."[14]

Keynes was really the first of a breed that we have come to know well: the government policy entrepreneur. He lived and breathed policy, loved being consulted, pursued, and even lion-ized by the political and business elite. Throughout his adult life, he worked himself to the point of nervous exhaustion to fulfill the demands of press and politicians along with those of his aca-demic colleagues and students.

Prior to Keynes, economists played a role in public life, but at a remove from the action. They were like biblical prophets of old who would appear from time to time to speak truth to the politi-cal leaders, but unlike the old prophets spoke quietly through their articles and books. The economists' job was to focus on what was best overall, not just for special interests, but for the whole nation, even for humanity as a whole; and not just for the short term, but for as far as they could see ahead, even into future generations. These economists were, above all, custodians of the future.

Politicians' eyes have always been fixed firmly on the next elec-tion, not the long-term. But they did not want to be scolded by economists guarding the public weal, and thus had to pay some heed. With Keynes this all changed. The lines became blurred, economists began working directly for politicians, and the pro-phetic custodians of the future completely disappeared.

Where Keynes Went Wrong has been written in five parts, this introduction being Part One. Part Two attempts to summarize what Keynes really said, frequently relying on exact quotation. This part is not meant to be a "hatchet job." It is meant to present Keynes honestly, wherever possible speaking for himself.

The aim has been to be fair, but also to be clear. Keynes himself is often obscure, even at first glance self-contradictory. In some cases, very close examination reveals that Keynes was not actually contradicting himself. Often he was simply being sloppy, although sometimes he seems to be intentionally opaque, rather like former US Federal Reserve Chairman Alan Greenspan used to be when testifying to Congress. Opacity has its uses in politics, especially when there is a logical difficulty to obscure or evade.

Keynes's arguments are presented without interruption in Part Two, because that is the fairest way to present them, and also the best way to understand them. The same arguments are repeated in Part Three, sometimes verbatim but usually in condensed form, so that they can be dissected, reviewed, discussed, and rebutted. A reader who does not want to read Keynes's ideas in full and without interrruption can skip Part Two and go directly from Part One to Part Three. Conversely, a reader interested only in what Keynes said can skip Part Three.

Part Four tells us more about Keynes, especially his methods of persuasion. Part Five explores the paradoxical nature of Keynesian economics and also explains why it has so much potential for harm.

It might be objected that this book treats only Keynes, not the Keynesians who have followed. There are several justifications for this. In the first place, Keynes himself is enough for one book. In the second place, it is Keynes who is cited as the towering authority for government money printing, borrowing, spending, and rescuing in the wake of the 2008 Crash. So, at least in this book, the spotlight will be narrowly focused on Keynes himself.

As we now turn to Part Two, we will begin by presenting what Keynes had to say about lending and borrowing. In someone else's hands, it might be a dry topic. What Keynes has to say about it is, on the contrary, quite startling.

Part Two

What Keynes Really Said

2

Drive Down Interest Rates

Keynes on Lending and Borrowing

1. Without government intervention, interest rates are almost always too high.

As Keynes says,

> The rate of interest is not self-adjusting at a level best suited to the social advantage but constantly tends to rise too high. . . .[1] [Interest] rates . . . have been [too high for] for the greater part of recorded history.[E 2]

2. This is the principal reason that humanity still remains mired in poverty.

> That the world after several millennia of steady individual saving, is so poor . . . is to be explained . . . by . . . high . . . rate[s] of interest.[3]

> High ... rate[s] of interest [are] the outstanding evil,
> the prime impediment to the growth of wealth [because
> they discourage borrowing and, by doing so, discourage
> investment].[4]

3. There is no good reason for interest rates to have been so high throughout human history, a few periods excepted, or to continue to be so high.

Why do interest rates tend to be higher than they should be? Partly because people "hoard" their money out of fear, which creates a shortage of lendable funds, and thus drives up interest rates.[5] Partly because it is expensive to "bring ... borrowers and lenders together," which also drives up rates.[6] Partly because there may be a "wide gap between the ideas of borrowers and those of lenders"[7] with the result that "wealth-owners" simply do not "accept" lower rates.[8]

4. Government can and should bring interest rates down to a more reasonable level.

If private "wealth-owners" withhold their funds from the loan market or refuse to accept reasonable rates, the government can help bring rates down by increasing the "quantity" of lendable funds.[9] This is done by printing new money which is made available to banks to lend.[*][10] The more money there is to borrow, the less it should cost to borrow:

> A change in the quantity of money ... is ... within
> the power of most governments. .... The quantity of
> money ... in conjunction with [lenders' willingness to
> lend] determines the actual rate of interest.[11]

---

* The government does not literally print money. See Note F for clarification.

5. Fears of government intervention and of a government-engineered increase in the amount of money circulating in the economy are ill founded.

New money that has been printed by the government and injected into the banking system is

> just as genuine as any other savings....[12] [Since] there is no special virtue in the pre-existing [high] rate of interest ... [there can be no] evil [in bringing it down by government intervention].c [13]

6. If the government reduces interest rates, the ultimate target level should be "zero."

This is both feasible and desirable. But it should not be undertaken abruptly:

> I should guess that a properly run community ... ought to be able to bring down the ... [general rate of business profit and interest rates] approximately to zero within a single generation.[14]

Eventually, provided that government supplies an inexhaustible well of capital, borrowers should not have to pay interest or businesses a dividend:

> [Our] aim (there being nothing in this which is unattainable) ... [should be] an increase in the volume of capital until it ceases to be scarce, so that the [owner of savings] will no longer receive a bonus.[15]

> The ... owner of capital [is] functionless.... [He or she] can obtain interest because capital is scarce. But ... there can be no intrinsic reason for the scarcity of capital [since government can always print and distribute more of

it]. . . .[16] [Making capital freely available] may be the most sensible way of gradually getting rid of many of the objectionable features of capitalism. The rentier [wealthy lender or investor] would disappear . . . and [so would] the cumulative oppressive power of the capitalist to exploit the scarcity-value of capital.[17]

Viewed in this light, it is an abomination for workers to remain unemployed, when there is much useful work to do, just because capital is made artificially scarce, interest rates too high, and investment consequently too risky. This is just

a desperate muddle.[18]

7. Should the government ever reverse gears and deliberately raise interest rates? No.

In this matter, like most matters, Keynes said different things to different people at different times.[19] But, at least in *The General Theory*, he was emphatically against raising interest rates. He was aware of the argument that a runaway economic boom could lead to inflation, and that higher interest rates could be used to dampen a boom and thus forestall inflation. But he thought it

extraordinary

that this line of argument

should exist,

or at least that anyone should regard punitive interest rates as the preferred way of combating inflation:[20]

The remedy for the boom is not a higher rate of interest but a lower rate of interest! For that may enable the boom to last. The right remedy for the trade cycle is not to be found in abolishing booms and thus keeping us permanently in a semi-slump; but in abolishing slumps and thus keeping us permanently in a quasi-boom.[H][21]

8. It was fear of the boom that led the US Federal Reserve to raise already too high interest rates in the late 1920s. This led directly to the Great Depression.

I attribute the slump of 1930 primarily to the . . . effects . . . of dear [expensive] money which preceded the stock market collapse [of 1929], and only secondarily to the collapse itself.[22]

9. Economic booms should be welcomed, not feared. To think otherwise is a "serious error."[23]

The problem with most booms is that businessmen become carried away by "overoptimism" and make investments which will not pay for themselves, given the "excessive[ly high] rate of interest."[24] If we lower the rate of interest, the same investments will earn a satisfactory rate of return. Since the human race is still poor, we should be encouraging, not discouraging, investment. There will always be some "misdirected investment," because people make mistakes, but this "happens . . . even when there is no boom."[25]

The correct conclusion is very simple:

We should avoid [high interest rates] . . . as we would hell-fire.[26]

10. Inflation is an "evil,"[27] but it is unlikely that a boom will lead to "true inflation."[28]

Booms may create

bottle-necks

in which the price of some products rise.[29] But we cannot

declare that conditions of inflation have set in

until unemployment has completely disappeared.[30]

Keynes's Cambridge University colleague, collaborator, disciple, and interpreter Joan Robinson wrote a 1937 book with Keynes's approval setting out her mentor's *General Theory* in simple terms. She explained that

> Wars and revolutions have frequently led to violent inflation, but in times of peace and with . . . competent . . . [policy] it is little to be feared.[31]

The real problem is unemployment, not inflation, since as Keynes said,

> Full or even approximately full employment is of rare and short-lived occurrence.[32]

11. In the rare event that full employment does arrive, there are better remedies than "clapping on a higher rate of interest."[33]

Instead of increasing interest rates, government should raise taxes, run a budget surplus, and keep the extra cash idle.'[34] In extreme cases, such as the onset of World War II, when the economy had to be run on hyper-speed, some inflation is unavoidable, but Keynes advocated raising taxes very high in advance of inflation to help control it.[35]

12. Progressive income taxes, in which the rich pay a higher and higher tax rate, also help to reduce economic inequality:

> [An] outstanding fault of the economic society in which we live [is] its arbitrary and inequitable distribution of wealth and incomes.[36]

Keynes thought that high income and estate (death) taxes had done much to make a more economically just society. But governments had hesitated to go further because the rich are best able to save, and their savings are needed to finance much needed investment.[37] Keynes's program of financing investment with newly printed money injected into the banking system helps solve this problem. Thanks to this innovation, society need no longer depend so heavily on the savings of the rich. If inflation does appear, the economy can be cooled by taxation without jeopardizing investment. Indeed, if the government raises taxes and runs a budget surplus, it will itself become a principle economic saver.[J]

13. If the government prints a great deal of new money and injects it into the banking system, interest rates should fall. But if they do not fall enough, other measures will be required to boost investment.

It is possible that cheap new money from the government might not fully succeed in driving interest rates down to the

> optimum [level].[38]

This is because "wealth-owners," who have not yet been completely displaced as lenders, might find low rates "unacceptable" and succeed in blocking them. If so,

> The State, which is in a position to calculate ... on long
> views and on the basis of the general social advantage, ...
> [will have to] directly organiz[e] ... investment.[39]

14. For now, national governments must take the necessary actions to bring interest rates down and keep them low. Eventually, global institutions might assist in this task.

Keynes hoped that what became known as the International Monetary Fund would instead be called a bank. He further hoped that it would act as a global central bank and have the power to print new money and inject it into the global economic system in order to reduce interest rates.[40]

15. We should pay our respects to the "army of heretics and cranks"[41] who in earlier periods argued for lower interest rates.

In *The General Theory*, Keynes acknowledged that he was refurbishing and updating

> sixteenth and seventeenth century ... [economic writers generally known as] Mercantilists.[42]

This was ironic, because Keynes's teachers in Britain, and Keynes himself early in his career, had regarded Mercantilist thought as a "fallacy" long since exploded.[43] Now Keynes saw an

> element of scientific truth in Mercantilist doctrine, [especially in their view] that an unduly high rate of interest was the main obstacle to the growth of wealth [and in their] preoccupation ... [to] increase ... the quantity of money [in order to] ... diminish the rate of interest.[44]

In addition to the Mercantilists, Keynes acknowledged his debt to the economist Thomas Malthus (1766–1834), a few other economists, and even some 20th century figures, Sylvio Gesell and Major C. H. Douglas, whom he had previously dismissed as

no better than … crank[s].[45]

In *The General Theory*, he described Gesell, best known for advocating stamped money whose value would expire if not spent by a certain date, as

an unduly neglected prophet … [with] flashes of deep insight.[46]

Douglas, another proponent of what is sometimes called easy money, he somewhat backhandedly praised as

at least … not wholly oblivious of the outstanding problem of our economic system.[47]

These people together Keynes called his

brave army of heretics[48]

in which classification he happily included himself.

3

Spend More, Save Less, and Grow Wealthy

Keynes on Spending and Saving

1. Consumption—to [state] the obvious—is the sole . . . object of all economic activity.[1]

This does not mean consumption someday. It means consumption now. It is rather easy to lose sight of this fundamental truth:

> The "purposive" man is always trying to secure a spurious and delusive immortality. . . . He does not love his cat, but his cat's kittens; nor, in truth, the kittens, but only the kittens' kittens, and so on forward forever to the end of cat-dom. For him jam is not jam unless it is a case of jam tomorrow and never jam today.[2]

2. 19th century capitalists turned self-denial and thrift into a kind of religion. But it was a religion based on "bluff or deception."[3]

> On the one hand the laboring classes accepted from ignorance or powerlessness, or were compelled, persuaded, or cajoled by custom, convention, authority, and the well-established order of Society into accepting, a situation in which they could call their own very little of the cake that they and Nature and the capitalists were cooperating to produce. And on the other hand the capitalist classes were allowed to call the best part of the cake theirs and were theoretically free to consume it, on the tacit underlying condition that they consumed very little of it in practice. The duty of "saving" became nine-tenths of virtue and the growth of the cake the object of true religion. There grew round the nonconsumption of the cake all those instincts of puritanism which in other ages has withdrawn itself from the world. . . . And so the cake increased; but to what end was not clearly contemplated. . . . Saving was for old age or for your children; but this was only in theory—the virtue of the cake was that it was never to be consumed, neither by you nor by your children after you.[4]

3. Christianity joined hands with the secular religion of saving.

Religious leaders such as John Wesley, the founder of Methodism, preached that: "You should save all you can."[5] In this way, as Keynes explained, the morals, the politics, the literature, and the religion of the . . . [19th century] joined in a grand conspiracy for the promotion of saving. God and Mammon were reconciled. Peace on earth to men of good means. A rich man could, after all, enter into the Kingdom of Heaven—if only he saved.[6]

"Classical" (18th, 19th, and some 20th century) economists played a pivotal role as secular priests charged with explaining and defending the dogma of saving.

Yes, they said, spending was needed to make an economy work. When the baker buys vegetables from the greengrocer, the greengrocer will then have money with which to buy bread from the baker. But saving was another, much more special form of spending. When we save, the money does not simply disappear. It is spent on expanding businesses, making them more efficient. If we work hard, produce, and save, we will enjoy a cornucopia of cheaper, better, and more abundant products.

Over time, compounding will start to work its magic. If saving and investment enable production to grow at only 3% a year, production will double in 25 years. In a lifetime we can be three times richer. With each doubling, we can eliminate some poverty. Within our children's lifetime, we might hope to eliminate poverty completely. Moreover, if we follow these simple principles of working, producing, and saving, we can have full employment, and we can do so without economic slumps.

This is a very appealing story, and it is not surprising that, as Keynes said, the cult of saving

conquered England as completely as the Holy Inquisition conquered Spain.[7]

Unfortunately, Keynes tells us, the story told by the "classical" economists is merely a fable. It does not capture what happens in real life. In real life, poverty persists. We are beset by unemployment. We are beset by economic slumps. There is clearly something very wrong with what the classical economists have told us.[8]

4. The principal error in the "classical" vision is that savings may not be channeled smoothly and fully into a widening stream of investment.

If savings are smoothly and fully invested, society will prosper. But that is the rub—there is no certainty whatever that savings will be invested.

Perhaps the savers will want too high a rate of interest, higher than the business owners can pay.[9] Perhaps business owners or managers are lacking in the confidence or conviction required to borrow and invest. Perhaps the saver will simply decide not to lend—to hoard cash instead. As Keynes observed,

> an act of individual saving means—so to speak—a decision not to have dinner today. But it does not necessitate a decision [either] to have dinner a week hence or a year hence [or to invest what is not spent].[10]

It is

absurd

to think that investment will be increased by one pound or one dollar for every pound or dollar that is not spent on consumption.[K]

5. Nor should we deceive ourselves that a mismatch between saving and investment is either a rare or an unlikely occurrence.

On the contrary:

> There has been a chronic tendency throughout human

history [for savings to exceed investment].[11]

And it has become more of a problem, not less of one, as societies have advanced.

We all know that becoming richer makes it easier to save. In the same way, a rich society tends to save more than a poor society. As the savings increase, so does the mismatch between savings and investment.

6. During an economic slump, we especially want to save more, because we fear losing our jobs.

This just makes things worse, because the additional savings are unlikely to find an outlet in investment at the moment. The unused savings sit idle, the flow of money through the economy slows further and the slump deepens.[L]

What we need to understand, under these circumstances, is that

> the more virtuous we are, the more determinedly thrifty, the more obstinately orthodox . . . the more our incomes will have to fall. . . . Obstinacy can bring only penalty and no reward. For the result is inevitable.[12]

7. There are better and worse ways to address the problem of a savings glut. (We will begin with some of the worse ways.)

We could hope for

> [enough] unemployment to keep us . . . sufficiently . . . poor . . . and [our] standard of life sufficiently miserable to bring savings [down][13]

We could instead hope that

millionaires [will stop their relentless saving and instead] find their satisfaction in [putting their savings to use by] building mighty mansions to contain their bodies when alive and pyramids to shelter them after death, or, repenting of their sins, erect cathedrals and endow monasteries.[14]

We could rely on the unexpected:

[Throughout history, natural disasters such as] earthquakes, even wars ... [have] serve[d] to increase wealth [by using up savings].[15]

We might petition governments, even those wholly devoted to free market ("laissez-faire") principles to

fill old bottles with bank notes, bury them at suitable depths in disused coal mines which are then filled ... with town rubbish, and leave it to private enterprise ... to [invest in] dig[ging] the notes up again.[16]

As Keynes says, it would be

more sensible to build houses ... but digging up bank notes is not so different from "gold mining" and would equally serve as a way to consume excessive savings.[17]

8. There are, of course, better ways to reduce unused savings.

One way is for society to bring interest rates down so that businesses can afford to borrow all of it. As discussed earlier, savers may try to block this by refusing to lower the rates they will accept. If so, government can overrule them by printing new money and injecting it into the loan market. This will add to the total available "savings," but if interest rates are lowered enough, the extra money will not hurt. At a sufficiently low rate, all of it will be used by investors.

An alternative to lowering interest rates (thereby increasing investment) in order to reduce unused savings is to

> consume . . . more [that is, spend more as consumers so that we save less] or work . . . less [that is, reduce our income and thus our ability to save].

Keynes said that this works

> "just as well" as more investment.[18]

A practical way for society to consume more is to tax the rich at high rates and redistribute the wealth to those who are needy and thus sure to spend it.[19] If we keep clearly in mind that

> the growth in wealth, so far from being dependent on the abstinence [savings] of the rich, as is commonly supposed, is more likely to be impeded by it,[20]

we will then see that "death duties" [estate taxes] as well as progressive income tax rates will help society prosper.

And what if the rich succeed politically in blocking these death duties and high income taxes? Well, governments can also borrow from the rich. This will soak up their excess savings. And, having borrowed the money, government can then spend it, which will get it into circulation and stimulate the economy. In this case, government becomes what might be called the spender of last resort.

But this reference to government spending gets us a bit ahead of our story. Before considering the role of government spending, we will digress for a moment to discuss Keynes's personal values, and how they both influence and reflect his economics.

4

The Immoralist

(A Digression to Discuss Keynes's Personal Values)

A VISITOR TO KEYNES'S London lodgings found the economist and his wife, the ballerina Lydia Lopokhova, in a state of mutual hilarity. Keynes pretended to instruct his wife in the logic of the Christian trinity, and she pretended to be his artless and uncomprehending student.[1]

Satire and intellectual burlesque were dear to Keynes's heart. Organized religion, with its "superstition" and "hocus-pocus," was a favorite target.[2] He had been

> brought up in a free air undarkened by the horrors of religion.[3]

About Soviet Communism, he remarked:

> To say that [it] . . . is the faith of a persecuting and propagating minority of fanatics led by hypocrites is, after all, to say no more nor less than that it is a religion.[4]

One wonders what (by then Lord) Keynes would have thought of his own memorial service in 1946, a very traditional service with age-old Anglican prayers and hymns held in Westminster Abbey and attended by the great of the land including several prime ministers.

Keynes's satire sometimes degenerated into what others regarded as ridicule or mockery, but it was not meant to wound. It was meant to be fun. Keynes deprecated seriousness, appreciated silliness, and said of some minor 16th and 17th century English authors that they were

> silly and neurotic in just that way I fancy.[5]

One Cambridge University economist, Dennis Robertson, referred to his colleague as "an imp."[6] Another fellow economist called him an "enfant terrible."[7] But those were just partial views. The "imp" and "enfant terrible" could, for the nonce, become sympathetic, authoritative, commanding, or combative. The combative Keynes once commented that

> over against us, standing in the path, there is nothing but a few old gentlemen tightly buttoned-up in their trade coats, who only need to be treated with a little friendly disrespect and bowled over like ninepins. Quite likely they will enjoy it themselves, when once they have got over the shock.[8]

Financially well-heeled Britons of the 20th century were very keen on clubs, and Keynes belonged to many of them, both formal and informal. He joined the Apostles, a secret organization of Cambridge undergraduates, in 1903. Along with fellow Apostle Lytton Strachey, he helped create what came to be called The Bloomsbury Group, an assortment of like-minded bohemian intellectuals and nonconformists that also included the painters

Vanessa Bell and Duncan Grant, as well as the novelists Virginia Woolf and, at a bit of a remove, Morgan Forster.

For many years Keynes participated in a Memoir Club comprised of Bloomsbury personalities. An essay entitled "My Early Beliefs," prepared for the group and read aloud one evening in 1938, describes how the youthful Apostles had completely rejected traditional values, especially those of their Victorian parents and grandparents:

> We repudiated entirely customary morals, conventions, and traditional wisdom. We were, that is to say, in the strict sense of the term, immoralists. The consequences of being found out had, of course, to be considered.... But we recognized no moral obligation on us, no inner sanction to conform or to obey.... [Others may regard this with] justifiable suspicion. Yet so far as I am concerned, it is too late to change. I remain, and always will remain, an immoralist.[9]

Keynes already had heart trouble by the time he composed this memoir. It required effort to present it, especially because it was so deeply felt, and he had to be helped to his bedroom to recover, while his wife served ham sandwiches and hot cakes to the guests.[10]

Was Keynes an immoralist? His brother Geoffrey sought to burn "incriminating" letters after his death,[11] but correspondence with Lytton Strachey and others was preserved. This revealed a youthful obsession with sex and sexually explicit language, both a sharp departure from Victorian moeurs, and much debate about the "higher and lower sodomy," culminating in rivalry between Keynes and Strachey for Duncan Grant's affections.[12]

Even before these letters came to light, Bloomsbury as a whole developed a degree of notoriety for partner swapping, whether homosexual, heterosexual, or bisexual. Initially this was not supposed to be about pleasure.[13] Pleasure crept in, but it did not erase the original high-minded zeal to reshape the world, first in the direction of sexual freedom, and then beyond. For most of Bloomsbury, beyond meant the world of art, literature, and culture; for Keynes it meant business and public life as well.

This difference led to conflict, not only between Keynes and his friends, but also within Keynes. During World War I, he held a Treasury post which kept him safe from the slaughter that consumed much his generation, but wrote to Duncan Grant,

> I work for a government I despise for ends I think criminal.[14]

He also asked a group of undergraduate Apostles at Cambridge,

> Is there any brother [Apostle] who would rather not be a scientist than a businessman, and an artist than a scientist?[15]

In time, Keynes became rich through his investments. This was neither incidental nor accidental. He wanted very much to be rich, worked assiduously at it, lost everything once and nearly everything again with the onset of the Great Depression, but recovered each time and died a multimillionaire in today's money. This very financial success, however, posed a problem. Apostles and then members of Bloomsbury were supposed to hold money in contempt. As Keynes said:

> The economic [motive was] ... less prominent in our philosophy than with St. Francis of Assisi, who at least made collections for the birds.[16]

The pursuit of money in general was regarded as

> the worm which is gnawing at the insides of modern civilization.[17]

In 1926, Keynes wrote that

> the essential characteristic of capitalism [is its] dependence upon an intense appeal to the money-loving instinct of individuals.[18]

Keynes thought this had an undeniable utility. It motivated people,

> it was "efficient."[19]

> No other system worked so well.[20]

But it was also

> "extremely objectionable."[21]

In "Economic Possibilities for Our Grandchildren," an essay written in 1930 at the beginning of the Great Depression, Keynes expressed the hope that one day, perhaps within a hundred years,

> The economic problem may be solved.[22]

By then there might be sufficient

> "economic abundance"

to meet everyone's legitimate needs. If so, we could then

> return to . . . the . . . sure . . . principle . . . that avarice is a vice, . . . the exaction of usury [high interest rates] is a misdemeanor, . . . the love of money is detestable, . . . those walk most truly in the paths of virtue and sane wisdom who take least thought for the morrow.[23]

In this context, he quoted with approval Jesus's admonition to

> consider the lilies of the field, how they grow; they toil not, neither do they spin.[24]

and would probably have agreed with Jesus's warning that "It is easier for a camel to go through the eye of a needle, than for a rich man to enter the Kingdom of God,"[25] not because the rich have too much money, but because they cling to it avariciously, and even when they do open their pocketbooks to spend, generally choose the wrong objects to spend it on.

Keynes complained that the behavior

> of the wealthy classes today . . . is very depressing. . . . [But] I feel sure that with a little more experience we shall use [wealth] quite differently from the way in which the rich use it today.[26]

He also expressed hope that humanity would employ its wealth

> to live wisely and agreeably and well,[27]

by which he meant that a surplus of funds would be spent on both the arts and the art of life, as defined by himself and his Bloomsbury friends.

It will be quite evident that Keynes did not want the masses of humanity, when finally rescued from poverty, to emulate the rich by going on a consumer-buying binge. The economic advice for society to focus on today—spend more, stop saving, and reduce interest rates to make debt more affordable—was not meant to engender mass consumerism.

Nor was Keynes saying that governments should go on a buying binge either. As early as 1909, the then president of Harvard University, Charles W. Eliot, had said in a commencement address that

the Religion of the Future should concern itself with ...
[public] needs ... with public baths, play grounds, wider
and cleaner streets and better dwellings.[28]

Harvard (and Keynesian) economist, John Kenneth Galbraith,
seconded this thought in books like *The Affluent Society* and *The
New Industrial State*. In Galbraith's version of Keynesianism, society needed to stop saving and spend more, but on public goods,
not on tasteless, mass produced, mass advertised consumer goods.

Would Keynes have backed this position? Perhaps in part. He
might have agreed that society has a greater need for public goods
than consumer goods. But the whole emphasis on goods, public
or private, would have struck him as unduly materialistic, part of
what he called the

Benthamite Calculus,

after the 18th and 19th century materialist philosopher Jeremy
Bentham.[M]

A jaundiced observer might find more than a touch of elitism
in this. If so, Keynes would not have denied it. Just as he simultaneously sought wealth and descried the love of money, he also
simultaneously backed

social justice

right alongside unabashed privilege.

We have already seen that he recommended high taxes and
death duties on the rich. He described himself as a "leveller":

I want to mold a society in which most of the existing
inequalities and causes of inequality are removed.[29]

But he also said about Soviet Communism:

> How can I adopt a creed which, preferring the mud to
> the fish, exalts the boorish proletariat above the bour-
> geois and the intelligentsia who, with whatever faults,
> are the quality of life and surely carry the seeds of all
> human advancement?[30]

And, in a similar vein, he said that he could not join the British
Labor Party because

> it is a class party, and the class is not my class.... The class
> war will find me on the side of the educated bourgeoisie.[31]

This sense of elitism carried Keynes into even more treacher-
ous waters:

> The time may arrive ... when the community as a whole
> must pay attention to the innate quality ... and [not]
> mere numbers of its future members.[32]

Keynes's values always had many facets. The central theme, the
rejection of Victorian "copybook morality"[33] as

> medieval [and] barbarous[34]

was clear. But even this was qualified.

For example, the Victorians exalted hard work, yet Keynes
worked as hard as any Victorian. Sometimes he was sly about it. Like
other upper class Englishmen of his time, he consciously sought to
make it all look as effortless as possible, because deliberate toil had
a proletarian tinge. Many mornings found him in bed until noon
(even before the heart troubles began). But after breakfast, brought
on a bed tray by a servant, there was reading, writing, and dictating,
and by the end of the morning a full day's work might be done.

Despite these unstinting if eccentric work habits, Keynes did
transvalue Victorian values, and was immensely successful in

doing so. Mr. Micawber in Charles Dickens's 19th century novel *David Copperfield* issues a stern warning:

> Annual income twenty pounds, annual expenditure nineteen, nineteen six, result happiness. Annual income twenty pounds, annual expenditure twenty pounds ought and six, result misery.[35]

Before the Keynesian revolution, the average Briton or American nodded his head in agreement with Mr. Micawber. Afterward everything changed and, especially in America, overspending, undersaving, debt, and disregarding the future became a way of life. As German economist Wilhelm Röpke said, Keynes "seduced" succeeding generations and persuaded them to "*pecca fortiter*, that is, do with a light heart what you have hitherto regarded as a sin."[36]

Keynes had justified his focus on the present by saying

in the long run we are all dead.[37]

This flip remark was all too true, but does it not represent an abandonment of the concept of prudence, of adult (as opposed to childish) thinking?

The ancient Greek philosopher Epicurus warned that

> the chief good is care in avoiding undesired consequences. Such prudence is more precious than philosophy itself, . . . all the other virtues spring from it. It teaches that it is impossible to live pleasurably without also living prudently. . . . For the virtues are closely associated with the pleasant life, and the pleasant life cannot be separated from them.[N38]

When contemporary environmentalists preach to us about sustainability, are they not making a similar point, that long-run effects matter, even very long-run effects? And if we escape the worst consequences of our own actions, can we rest easy about what we are passing on to posterity?

Austrian economists such as Ludwig von Mises and Friedrich Hayek were especially critical of Keynes's focus on the present at the expense of the future. Hayek regarded Keynes's stance as "a . . . betrayal of the main duty of the economist and a grave menace to our civilization."[39]

Before leaving Keynes's values, we must ask ourselves: do they really matter to our larger task, which is to understand and evaluate Keynes's economic policy prescriptions? Economics is a science, is it not? And, as such, why would the economist's personal values concern us?

The question of whether economics is a science is briefly discussed in this author's *Are the Rich Necessary?* The conclusion reached there is that economics is not and never shall be a science. Why? In the first place, when we observe an apple fall from a tree, or deduce the force of gravity, it will not affect what the apple does. But human action, the subject of economics, is entirely different. It is very changeable; it is even changed by what economists tell us about ourselves.

If economists tell us that stocks are the most reliable long-term investment, we will all buy stocks and the prices will soar. Eventually there will be no sellers, the price will collapse, and we will discover that we have made a very bad investment. We saw that well enough in the 1920s and 1990s. So, on the whole, it is much better to accept that economics is trying to sort out probabilities, not truths, and is most closely aligned with moral philosophy, also known as values.

Keynes, it must be said, was an important moral philosopher. His essay "My Early Beliefs," which we have quoted, is a philosophical gem. Keynes also wrote *A Treatise on Probability* (his first book) which has a place in the history of moral philosophy.

On the subject of whether economics could be a science, Keynes was ambivalent, or perhaps coy. It was, after all, useful to claim economics as a science. That made an economist's prescriptions more likely to be followed. Either for this reason, or from convention, Keynes wrote of:

■■ Economics [as] a technical and difficult subject [which] ... is ... becoming a science.[40]

■■ Scheme[s] of [economic] management drawn up scientifically.[41]

■■ The latest scientific improvements devised in the economic laboratory of Harvard.[42]

In the same general spirit, Keynes wrote that

I believe ... the right solution [to the economic questions of the day] will involve intellectual and scientific elements which must be above the heads of the vast mass of more or less illiterate voters.[43]

On the other hand, Keynes admitted that

economics is ... not a natural science [but rather] employs ... judgements of value.[44]

He told the Archbishop of York that

economics—more properly called political economy— is a side of ethics.[45]

So it is fair to conclude that Keynes did not think his economics and his values existed in separate spheres. On the contrary, he thought that it is

painful and paralyzing ... [for] our sympathy and our judgement ... to be on different sides,[46]

and he constantly struggled to integrate his values and his economics into one solid whole.

5

What to Do about
Wall Street?

A Recapitulation

To review what was covered before our digression on Keynes's
values:

- Humanity has focused too much on the future and has
  consequently spent too little and saved too much.
- A society saves too much when the amount of savings
  exceeds what can be invested. For most of human history, this has been the case.
- Unused savings, sitting idle, interrupt the flow of
  money through the economy and lead to unemployment. Unemployment reduces society's income. A
  lower income eventually reduces the amount saved, but
  at a great cost in human suffering and lost opportunity.
- Either more spending or more investment will solve the
  problem. More spending will reduce the level of savings. More investment will absorb all the savings.

Keynes recommended a combination of approaches, seemed to favor more investment, but also said, as we have seen, that spending was just as good.[1]

■■ The fundamental reason that investment is too low is that interest rates tend to be too high. This is the root cause of human poverty.[2]

■■ Government can help bring interest rates down by printing new money and injecting it into the economy through the banks as lendable funds.

Keynes on the Stock Market

1. Unfortunately lower interest rates alone will not guarantee more investment in a market system.

When business owners and managers consider a new investment, perhaps in a new facility, they are much influenced by interest rates. If they can borrow money at 2%, and the facility is expected to return 6%, this looks good. If interest rates rise to 5%, it does not look so good, and at 6% it does not make any sense. But it is not just the rate of interest that counts. It is also the investor's expectations. Expectations in turn depend heavily on a purely psychological factor, the state of business confidence.

2. Unfortunately business confidence is generally weak.

The average person thinks that business owners and managers know what they are doing and, in particular, know a great deal about the future return of a factory, a mine, a product, or a service. But this is not so. All human beings, even so-called experts, are mostly in the dark about the future. Their knowledge of the future amounts to little and sometimes to nothing,[3] and their ability to make accurate, especially pinpoint, forecasts is usually nil.

People in general and business investors in particular cope with their ignorance of (and anxiety about) the future by falling back on a simple convention. They assume that what has happened in the recent past will continue to happen.[4] Unfortunately this device is

> arbitrary . . . weak . . . [and] precarious.[5]

It often fails, and failure brings with it a psychological shock.

3. Even if some business owners or managers guess right about the future, many will not.

It is "probable" that business returns on average "disappoint,"[6] especially in relations to the "hopes" which precede them.[7] Why then do business investors keep wanting to play the "game"? Not presumably out of "cold calculation," but rather out of

> animal spirits.[8]

Unfortunately, "animal spirits" depend on

> the nerves and hysteria and even the digestions [of the players].[9]

4. This is already a weak foundation on which to build a modern economy. But it is made even weaker by the pernicious influence of the stock market.

The stock market is not all bad. It is a way to finance companies. By offering "liquidity," the ability to buy and sell investments, such markets may also persuade the timid investor to pull money out from under the mattress and actually make an investment. Of course the liquidity is largely illusory. People cannot all get in or get out at the same time, which they typically want to do.

Then too, if money is invested in existing stocks, it will not be invested in new plant, equipment, employees, products, and services, which is what real investment is about. Much stock market investment is really sterile, not much better for society than keeping the money under a mattress.[10]

The pricing of shares on a public market is often "absurd."[11] For example, Keynes has heard that the shares of ice companies sell at a higher price in the summer (when profits are seasonally higher) than in winter. A rational market would know that seasons alternate and that profits for the year are what count.

If the stock market rises, this will have the beneficial effect of boosting business confidence. But a fall will depress it. And in a stock market oriented country such as the US, a falling market will not only depress business investment. It will also depress consumer demand as well, because consumers who have invested will feel less rich, and even those who have not invested will fear for their jobs.[12]

5. The worst aspect of the stock market is its "casino" atmosphere.[13]

The ostensible purpose of a stock market is to channel private savings into the most socially useful (and thus profitable) investments.[14] This requires a "long-term" point of view.[15] The "best brains of Wall Street," however, are completely unconcerned with the long-term. They are not even concerned with learning very much about the companies they buy.[16] Their "game," which they play with the utmost "zest" is to identify those stocks which will become popular and to buy them first.[17] Since everyone else is playing the same game, this means, in effect,

> anticipating what the average opinion [will] expect...
> the average opinion to be,

and then profiting from a correct guess.[18]

Under these circumstances, genuine long-term investing becomes so difficult . . . as to be "scarcely practicable" and anyone who attempts it will, paradoxically, seem "unconventional" and therefore "rash."[19] Even the most conservative investment committees will be uncomfortable with a long-term approach because

> worldly wisdom teaches that it is better for reputations to fail conventionally than to succeed unconventionally.[20]

Wall Street might seem to be merely a "spectacle," but its disfunctionality has serious consequences:

> Speculators may do no harm as bubbles on a steady stream of enterprise. But the position is serious when enterprise becomes the bubble on a whirlpool of speculation.[21]

Under these circumstances, capital will not only be misallocated. Average citizens will also lose faith in the system.

It is one thing to watch some people get unimaginably rich, if extremes of wealth are thought to reflect hard work, astute judgement, and the production of vital goods for society as a whole. Even then, the winners are getting far too much, whether from the point of view of justice or from the point of view of providing useful incentives.[22] But it is quite another thing if vast rewards go not to the disciplined and deserving, but only to the lucky gamblers. In time, the social system will unravel, no one will want to work, and everyone will want to gamble.[23]

6. The only real remedy for stock market failure is for government to allocate capital itself.

As we have seen, the problem of converting savings into investments has two components. The first obstacle is that interest rates tend to be chronically too high, which discourages investment, and leaves large amounts of savings unused. Government can alleviate this by printing more money and injecting it into the banking system to bring interest rates down.

But this solves only half the problem. The other problem is that

> the psychology of [private investors, both in business and on Wall Street or other stock markets, is] disobedient . . . and . . . uncontrollable.[24]

Operating in a cloud of ignorance, private investors tend to manic highs and morose lows. When morose they cannot be prodded to take advantage of even the most attractive interest rates. The entire system of private investment

> is not intelligent . . . [,] is not virtuous. . . . [It] doesn't deliver the goods.[25]

We can only conclude that

> the duty of ordering the current volume of investment cannot safely be left in private hands.[26]

6

Look to the State for Economic Leadership

Keynes on the Economic Role of the State

1. The state should decide on the "volume of investment."

This means that if investment is too low to absorb all savings, and if lower interest rates do not bring up investment sufficiently, the state should make investments itself.

How will the state know that lower interest rates are not enough, that direct investment is needed? The key indictor is employment. If cheap money produces "full" employment, direct investment is not needed. If unemployment persists, then it is.

The state will not print the money to invest. It will get the money either by taxing wealthy individuals or by borrowing. If it borrows, this will not necessarily cause a government budget deficit; government investment may be kept off-budget or in a separate capital budget.[1]

2. The level of government investment should be carefully calibrated in order to foster a perpetual "quasi-boom."

It is widely assumed that Keynes meant the state should "balance" what private investors are doing. Walter Lippmann described this idea of the state providing "balance" as follows:

> An uncoordinated, unplanned, disorderly individ-
> ualism . . . inevitably produces alternating periods
> of boom and depression . . . . The state [should] un-
> dertake . . . to counteract the mass errors of the in-
> dividualist crowd by doing the opposite of what the
> crowd is doing; it saves when the crowd is spending
> too much; it borrows when the crowd is saving too
> much; it economizes when the crowd is extravagant,
> and it spends when the crowd is afraid to spend. . . .
> [This] compensatory method is, I believe, an epoch-
> making invention.[2]

Leaving aside, for the moment, whether this "compensatory method" is actually feasible, the more immediate question is: did Keynes endorse it? Most people think so.° But the answer would seem to be no, Keynes did not endorse it, or at least did not fully endorse it at the time of *The General Theory*. He did say in *The General Theory* that the state enters as a

balancing factor.[3]

But by this he primarily meant that the state should top off invest-ment when it is too low.

As we saw in chapter 2, Keynes did not agree with the idea that both booms and busts are bad, that boom leads to bust, that we should avoid both extremes and strive for a happy middle. On the contrary, he believed that

> the right remedy for the trade cycle is not to be found
> in abolishing booms and thus keeping us permanently
> in semi-slump; but in abolishing slumps and thus keep-
> ing us permanently in quasi-boom."[4]

All of this follows from Keynes's view that, most of the time, investment lags savings, so that money remains idle, and the economy falters. A boom should therefore be nursed and kept going as long as possible.

One must ask—is it not conceivable that, at least in some instances, the reverse could be true? Might not the combination of consumer demand and investment run so strong that the boom finally does get out of control? If all available resources are being used to the utmost, if every willing worker is employed, if demand and investment still surge, would that not overheat the economic machine, even cause inflation?

As we have seen, Keynes acknowledged that this could conceivably happen. Even in this case, however, he did not want to increase interest rates. As he said:

> We must find other means of [cooling the economy]
> than a higher rate of interest. For if we allow the rate
> of interest to [rise], we cannot easily reverse the trend.[5]

In particular, he feared that investors, if they thought that interest rates would rise from time to time, might hoard their funds in hopes of catching a rise.

3. The state's usual job is to fill up the investment tank, not to drain it. Keeping it full is what matters most. But there are other reasons to welcome a larger role for the state in investment.

On the whole, Keynes appeared to sympathize with the idea that government would do a better job of investing than private markets. As we have seen, he painted a bleak portrait of private investment, handicapped (he said) by profound ignorance, uncontrollable emotion, and speculative tendencies. By contrast, as we have also seen, he thought the state able to decide matters based on

> long views . . . the . . . general social advantage . . . and . . . collective wisdom.[6]

In 1932, he criticized Harold Macmillan, later a British prime minister, for not being

> nearly bold enough with your proposals for developing the [direct] investment functions of the state.[7]

In 1936, in *The General Theory*, he said that he favored

> a somewhat comprehensive socialization of investment.[8]

In 1937, he suggested in the *London Times* that the British government set up a formal Public Office of Investment.[9] And in 1939 he enthusiastically promoted an

> amalgam of private capitalism and state socialism.[10]

These and other statements would seem to support the proposition that Keynes wanted government investment for its own sake, not just to top off private investment. He did also say that

> I see no reason to suppose that the existing [private]

system seriously misemploys the factors of production which are in use.[11]

But this seems to mean that private enterprise is well equipped to run the show after the investment is made, not that private enterprise is necessarily better at choosing the investment in the first place.

4. The state's control of the economy should not stop with interest rates, investment, taxation, and exchange rates.

In 1940, Keynes said that free prices were indispensable, but that he also favored setting up public boards to manage the prices of commodities.[12] In 1943, looking ahead to the post-war period, he said that

> I am ... a hopeless skeptic about [any] return to nineteenth century laissez-faire. I believe that the future lies with—(i) state trading for commodities; (ii) International cartels [government sanctioned monopolies] for necessary manufactures; and (iii) Quantitative import restrictions for nonessential manufactures. . . . [These are the] instrumentalities for orderly economic life in the future. . . .[13]

> [In general], state planning, ... intelligence and deliberation at the center must supersede the admired disorder of the 19th century.[14]

In describing all this, Keynes acknowledged that the state would involve itself in

> many of the inner intricacies of private business[15]

But even so, a

> wide field ... of [private] activity [will be] unaffected.[16]

Moreover, over time, the very distinction between private and public economic activity will gradually fade. Private companies will become

> semi-socialized

and eventually "Public Boards" and "Private Companies" will only differ with respect to how the directors are appointed.[17]

5. State planning is not to be confused with Fascism or Communism.

Keynes always took pains to differentiate his ideas from those of a totalitarian system:

> We can accept the desirability and even the necessity of [economic] planning without being a Communist, a Socialist, or a Fascist.[18]

But he did not completely disparage Fascist or Communist economic management:

> Italian Fascism . . . seems to have saved Italy from chaos and to have established a modest level of material prosperity. . . .[19]

And in his foreword to the German edition of *The General Theory* (published in Nazi Germany and not included in *The Collected Works*), he noted that his ideas could be applied to a completely controlled economy, although not worked out with that in mind.[20]

As we saw in our earlier discussion of Keynes's values, he found much that was

> detestable

about Soviet Russia. At best he regarded Communists as a species of deranged "Methodists."[21] But what Soviet planners had achieved by 1936 was

impressive

They were

disinterested administrators . . . [who had put] in operation . . . the largest scale empiricism and experimen-
talism which has ever been attempted.[22]

He went further in his praise:

Let us not belittle these magnificent experiments or refuse to learn from them. . . . The Five Year Plan in Russia, the Corporative state in Italy; . . . and state planning [under] democracy in Great Britain. . . . Let us
hope that they will all be successful.[23]

It is important to recall, in assessing this, that many intelligent
and otherwise decent people in the 1930s were admirers of Fascism and Communism. Keynes was neither.[P] Instead, he sought
what he called

new wisdom for a new age,

and did not in the least mind appearing

unorthodox, troublesome, and dangerous[24]

to conventionally minded capitalists who failed to see their own peril
or to understand that a Keynesian "third" way was their only hope.

6. State-run capitalism must be run by the right people.

At this point, it is necessary to ask how a self-described unorthodox thinker and rebel could put so much faith in government. Is
not government, like other established social institutions, usually
the embodiment of conventional wisdom?

We have previously noted Keynes's statement that

> I believe the right solution [to the economic questions
> of the day] will involve intellectual and scientific ele-
> ments which must be above the heads of the vast mass
> of more or less illiterate voters.[25]

But are political leaders, even heads of government, any less
economically illiterate than the voters? Did not Keynes himself in his second book (about the Versailles Peace Treaty) ridicule the leaders of Britain, France, and the United States, along
with all the other old and blinkered men who have traditionally led nations?

The answer to this conundrum is that, under Keynes's system,
government will turn over the economic reins to experts:

> [The economy] is a matter which ought to be left to
> the experts. They ought to understand the machine.
> They ought to be able to mend it when it goes wrong.[26]

As early as 1914, a young Keynes had concluded that experts
have

> solved . . . the intellectual and scientific part of the
> problem [of how to run an economy].[27]

This was premature, but by the 1930s Keynes was convinced that
he really did have the answers, that the problem of economic
management could simply be turned over to himself and his disciples. At the same time, he enjoyed intellectual novelty, and thus
liked to think there was always more to discover. On a radio
broadcast during World War II, he said that

> we may learn a trick or two from the economic manage-
> ment of the war that could be applied in peacetime.[28]

Keynes's biographer Robert Skidelsky observed that a belief in expert opinion "runs like a leitmotiv through [his] work and is the important assumption of his political philosophy."[29]

Since Keynes was the dominant economic expert of his era, both in Britain and the US, this faith in expert opinion was, at least in part, simply faith in himself, and a manifestation of his unflagging self-confidence.

7. These experts, however, will be more than experts.

Keynes was not satisfied that experts qua experts should be in charge. He wanted experts who also had the right values, people who might be described as platonic guardians. In a letter to Friedrich Hayek, a critic of state-run capitalism, he said that state-appointed guardians of the economy had to have the right

> moral position,

which would include a commitment to individual freedom. This was essential because:

> Dangerous acts can be done safely in a community which thinks and feels rightly which would be the way to hell if they were executed by those who think and feel wrongly.[30]

Although the guardians must be exceptionally moral, this does not necessarily refer to conventional Judeo-Christian morality. Most economic issues by their nature are simply over the head of the average voter. It is, therefore, not inappropriate for economic managers to resort to sleight of hand or even mild deception in order to obtain the consent of the governed for essential actions.

In a passage in *The General Theory*, Keynes notes that the public wants

> the moon,

by which he means perennially high wages, and that to maintain high wages there must be plenty of money in circulation. The "remedy" is thus to

> persuade the public that green cheese [government printed money] is practically the same thing [as real money] and to have a green cheese factory (i.e. a central bank) under public control.º [31]

7

In an Economic Crisis, Print, Lend, Borrow, and Spend

Keynes on How to Handle an Economic Crisis

1. It is sometimes alleged that economic crises, recessions, and depressions serve a useful purpose. This is false.

Keynes is aware that booms bring some

misdirected investment,[1]

and that slumps may help to

get rid of a lot of deadwood.[2]

But even misdirected investment is better than no investment at all.[3]

It is a

serious error

to think that slumps are in some sense necessary to economic progress, either because of their purgative role, or because they moderate speculation and reckless risk-taking by introducing an element of fear. On the contrary, as we have seen, we should

abolish slumps[4]

and instead seek to maintain a perpetual

quasi-boom.[5]

2. An incipient financial crash, an economic slump, or first one and then the other, require prompt and decisive government intervention.

Crashes and deep slumps tell us that we have made a

colossal muddle,

that we have

blundered in the control of a delicate machine,[6]

and that repairs are urgently needed. Bold, strong, corrective action should be administered at the first sign of trouble. It should be as

radical

as necessary.[7]

In early 1932, more than two years into what became the Great Depression, Keynes warned that

a collapse of this kind feeds on itself,[R]

and complained that

it is very much more difficult to solve the problem today than it would have been a year ago. . . . The . . .

authorities of the world have lacked the courage or conviction at each stage of the decline to apply the available remedies in sufficiently drastic doses.[8]

Keynes went on to state that a point of no return might be reached, where the system would lose its

capacity for a rebound.[9]

3. The script for preventing a financial crash was written long ago. We need to follow it.

In 1873, Walter Bagehot, editor of *The Economist* magazine, published a book called *Lombard Street*. This book argued that the Bank of England, then a private institution although with semi-official status, should stand ready to act as the "lender of last resort." If the public is nervous and starts withdrawing funds from a bank, that bank would be able to replace those funds by borrowing from the Bank of England.

Of course there were rules. The borrowing bank must still be solvent, it must give the Bank of England sound securities as collateral for the loan, and it must pay a stiff interest rate. The sound collateral meant that, no matter what happened, the Bank of England should not lose money.

Here is where Bagehot became controversial: he said that the Bank of England should stand ready to make as many of these loans as necessary to reassure the public and stop bank runs. It should stand ready to make these loans even if it had already made as many loans as its own reserves, under then banking law, allowed. In other words, the Bank of England should do whatever it took to stop a bank run, even if it had to abandon sound banking procedure or even, technically, violate the law.

Bagehot's ideas were not without critics. One, Thomas Hankey, thought that a "lender of last resort" system would lead banks to take on riskier loans, or otherwise behave recklessly, because they would expect to be bailed out, even if at a penalty interest rate.[10]

Bagehot's ideas triumphed over those of his friend Hankey. Keynes also sided with Bagehot, but worried that his ideas may be applied too late or timidly. The way to stop a financial crisis is for the government to step in decisively. If unlimited funds are made available to threatened financial institutions, a downward spiraling mass panic can be stopped. Individuals, confident of the government's support, will no longer rush to protect themselves in ways that quickly backfire by bringing down the system and guaranteeing a bad outcome for all.

4. Bagehot's approach, if applied with vigor, is generally correct, but still needs further refinement. In particular, interest rates need to be lower, lending standards lower, and the scale of overall government assistance higher.

As we have noted, Bagehot wanted the "lender of last resort" to lend at rates high enough to impose a penalty. Keynes, on the other hand, wanted low interest rates to prevail throughout the financial system at all times, both in regular loans and, presumably, in emergency loans as well. Nor should the "lender of last resort" be so choosy about who is helped.

Keynes also recognized that if interest rates are already low when the crisis strikes, there is only so much that cheap credit can do. In addition, no matter how cheap the credit is, people may be too frightened to borrow. In this case,

> direct state intervention is needed.[11]

This intervention may take the form of subsidized long-term loans at very low rates or other subsidies to industry.[12] In addition, the state should prepare plans to expand and accelerate its own direct investment program, and put the plan into effect at the first sign of need.[13]

5. Can a country spend its way into recovery? Yes.

Keynes wrote an article in 1934 for the popular American magazine *Redbook* entitled

"Can America Spend Its Way Into Recovery?"

and opened the article with

Why, obviously![14]

The article continued: The very behavior that would make

a man poor

could make

a nation wealthy.[15]

Yes, the extra government spending needed during a slump will exceed tax revenues, no matter how high tax rates are, because taxes fall during an economic contraction. There would necessarily be a government budget deficit and a need to borrow. But the nation's debt would usually be to its own citizens.[s]

Moreover, tax rates should never have to be increased to pay for the new debt. The money borrowed and spent will revive the economy. A revived economy requires less government spending on the "dole" (unemployment insurance) and generates a stream of new tax revenue. Together, the savings and the new taxes will more than cover the debt service. So, in sum, government spending of borrowed money under conditions of less than full employment is (what economists after Keynes came to call) a free lunch.[16]

6. There is no shortage of useful projects for government to spend money on.

Keynes noted that any spending under dire economic circumstances was better than no spending. The main thing is to

get the money spent.[17]

It will always be hard to get the

dead-heads[18]

to agree that any project is legitimate, but in truth such projects abound.

Roads are a good choice and Keynes liked a proposal he had heard to build a "broad boulevard" along the south side of the Thames in London. He also liked housing projects and asked why the whole of South London should not be torn down and replaced with

far better buildings.[19]

In general, as noted in our chapter on values, he always liked schemes that combined art and commerce to produce something both beautiful and useful.[T]

7. The impact of government spending during a slump is magnified by the "investment or employment multiplier."

The Keynesian multiplier springs from the initial observation that a newly employed person will start to spend money. This spending will in turn help employ others. Employment leads to further employment, just as unemployment leads to further unemployment. If an economy is near full employment, the spending of one more newly employed person will not matter much. If unemployment is widespread, each increment of new employment and new spending will matter more.

Keynes gives an example in which 5,200,000 persons are employed. 100,000 new jobs are created by a government public works program. These new jobs then lead to more new jobs until total employment rises to 6,400,000, which is 1,200,000 more jobs. In this instance, the employment multiplier is 12.[20] Although the actual multiplier will vary, it should be

at least three or four times[21]

on public works expenditure.

The concept of the multiplier is critical because it refutes the criticism that public works programs will never be large enough to make much of a difference in a developed economy. As Keynes says:

> Public works even of doubtful utility may pay for themselves over and over again at a time of severe unemployment, if only from the diminished cost of relief expenditure.[22]

8

Markets Do Not Self-Correct

Keynes on the Defects of Free Markets

1. It is an especially grave mistake to think that a malfunctioning economic machine can be left alone.

Economies are not, as the "classical" economists thought,

> self-adjusting;[1]

they do not fix themselves.[2] On the contrary, without government intervention markets are more likely to cycle down and establish a new

> equilibrium[at a] sub-normal [level of] employment [and remain there] in a chronic condition.[3]

2. "Classical" economists thought that economies were self-adjusting and therefore advised governments confronted with a slump to: Do Nothing. But (as Keynes saw it) Do Nothing really meant: Drive Wages Down.

These two positions—Do Nothing and Drive Wages Down—were not necessarily inconsistent. Classical economists thought that markets suffering from a slump would drive wages down on their own. Action by government to achieve this was neither necessary nor desirable.

What was the rationale for such a policy? Did not working people suffer enough during slumps from job loss? Why would it be desirable to drive wages down? The classical response (the response Keynes was taught in his youth) runs as follows:

During a slump, people buy less. This reduces business revenues. Because revenues fall first, before expenses, profits fall. Business owners then lay off employees to reduce costs and restore profitability. If, instead, wages fall, profitability can be restored without layoffs.

This is especially necessary if prices start falling all over the economy. If people are buying so much less that almost all prices start to fall, business revenues will be especially hard hit. Not only will fewer widgets be sold, but each individual widget will be sold for less. Under these circumstances, if wages do not fall with prices, businesses will certainly face bankruptcy. On the other hand, if both prices and wages fall together, workers should be no worse off. Although wages are lower, the consumer products workers buy will also cost less. It will be a wash.

Keynes agreed that lowering wages along with prices during a depression could save jobs. But, even so, he strongly objected to lowering wages, for a variety of different reasons.

3. Even if ultimately successful, a policy of Drive Wages Down takes too long to cure unemployment during a slump.

In 1930, Keynes wrote:

> The correct answer [to deep unemployment] along austere lines is as follows: A reduction of money wages by 10 percent will ease unemployment in five years' time. In the meanwhile you must grin and bear it. If you can't grin and bear it, and are prepared to have some abandonment of laissez-faire [i.e., let the government take charge of the economy in different ways], then you can hope to get straight sooner. You will also be richer ... five years hence. You may, moreover, have avoided a social catastrophe.[4]

4. Even if one has the patience for market solutions, there are reasons to doubt that lower wages will actually solve unemployment.

We must keep clearly in mind that

> one man's expenditure is another man's income.[5]

A business owner will readily see

> the obvious great advantages to ... a reduction of the wages he has to pay.[6]

But will not see

> so clearly the disadvantages he will suffer if the money incomes of his customers are reduced.[7]

If consumer spending falls with wages, we could find ourselves in a situation where both spending and wages fall in a vicious downward spiral. According to Keynes, there is no theoretical reason why wages might not just fall and fall

without limit.[8]

5. Although falling wages are not good medicine for a slump, it does not follow that rising wages would help.

Prior to the Great Depression of the 1930s, a popular argument held that capitalism chronically falls into crisis because workers are not paid enough. Because they are not paid enough, they cannot afford to buy enough of the goods they are making. The result is a tendency for production to outstrip consumption. In economic jargon, there is an underconsumption gap.

Rich business owners partly close the underconsumption gap by spending extravagantly. But they are too few to close it completely. The result is that the economic system sputters. From time to time it stops altogether. Famed newspaper columnist Walter Lippmann seemed to think that something along these lines had been responsible for the Great Depression: "The heart of the problem . . . [has been] . . . an insufficiency of consumer . . . purchasing power."[9]

President Herbert Hoover probably did not accept the underconsumption theory, at least not in full, but he did believe that falling wages would be disastrous for an economy. After the 1929 Crash, he worked assiduously to secure pledges from leading businessmen that they would not cut wages.

Franklin Roosevelt also opposed wage cuts, and used the National Recovery Act (NRA) to prohibit them. By passing the Wagner Act and other labor legislation, he actually helped push many wages up. Keynes agreed that wage cuts were inadvisable, but did not endorse wage increases either. In his view, rising wages were a positive insofar as they increased consumer purchasing power, but a negative insofar as they increased labor costs. As he said, increasing labor costs would lead to a less

> optimistic tone[10]

among business people. Keynes concluded that

> the net result of the two opposing influences [from rising wages] is to cancel out.[11]

The best policy was therefore neither to cut nor to increase wages in a depression, but rather to leave them where they are.

6. A better case could be made for wage cuts if they could be mandated across the board for all workers.

Keynes noted that

> Except in a socialized community where wage-policy is settled by decree, there is no means of securing uniform wage reductions for every class of labor. . . . It is only in a highly authoritarian society, where sudden, substantial, all-around changes could be decreed that a flexible wage policy could function with success. One can imagine it in operation in [then Fascist] Italy, [then Fascist] Germany or Russia, but not in France, the United States or Great Britain. . . . [Wage reductions that are not across the board] can only be brought about by a series of gradual, irregular changes, justifiable on no criterion of social justice or economic expediency. . . .[12]

7. Whatever the theoretical arguments for or against reducing wages in a depression, it is a completely impractical idea.

In the 19th century, workers accepted wage cuts in order to keep their jobs during a slump. Today this is no longer true. Partly because of the power of labor unions, partly because of unemployment insurance, partly because of a change in expectations, layoffs are the only practical way to reduce labor costs.

8. Wage reductions, even if practicable, would not be fair.

Market forces cannot be relied upon to allocate society's wealth in a just way. The market's

> juggernaut … settle[s the issue] by economic pressure.

The right way to go about it is to fix wages based on

> what is "fair" and "reasonable" … having regard to all
> the circumstances … between classes.[13]

Presumably Keynes would have his expert economic planners decide what wages are "reasonable," but he does not specifically say.

9. Fortunately, it is not necessary to reduce wages (to offset falling prices) during a depression in order to prevent business bankruptcies. There is a better way.

Let us remember that the starting problem is not high wages. It is, rather, that prices have fallen.[ᵘ] The primary lesson to be drawn from this is that prices should never be allowed to fall in the first place. Deflation is poison to an economy. It threatens not only debtors, but everyone.

If preventative measures have failed, and prices are falling, the fall should be promptly arrested. The previous price level should be restored. Once this has been done, wages will not have to be cut and neither profits nor employment will be threatened by unstable prices.

So far so good. But how will prices be prevented from falling, or if they have fallen, restored to the previous level? The answer is simple: government should engineer enough inflation to counteract deflationary forces and thus either maintain or restore previous prices. There are different ways to accomplish this, but the easiest way is for the government to print more money and inject it into the economy.

To see how this might work, take the simple case of two shipwrecked people living on an isolated tropical island. Their "economy" consists of two knives and two dollars rescued from their lost ship. Under these circumstances, we might expect that each knife would be worth $1.

Next assume that two more dollars wash ashore inside a bottle. As a result of this money infusion, each knife is now worth $2. In the same way, government can pull prices up by printing a large amount of new money and injecting it into the economy through any number of channels (lending it through banks, giving it as cash grants, or spending it through the government's budget).

Keynes sums this up by stating that:

> Having regard to human nature and our institutions, it can only be a foolish person who would prefer a flexible wage policy to a flexible money policy.[14]

Keynes thought that the primary purpose of a "flexible money policy" would be to combat deflation, but he thought that it would have other uses as well. In particular, it could be used to manage labor demands. If, during normal times, labor productivity was increasing at 2%, but unions insisted on a 4% wage increase, a 2% inflation would ensure that labor's real (inflation adjusted) raise was not 4%, but rather 2%. As Keynes saw it, workers were mainly concerned with the nominal level of wages, not the real (inflation adjusted) level.[15]

For all of these reasons then, but especially to control hyper-deflation, Keynes called for a policy of

> price raising—which one can call inflation for short—throughout the world.[16]

9

Yes, No, and Again Yes to Economic Globalization

(If this sounds like a mixed message, so it is.
But we will try to sort it out.)

Keynes on a Global Economy and Free Trade

1. Gold is a "barbarous relic."[1]

In his first book, Keynes described the wonders and pleasures of the first real global economy, the one that flourished in his youth before the beginning of World War I. It was a golden age, both metaphorically and materially, since its monetary system rested firmly on a foundation of gold:

> What an extraordinary episode in the economic progress of man that age was which came to an end in August, 1914! The inhabitant of London could order by

telephone, sipping his morning tea in bed, the various products of the whole earth, in such quantity as he might see fit, and reasonably expect their early delivery upon his doorstep; he could at the same moment and by the same means adventure his wealth in the natural resources and new enterprises of any quarter of the world, and share, without exertion or even trouble, in their prospective fruits and advantages; or he could decide to couple the security of his fortunes with the good faith of the townspeople of any substantial municipality in any continent. . . . He could secure forthwith, if he wished it, cheap and comfortable means of transit to any country or climate without passport or other formality, could dispatch his servant to the neighboring office of a bank for such supply of the precious metals as might seem convenient, and could then proceed abroad to foreign quarters, without knowledge of their religion, language, or customs, bearing coined wealth upon his person, and would consider himself greatly aggrieved and much surprised at the least interference. But, most important of all, he regarded this state of affairs as normal, certain, and permanent, except in the direction of further improvement, and any deviation from it as aberrant, scandalous, and avoidable. The projects and politics of militarism and imperialism, of racial and cultural rivalries, of monopolies, restrictions, and exclusion, which were to play the serpent to this paradise, were little more than the amusements of his daily newspaper, and appeared to exercise almost no influence at all on the ordinary course of social and economic life, the internationalization of which was nearly complete in practice.[2]

The classic gold standard of this first global economy meant that the world shared one money. The dollar might represent one fraction of an ounce of gold, the British pound another fraction, the French franc another, but it was all really just the same thing, gold. A few countries relied on silver, but the United States rejected bimetallism (using both metals), so world money became gold.

Despite the advantages of having one world money, Keynes considered the gold standard to be unduly restrictive. It gives a national government little or no control over its own money supply. When interest rates are too high, which, according to Keynes, they tend chronically to be, additional money cannot be printed in order to bring interest rates down.

Keynes thought that our belief in gold is also irrational. He said that its

> prestige [depends on]...color...[even] smell....Dr. Freud related that there are peculiar reasons deep in our subconscious why gold in particular should satisfy strong instincts.[3]

Our primitive relationship with gold had, over the years, been encrusted with rationalizations and evolved into an elaborate yet

outworn dogma.

The challenge for contemporary society is to pierce the veil of ancient superstition in order to fashion

a more scientific [exchange] standard.[v][4]

2. A "gold exchange standard" is better than a "classic gold standard," but not much better.

The classic gold standard was abandoned at the onset of World War I in 1914. It was succeeded in the mid 1920s by a very diluted version called the "gold exchange standard." The "gold exchange standard" gave governments much more control over money, but Keynes still felt that it was a

shackle[5]

and greeted its abandonment during the Great Depression as

the breaking of our gold fetters ... and [a] blessed event.[6]

Efforts to establish a new global monetary and trade system during the Depression failed, primarily because President Roosevelt sent a letter torpedoing the idea at the London Conference of 1933. Many people felt that the Great Depression was thereby deepened and prolonged, but Keynes responded that

President Roosevelt is magnificently right.[7]

At this juncture, Keynes was operating more or less as an economic nationalist who wanted as much freedom of action as possible for Britain.

By the end of World War II, Keynes agreed that a new global monetary and trade system was needed. The system that emerged, named "Bretton Woods" for the New Hampshire resort where it was formally adopted, was yet another gold exchange standard. Keynes reluctantly went along with this because the Americans wanted a gold link. A quarter century later, the US also found gold to be a "shackle" and cast it off in favor of unrestrained paper money system.

3. What is actually needed is a single world monetary authority run on scientific lines.

When "Bretton Woods" finally collapsed in 1971, it was replaced by a "dirty" system of floating rates, that is a system of floating national currency rates that governments increasingly manipulated.

Although Keynes died in 1946 (of chronic heart trouble), he had at different times said both negative and positive things about the concept of floating rates.[8] What he actually preferred, and tried unsuccessfully to establish within the Bretton Woods system, was a supranational agency authorized to create its own paper money:

> We have reached a stage in the evolution of money when a "managed" currency is inevitable, but . . . [this is best entrusted] to a single authority . . . with [the] plenary wisdom [and] scientific management . . . [of] a supernational authority.[9]

Robert Mundell, the Columbia University economist who founded what came to be called supply-side economics, later agreed with Keynes that a single world money system (other than gold) would be desirable: "Ideally the [global] economy ought to have one money, with one central bank, perhaps. [In the meantime], a system of truly fixed exchange rates would simulate a world money. . . ."[w][10]

4. The first global economy, the one that ended with World War I, depended on the classic gold standard, but also on a strong commitment to international trade. In Britain's case, a commitment to international trade meant a commitment to free trade.

Keynes was all over the map about free trade, and he acknowledged as much. He agreed that free trade encouraged nations to specialize, and that a high degree of specialization could make us all much richer. As a young economist, he regarded departures from the free trade doctrine as an

imbecility and . . . outrage.[11]

In 1923, he wrote that

> we must hold to Free Trade, in it widest interpretation,
> as an inflexible dogma.[12]

And also:

> If there is one thing that Protection cannot do, it is to
> cure Unemployment.... The claim to cure Unemploy-
> ment involves the Protectionist fallacy in its grossest
> and crudest form.[13]

Keynes himself cited this last passage in *The General Theory* to
show how far his ideas had changed by 1936.

What changed Keynes's mind was the Great Depression and
the protectionist tide that followed its onset. The United States
passed the infamous Smoot-Hawley Tariff Act (raising trade barriers) in 1930. A thousand American economists condemned it
at the time. Most economists condemn it today for at least deepening and possibly even precipitating the Depression. (It might
have helped precipitate the Depression since hearings on the bill
were underway before the Crash of 1929).

America was already the greatest economy in the world. Its
actions mattered enormously. But America also had a strong tradition of protectionism, at least since the Civil War. Britain, on
the other hand, was by far the leading practitioner and defender
of free trade. How would it respond to the Smoot–Hawley
tariffs?

It was a close thing. Some commentators believe that Keynes's
about face on free trade, his endorsement of protectionism in
the early 1930s,[14] turned the tide.[15] Whether or not this is accurate, Britain did abandon free trade in 1932 in favor of Imperial Preference (free trade within the Empire). This meant that
world trade suffered yet another major blow, and the Depressions deepened.

By 1936, in *The General Theory*, Keynes was reappraising 16th and 17th century Mercantilist doctrine, which had been protectionist, and finding in it an

> element of scientific truth,[16]

but also insisting on

> the ... real and substantial ... advantages of the international division of labor ... [albeit] advantages [that have previously been] overstressed.[x] [17]

On the question of globalization, it seems that Keynes generally approved of a global economy, even though, from time to time, he endorsed economic nationalism, protectionism, capital controls,[18] and so on. He certainly wanted a single world monetary authority, presumably with free trade, so long as someone like himself could run it.

Part Three

Why Keynes
Was Wrong

In Part Three we will begin the process of refuting Keynes's arguments. We will do so by revisiting each chapter and argument from Part Two, repeating Keynes's arguments, sometimes verbatim but usually in condensed form. In each case, we will try to explain what is wrong and *why* it is wrong.

10

"Drive Down Interest Rates"
(and Reap a Whirlwind of Inflation, Bubbles, and Busts)

1a. Keynes: Interest rates are too high.

> The rate of interest is not self-adjusting at a level best suited to the social advantage but constantly tends to rise too high. . . .[1]

1b. Comment: This is a frontal assault on the entire price system.

Keynes does not define any of his terms. He does not say what the "social advantage" is. He does not tell us how we will know when interest rates have fallen far enough. Nevertheless, he has told us something important—that the price system cannot be trusted.

It is important to keep in mind that interest rates are a price, the price of borrowed money. They are not only a price; they are one of the most important prices in an economy. All prices are interconnected, but this price in particular affects all other prices.

Businesses depend on prices to give them the information with which to run the economy. If the price system for interest rates is broken, no part of the price system is unaffected. If the price system is hobbled, it is a very serious matter because attempts to replace market prices with government-imposed prices have not generally been successful. As Oysten Dahle, a Norwegian oil executive, said about the Soviet Union, "[It] collapsed because it did not allow [market] prices to tell the economic truth."[2]

As a rule, we should be extremely wary of any argument that begins by throwing the market price system out the window, but for the moment we will withhold further judgement and see where Keynes is going.

2a. Keynes: High interest rates keep the world poor.

> That the world after several millennia of steady individual saving, is so poor ... is to be explained ... by ... high ... rate[s] of interest.[3]

2b. Comment: Fear of theft, including theft by government, is a more likely explanation.

Why is humanity still so poor? It is a good question. As noted in this author's *Are the Rich Necessary?*, even the tiniest sums, compounded over long periods, become unimaginably large. $10 compounded at 3% a year for 1,000 years would produce a sum over two times the world's total wealth today. Why then has humanity not done better? What has held us back?

Any answer to this question has to be a guess. It is not really a fault of Keynes that he offers no evidence for his particular guess. But are high interest rates really the heart of the matter?

Even Keynes admits that there was always an issue of safety, that rates were high in part because it was not safe to lend.[4] Would it not be reasonable to regard lack of safety as the primary variable here, with high interest rates just a secondary symptom? In most societies throughout history, it was not safe to own property, much less to lend it. The best way to safeguard property was to hide it, which made investment difficult. Why invest if someone else will shortly steal the fruits?

Moreover, throughout history, that someone else was often neither a thief nor a "strongman." It was often the state itself. A well functioning state monopolizes the use of force. It can and does use that force to tax or even to expropriate. Is this not one of the principal reasons that humanity has remained so poor—paralysis of private investment because of fear of seizure by the state? If so, should we not pause before asking the state, as Keynes does, to take a larger and larger role in the economy?

3a. Keynes: Interest rates are high because people refuse to lend or refuse to lend on reasonable terms.

Interest rates are higher than they should be partly because people "hoard" their money out of fear, which creates a shortage of lendable funds and thus drives up rates. Partly because "wealth-owners" simply do not "accept" reasonable rates.[5]

3b. Comment: These are Keynesian flashes (intuitions, hunches), unsupported by any real evidence.

The idea that lenders are obstinately holding out for exorbitant rates is particularly odd. It suggests a one-sided market in which the lenders have all the power and borrowers have little or none. Perhaps Keynes is thinking in Marxist terms, that lenders are powerful because they are rich and borrowers powerless because they are poor. But this is not true. Lenders are not necessarily rich nor borrowers poor.

Most borrowing requires collateral, something that the lender can take in the event of default. To borrow money, one must therefore usually have money. The vast majority of borrowing is done by wealthy people and firms, because they can offer the necessary collateral. Since borrowers are often rich and powerful, why should lenders be able to "rig" the market in their favor?

In many instances, of course, people are both lenders and borrowers, sometimes consecutively, sometimes simultaneously. For example, they may borrow to buy a home, but also lend from their retirement accounts. The market sorts out supply and demand and sets the rate. A refusal to lend at the market rate by any single lender will not make the slightest difference. Neither lender nor borrower can dictate terms in the market for money any more than in the market for other products or property. [Y]

4a. Keynes: The way to bring interest rates down is to create more money.

Government can and should bring interest rates down to a more reasonable level by increasing the "quantity" of lendable funds. This is done by creating new money that is made available to banks to lend. [E] [6]

4b. Comment: Keynes's policy of creating new money to reduce interest rates ultimately backfires. Why? We will explore the reasons step by step.

i. The new money is inflationary.

Keynes is correct that pouring new money into the banking system should, at least initially, bring down interest rates. There is, however, a hitch. As soon as the new money has been borrowed, it will move out into the economy. Once there, it will tend to raise other prices. In other words, it will tend to create inflation.

If the world consists of a knife and two dollars, we may say the knife is "worth" $2. But if the government adds two more dollars, now the knife is worth $4. If the government could inject both "things" and money into the economy, then prices need not rise. But injecting money alone in order to bring down one price (interest rates) will as a general rule just raise other prices.

This is why leading American economists Frank Knight and Jacob Viner, in their reviews of Keynes's *General Theory* in the 1930s, said that it was proposing "inflationary remedies." Economist Melchior Palyi was more blunt: "Stripped of crypto-scientific semantics, the Keynesians's medicine is inflation."[7] This was somewhat ironic, because Keynes had begun his career as an articulate foe of inflationary policies.[z]

ii. Inflation leads to higher, not lower, interest rates.

There is a further hitch. What will happen to interest rates when other prices start to rise? Lenders will of course notice that the money coming back to them at the end of the loan will not buy as much as it once did. This will cause them to stop lending or lend less, which would tend to raise interest rates. Rates may even rise before inflation appears if lenders look into the future and take steps to protect themselves.

This is especially ironic, an example of what economists call an "unintended consequence." The quest to lower interest rates by injecting new money into the economy tends to lead, sooner or later, to higher rates. Swedish economist Knut Wicksell (1851–1926) initially developed this point. No one, including Keynes, has ever refuted it.

iii. The 1970s illustrate how inflationism leads to higher interest rates.

In the United States and elsewhere, printing money throughout the 1960s and 1970s led to very high inflation, which in turn led to very high long-term interest rates. Only decisive action by the chairman of the US Federal Reserve, Paul Volcker, finally broke the inflationary spiral. Volcker stopped printing money, stopped holding short interest rates down, deliberately let the economy plunge into severe recession, suffered intense criticism from national politicians, but was vindicated as inflation receded and the economy bounced back. By the early 1980s, Keynes appeared to be a false prophet, one whose recommendations had led the world to the brink of economic ruin.

iv. The deceptive 1990s.

Did the next decade the 1990s, contradict our arguments and vindicate Keynesian ideas? No. In this case Keynesianism led to bubbles and crashes. But events were genuiniely confusing.

After the deep recession of the early 1980s, governments went back to printing money. Consumer prices rose (doubled in the quarter century after Volcker's recession), but the rise seemed moderate enough by the standards of the 1970s. Interest rates did not rise as the pace of government money printing picked up in the 1990s and beyond; on the contrary, they fell. Without the drag of higher interest rates or a recession, the economy boomed.

Many people thought that this proved Keynes right. Contrary to the evidence of the 1970s, it was possible to inject new money into the economy and reduce interest rates without triggering inflation and then higher interest rates. To see why this is incorrect, we need to look a little more deeply into the 1990s.

a. Masked inflation.

Economist Ludwig von Mises (1881–1973) pointed out that there are times when consumer price inflation is harder to discern. Mises was thinking of the 1920s (before the Crash), but his observations apply to the 1990s and much of the 2000s as well. At these times, the economy is highly productive, which means that business costs fall. In addition, globalization of the labor market brings in cheap goods from countries with lower labor costs. For both reasons, consumer prices should steadily fall. This should especially help poor people, who will be able to buy more with their limited incomes. But everyone should benefit from being able to buy more with less.

If prices should fall by, say, 3% a year, but in fact rise by 3%, what is happening? The explanation is that government is creating (and injecting into the economy) enough new money to raise prices 6%. Of course, this is masked. It appears that prices are only rising 3%, when they are actually rising 6%.

b. Underreported inflation.

Government inflation statistics may also mislead. Under the Reagan administration in the 1980s, Social Security benefits and other government programs became linked to the calculation of consumer inflation. Coincidentally or not, new procedures for calculating inflation were developed under the Clinton administration in the 1990s which generally resulted in a lower inflation rate. Even the old method excluded house price changes, so none of the housing bubble showed up in reported consumer prices.[AA]

c. Asset inflation.

Government inflation indexes only track the prices of consumer goods. But new money from the government does not flow solely into consumer goods. It may flow into stocks, as it did in the 1990s.

It may flow into homes, as it did in the 1990s and 2000s. It may flow into other investment assets, as it did in both periods. It may flow into art and collectibles. Since the government's new money enters the economy through banks as lendable funds, it all depends on who borrows the money and how they use it.

d. Bubbles.

Masked inflation, underreported inflation, and asset inflation all work together to create a bubble. What looks like moderate consumer price inflation helps keep interest rates down. This in turn makes it easier to borrow greater and greater sums of money to invest in assets such as stocks or real estate. As the prices of these assets rise because of all the borrowed money being funneled into them, lenders are all the more willing to lend against the assets, and borrowers are all the more willing to borrow to buy more of them. Before long, all the new money channeled into investment assets has created a full-scale bubble.

e. The dot-com and housing bubbles.

In the 1990s, corporations borrowed much of the new money flowing into the economy and used it to buy up their stock. Stock prices soared; the public noticed and started buying stocks too. Fed Chairman Alan Greenspan said we were in a "new era," the bubble grew and grew until finally consumer price inflation began to move up, interest rates rose (a bit), and the bubble popped.

The Fed responded along Keynesian lines by driving interest rates down to 1%. It held them there for a year and below the rate of reported consumer inflation for three years. This was tantamount to giving money away. It led inexorably to the housing bubble and then the collapse of the housing bubble starting in 2007. Toward the end of the housing bubble, interest rates finally began to rise.

v. The bottom line: government efforts to reduce interest rates create conditions that lead to crashes.

Newly "printed" money, injected into the economy through the banking system by government always leads to inflation, if inflation is properly understood and properly defined. This inflation will in turn lead to crashes.

As Ludwig von Mises, Keynes's most systematic critic, concluded,

> The cyclical fluctuations of business are not an occurrence originating in the sphere of the unhampered market, but a product of government interference with business conditions designed to lower the rate of interest below the height at which the free market would have fixed it.[BB] [8]

This means that artificially low interest rates will, in the long run, lead not to boom, but to boom and bust, although the path to bust may lead either through consumer price inflation or through an economic bubble.

One might object to Mises's argument on the following grounds. Since economic boom/bust cycles have been a feature of economic life for centuries (if not longer), how can Keynesian policies be blamed for them? The short answer is that Keynes did not invent inflationism. Although boom/bust cycles predated Keynes and his particular inflationary policies, government efforts to thwart the price system and reduce interest rates are as old as human recorded history. Indeed price controls and interest rate controls are inscribed (literally on stone) in the ancient Babylonian law code of Hammurabi.

There have been eras of less government interference and more government interference with prices and interest rates. But even in the so-called era of laissez-faire that ended with World War I, banking laws and regulations expanded the money supply, artificially reduced interest rates, and thus destabilized the economic environment. We will discuss this further in a later chapter.[cc]

5a. Keynes: Money injected into the economy is no different than traditional savings.

Fears of government intervention and of a government-engineered increase in the amount of money circulating in the economy are ill founded. New money that has been injected into the banking system is

> just as genuine as any other savings.[9]

5b. Comment: Money created by the government is not savings; it destroys savings.

It is Orwellian to refer to newly printed government money as "savings." Whatever the merits or demerits of "printing press" money, it is not the same as savings. The word savings describes money that has been earned, and having been earned, is not spent but rather is set aside for emergency or investment use.

Nor should we imagine that the government's newly printed money will just augment or "top off" traditional savings. This concept is completely erroneous. The government's new money will eventually destroy traditional savings. This is true because the resulting inflation, whether overt or stealthy, will ultimately erode the purchasing power of traditional savings and thus ruin the saver, especially the small saver.

This is why Malcolm Bryan, president of the Federal Reserve Bank of Atlanta, said in 1957:

> If a [government] policy of active or permissive inflation is to be a fact . . . we should have the decency to say to the money saver, "Hold still, Little Fish! All we intend to do is to gut you."[10]

6a. Keynes: There is nothing special about existing interest rates.

> [Since] there is no special virtue in the pre-existing [high] rate of interest . . . [there can be no] evil [in bringing it down by government intervention].[11]

6b. Comment: There is something very special about existing interest rates if they are market rates.

The price system is essential. It communicates reliable supply and demand information to all market participants and thus coordinates the entire economy. Together with the carrot of profit and the stick of business failure and bankruptcy, it helps us achieve the largest amount and the highest quality of production at the lowest possible cost.[12] If one accepts this basic point, then all free prices are "special," but the price of borrowed money is, if anything, even more "special," because of the central role it plays in the economy.

If one rejects the price system, it is logically necessary to suggest an alternative. Economist Ludwig von Mises, in his book *Socialism*, suggested that there is no conceivable (workable) alternative. If so, we must be careful about deranging the price system.

7a. Keynes: Interest rates (and stock dividends) should be brought to zero.

> I should guess that a properly run community . . . ought to be able to bring down the [general rate of business profit and the prevailing interest rate] approximately to zero within a single generation. [The owner of capital would then] no longer receive a bonus. [13]

> The . . . owner of capital [is essentially] . . . functionless. . . . [He or she] can obtain interest because capital

is scarce. But . . . there can be no intrinsic reason for the scarcity of capital [since government can always print and distribute more of it].[14]

[Making capital freely available] may be the most sensible way of gradually getting rid of many of the objectionable features of capitalism. The rentier [wealthy lender or investor] would disappear . . . and [so would] the cumulative oppressive power of the capitalist to exploit the scarcity-value of capital.[15]

7b. Comments:

i. Zero interest rates are nonsensical.

It could be argued that the US Federal Reserve, by setting short-term interest rates below the rate of inflation during the housing bubble years, has already experimented with the concept of lending for free. But Keynes was advocating something even more extreme: interest rates at zero. Is this realistic? Can interest rates ever be brought down to zero, much less within a generation?

If we can borrow money for free, it implies that money has no value. If it can be borrowed at no cost, why even bother to pay it back? Is there really any difference between giving money away and lending it at no interest? Economist Ludwig von Mises explains how utterly nonsensical this is:

There cannot be any question of abolishing interest by any institutions, laws, or devices of bank manipulation [such as the government injecting new money into the lending system through banks]. He who wants to "abolish" interest will have to induce people to value an apple available in a hundred years no less than a present apple.[16]

ii. This is like Marxism, but with the lender rather than the business owner as villain.

Keynes's glancing reference to the "oppressive power of the capitalist to exploit" is also interesting. What exactly does it mean? Does it mean that the charging of any interest is illegitimate or immoral?

Economic writer Henry Hazlitt says about Keynes's passage:

> This, of course, is a naked class theory of the business cycle . . . strikingly similar to Marx['s]. As with Marxism, the tacit assumption is that these government policies are necessary to protect the poor and discomfort the rich. But as also with Marxism, there is the pose that morality has nothing to do with it; that the existing "system" just won't work and must break down.
>
> The chief difference between Marxism and Keynesianism is that for the former the employer is the chief villain, and for the latter the lender.[17]

iii. Keynes and Proudhon

Marx of course did not invent socialism, and Keynes has features in common with other socialists. One of them, Pierre-Joseph Proudhon (1809–1865), is best known for saying that "property is theft." But he also invented the idea of "credit gratuit," free loans, the very idea which Keynes promotes.

iv. What "credit gratuit" really means.

There is a further point to be made about Keynes's version of "credit gratuit," a point also made by Hazlitt. If business profits and interest rates reach zero, as Keynes hopes they will, this implies that nothing will cost much. Humanity will have achieved an economic utopia with scarcity abolished.

v. Can scarcity be abolished through the Keynesian program of driving down interest rates?

To try to answer this question, consider two variant views on human poverty:

>   A. Billions of human beings live in poverty because food, clothing, shelter, and amenities are still scarce, which makes them expensive. In order for the entire human race to escape poverty, we need to work hard, save, and invest in order to produce more and better goods more cheaply.

>   B. The problem is not that goods are scarce. It is that money is scarce. Government should distribute more cash so that everyone has enough.

Most people will readily see that B is a fallacy. It will not work. Even if we gave every poor person $1 million a year, it would not help them, because there would be more money in the world, but there would be no more food, clothing, shelter, and amenities. The only result from a flood of new money would be soaring prices. People who had been poor on $300 a year would now be poor on $1 million a year.[DD]

Now let us consider a third alternative:

>   C. The problem is not that goods are scarce. It is that lendable money is scarce. If government will provide unlimited funds to borrow, we can invest those funds in new factories and businesses and, within a generation, nothing will be scarce.

C is Keynes's solution, and unfortunately it is just as much of a fallacy as B. Printing money and lending it to people will have the same result as printing money and giving it to people. It will either make existing goods and services cost more, in which case we will call it inflation. Or it will make assets cost more, in which case we will call it a bubble. Either way, it is really inflation.

vi. It is rich, not poor, people who benefit from inflation.

We know that inflation does not end poverty. It just makes poor people poorer, as numerous economic studies attest.[18] If anyone is going to make money from inflation, it is rich people, especially Wall Streeters and other financial insiders.

Rich people (or their advisors) understand what is happening. They understand the system. They are also, usually, the people who receive the government's new money first, the initial borrowers. They then lend it to others and make exorbitant profits in the process. President Andrew Jackson foresaw all this in the 19th century. He abolished the United States' first central bank because he observed rich people taking control of it and using it for their own ends.

vii. The creation of modern central banks has facilitated Keynes's inflationism.

The basic Keynesian fallacy expressed here—the idea that the government can create prosperity by printing money and lending it—was embodied in the very legislation that created the United States' second central bank, the Federal Reserve, in 1913. As Federal Reserve Chairman Alan Greenspan described the legislation in a youthful essay:

> If banks can continue to loan money indefinitely—it was claimed—there need never be any slumps in business. [The legislation was intended to ensure that] banks [would] never be short of cash [for loans].[19]

Before the creation of the Federal Reserve, there were episodes of American inflation (such as the Civil War), but over time the dollar kept its purchasing power. By contrast, since the creation of the Fed, the dollar has lost over 95% of its purchasing power.

8a. Keynes: By continually lowering interest rates, we can abolish slumps and enjoy a state of perpetual quasi-boom.

> It may appear extraordinary that a school of thought should exist which finds the solution for the trade cycle in checking the boom in its early stages [before problems arise] by a higher rate of interest. . . .[20] The remedy for the boom is not a higher rate of interest but a lower rate of interest! For that may enable the boom to last. The right remedy for the trade cycle is not to be found in abolishing booms and thus keeping us permanently in a semi-slump; but in abolishing slumps and thus keeping us permanently in a quasi-boom.[21]

8b. Comments:

i. As we have seen, this is a formula for creating inflations, bubbles, and crashes.

Is it possible to abolish slumps and live forever happily in a state of quasi-boom? US Federal Reserve Chairman Alan Greenspan experimented with this idea in the 1990s and 2000s and just produced bubbles.

Paul Krugman, Nobel Prize winning economist and fervent Keynesian, agrees that it should be possible to avert slumps, and if necessary to cure them, by running the government's printing press to reduce interest rates, and thereby to increase the demand for loans. He writes that "to many people it seems obvious that massive economic slumps have deep roots. To them, [the argument] that they can be cured by [the government] printing a bit more money seems unbelievable."[22]

In reading this, we should pay close attention to the words "a bit more money." If printing "a bit more money" will "cure" a "massive economic slump," then only the tiniest amount of newly printed money should be needed to keep a boom going. But this has not proved to be the case. In fact, larger and larger amounts of new money are needed to keep a bubble from popping. Eventually all the debt associated with the new money becomes too great a burden for the economy and everything collapses.

ii. There is a diminishing return to taking on debt.

In the United States, we have operated on Keynesian principles since World War II. The government has printed money. Debt levels have grown. We have not only gotten inflations and bubbles. We have also gotten less and less growth for each increment of debt.

During the decade 1950–1959, we added $338 billion in debt, and we got 73¢ in economic growth (increase in gross domestic product) for each $1 in new debt. For the decade 1990–1999, we added $12.5 trillion in debt, but got only 31¢ of growth per dollar of debt. For the seven plus years 2000–2008 (1st quarter), we added $24.3 trillion in debt, but got only 19¢ in growth for every dollar of debt.[23] It thus required more and more debt to generate further growth.

iii. Eventually the return on debt becomes negative.

By the end of 2007, the debt machine shuddered and threatened to fail. Fed Chairman Bernanke immediately reduced interest rates to emergency levels. Wall Street took one last gulp of cheap credit. But it did not work. The crash came anyway.

What is actually happening here? Henry Hazlitt again explains:

> If one truth concerning economic crises has been es-
> tablished . . . it is that they are typically brought on by
> cheap money—i.e., low interest rate policies that en-
> courage excessive borrowing, excessive credit expan-
> sion, imprudent speculation, and all the distortions
> and instabilities in the economy that these finally bring
> about. . . . A policy of perpetual cheap money [pro-
> duces] boom and bust, [not the perpetual quasi-boom
> that Keynes promised].[24]

9a. Keynes: High interest rates caused the Depression.

> I attribute the slump of 1930, [the Great Depression]
> primarily to the . . . effects . . . of dear [expensive]
> money which preceded the stock market collapse [of
> 1929], and only secondarily to the collapse itself.[25]

9b. Comment: On the contrary, cheap loans produced, first a bubble, and then a Crash in 1929.

In Keynes's version of events, it was fear of the boom that led the
US Federal Reserve to raise already too high interest rates in the
late 1920s. This supposedly choked off the boom and led to the
Great Depression.

The best short account of what really led to the Great Depression is found in Paul Johnson's *Modern Times*. Johnson in turn
drew heavily on economist Murray Rothbard's *The Great Depression*, the most authoritative source. Rothbard drew to some
degree on Lionel Robbins's book of the same title.

Both Rothbard and Robbins were in turn influenced by Austrian economists Ludwig von Mises and his protégé Friedrich

Hayek, although Robbins later converted to Keynesianism. An excellent recent account of the Depression is Amity Shlaes's *The Forgotten Man*.

What these books reveal is that the US Federal Reserve did indeed bring us the Great Depression, but not in the way that Keynes said. The Crash of 1929 was caused by the US Federal Reserve's cheap loan policy throughout the 1920s. Low interest rates blew up a bubble remarkably similar to the US stock market and housing bubbles that began in the 1990s. The Crash of 1929 presaged the Crash of 2008 seventy-nine years later.

There are indeed many parallels between the two crashes. In both cases, the primary cause was reckless central bank policies that blew up unsustainable bubbles. In both cases, central banks were following what came to be known as Keynesian policies. We will discuss the Depression further in subsequent chapters.[EE]

10a. Keynes: Booms are not wasteful.

The idea that investment funds will be wasted on unsound and speculative ventures during a boom is a

> serious error.[26]

Businesses may get a bit carried away and invest in ventures which will not earn enough to cover

> excessive[ly] high [interest costs].[27]

But the solution to that problem is to lower interest costs. In general, so long as humanity remains poor, almost any investment is better than no investment at all, which is what a slump will bring.[28] The conclusion is simple:

> We should avoid [high interest rates] . . . as we would hell-fire.[29]

10b. Comment: Contrary to Keynes, bubbles are extremely wasteful.

A large quantity of investment, all else being equal, is a plus. Investment raises our standard of living and helps eliminate poverty. But it is quality of investment that counts most.

Business investments that are unproductive, or that fail to pay for themselves, are wasteful. Unfortunately, these are just the kind of investments that we get during a bubble. We get "dotcom" businesses with no earnings and no prospects for future earnings. Or we get masses of housing that will not improve productivity and that, even worse, will turn out to be unneeded or unaffordable.

A rational and useful investment meets the test of paying for itself under a regime of normal, market interest rates. That is what the market test is for—to help weed out irrational and wasteful ideas.

11a. Keynes: We need not worry that creating and sustaining booms with low interest rates will lead to inflation.

It is unlikely that a boom will lead to true inflation.[30]

Booms may create

bottle-necks

in which the price of some products rise.[31] But we cannot

declare that conditions of inflation have set in

until unemployment has completely disappeared.[32]

11b. Comment: The idea that inflation appears all at once when the last unemployed person gets a job is preposterous. The record of the 1970s refutes it.

Characteristically, Keynes did not define full employment. Sir William Beveridge, a Keynesian whose "Beveridge Report" laid the foundation for the British welfare state after World War II, defined full employment as more job openings than people. Keynes offered different definitions at different times, and left the impression that the definition would depend on circumstances.

Followers of Keynes in the 1950s often shifted the focus from employment, which can be defined in many ways, to industrial production. So long as industrial production remained below some specified number (such as 80%) they thought there was virtually no chance of inflation, not even if the government injected a lot of new money into the economy. All the new money would just raise industrial production or employment, not prices.

Later, as the industrial sector of the economy declined, Keynesians's focus shifted from industrial capacity to an economy wide "output gap," defined as the difference between actual gross domestic product and "potential" GDP. Using this concept, inflation, if it came, would arrive after the output gap (and potential employees) had all been utilized.

The trouble with all these concepts is that neither idle capacity nor idle employees soak up newly printed money. That money still creates inflation, whether of the visible or the disguised kind. Inflation may help create an artificial boom, with temporarily lower unemployment, but it will not be sustainable.

In the 1960s and 1970s, Keynesians were chagrined by the increasingly rampant inflation at a time when capacity was not fully utilized. They were equally dumbfounded by the appearance of stagflation, the combination of unemployment and inflation.

12a. Keynes: If necessary, inflation can be controlled by taxes.

In the unlikely event that full employment does arrive (accompanied by inflation), there are better remedies than

clapping on a higher rate of interest.[33]

Instead of increasing interest rates, government should raise taxes, run a budget surplus, and keep the extra cash idle.[34] This will drain purchasing power out of the economy and bring prices back down.

12b. Comment: The idea of governments successfully creating a budget surplus in order to combat inflation is completely fanciful.

Very high taxes actually make a budget surplus harder to achieve, because they reduce economic output and thus reduce government tax revenues. The Great Inflation of the 1970s again provides some real life evidence.

The US government's so-called policy mix through most of the 1970s was completely Keynesian: low interest rates (in relation to inflation) combined with very high tax rates (over 70% at the top bracket). If Keynes was right, the high taxes should have braked inflation, but instead it was spiraling out of control.

As previously noted, the new chairman of the Federal Reserve, Paul Volcker, abandoned Keynesian orthodoxy in the late 1970s by curtailing the printing of money. President Ronald Reagan meanwhile persuaded Congress to reduce taxes dramatically, which further broke the Keynesian mold. Most Keynesian economists warned that it would not work. But the inflationary spiral subsided, the economy recovered, and Reagan was reelected in a landslide.

The 1980s stand out as the decade when the US, and also Britain, appeared to take a post-Keynesian course. Policy changed in important respects. At the same time, key Keynesian assumptions remained. The Federal Reserve, that is, government, still controlled and managed interest rates. Governments still ran massive budget deficits, even if the deficits were now driven by a combination of tax cuts and government spending rather than by government spending alone.

By the end of the 1980s, conventional Keynesians once again took command of the American economy. One of the most prominent of them, Alan Greenspan, was appointed Federal Reserve Chairman by Ronald Reagan himself.

13a. Keynes: High tax rates also contribute to a more just society.

Progressive income taxes, in which the rich pay a higher and higher tax rate, help to reduce economic inequality:

> [An] outstanding fault of the economic society in which we live [is] its arbitrary and inequitable distribution of wealth and incomes.[35]

Keynes thought that high income and death (estate) taxes had already done much to make a more economically just society. But governments had hesitated to go further because they were persuaded that the rich are best able to save, and that their savings are needed to finance much-needed investment.[36] Keynes's program of financing investment with newly printed money injected into the banking system helps solve this problem. Thanks to this innovation, society need no longer depend on the savings of the rich.

13b. Comment: High tax rates are economically counterproductive.

We will not attempt to sort out the equity versus inequity of wealth inequalities (see this author's *Are the Rich Necessary?*).

With regard to high taxes, as usual Keynes does not tell us what "high" means. He seems to have said different things about it at different times.

The heart of Keynes's argument is that newly printed money can take the place of traditional savings. We have already seen that this is fallacious. Printing more and more money just brings inflation or bubble followed by crash and slump, not perpetual "semi-boom." We need traditional savings. Without traditional savings, there will be no real funds to invest. The savings of the rich are especially important because they save the most. High tax rates are inadvisable for this reason alone.

Yes, a country may be able to borrow traditional savings from abroad. The United States did so for decades. If the borrowed funds are put into productivity-enhancing investments with a high return (not the case with the US), it may work out well, at least for a time. But in the long run, no country can escape the need for traditional savings, at least if it wishes to grow and prosper.

There are many other arguments against high taxes: that they will destroy economic incentives, that they will be evaded, that they will be wasted, that they will lead to government corruption as tax relief is exchanged by politicians for campaign contributions.* But, above all, there is the need for savings. No government ever saves, so if we want savings, we had better control taxes.

---

* See Note FF and chapter 14

14a. Keynes: As important as low interest rates are, they may not be enough.

If the government prints a great deal of new money and injects it into the banking system, interest rates should fall.[GG] But if they do not fall far enough, other measures will be required to boost investment.

Keynes thought it possible that cheap new money from the government might not fully succeed in driving interest rates down to the "optimum" low level.[37] This is because "wealth-owners," who have not yet been completely displaced as lenders, might find low rates "unacceptable" and succeed in blocking them. If so,

> the State, which is in a position to calculate ... on long views and on the basis of the general social advantage ... [will have to] directly organiz[e] ... investment.[38]

The application of cheap loan rates along with direct government investment is also the essential prescription for handling an economic crash, an idea that will be further developed in later chapters.

14b. Comment:

To be discussed in chapters 12, 13, and 15.

15a. Keynes: If low interest rates could be orchestrated at the global level, that would be even better.

For now, national governments must take the necessary actions to bring interest rates down and keep them low. Eventually, global institutions might assist in this task.

Keynes hoped that what became known as the International Monetary Fund would instead be called a bank. He further hoped that it would act as a global central bank with the power to print new money and inject it into the global economic system in order to reduce interest rates.[39]

15b. Comment:

To be discussed in chapter 17.

16a. Keynes: The need for lower interest rates is not a completely new idea.

We should pay our respects to the army of heretics and cranks,[40]

who in earlier periods argued for lower interest rates.

Among these in particular are sixteenth and seventeenth century Mercantilists whose doctrines contained an

element of scientific truth.[41]

16b. Comment: There are several ironies here.

Keynes is supposed to have invented a "new economics." He leads us to think so in the earlier chapters of *The General Theory*. He then confusingly tells us later in *The General Theory* that he is really reviving and refurbishing Mercantilist ideas from the 16th and 17th centuries, ideas that economists over the years had come to dismiss as gross fallacies. The truth is that Keynes's ideas are neither new nor correct.

It is also ironic that Keynes, who liked to number himself among the heretics and cranks, has now become so deeply entrenched in the conventional wisdom of world governments. There are those who think that, if alive today, he might not have become a Keynesian heretic, if only to keep fresh waters flowing. Perhaps. We shall have more to say about that in chapter 18. But, for the moment, it is Keynes's critics who must face dismissal and scorn as "heretics and cranks."

It is always a perilous business to point out that "the emperor has no clothes." If one dares to look, Keynes is an especially naked figure, in the sense that his work is so remarkably unsupported by evidence or logic. What he really offers (when the opaquely jargonish arguments are finally parsed) is a kind of shamanic utterance that we are supposed to take more or less on faith.

11

Spend More, Save Less, and Grow Poorer

1a. Keynes: We need more consumption.

Consumption—to [state] the obvious—is the sole ... object of all economic activity.[1]

The "purposive" man is always trying to secure a spurious and delusive immortality. ... He does not love his cat, but his cat's kittens; nor, in truth, the kittens, but only the kittens' kittens, and so on forward forever to the end of cat-dom. For him jam is not jam unless it is a case of jam tomorrow and never jam today.[2]

1b. Comments:

i. Keynes did not practice what he preached.

Perhaps Keynes was preaching to himself. He was certainly "purposive." He was himself (dare we say it?) a saver. His investment capital did not have an immaculate conception—the original stake was mostly saved prior to 1919.[3] Keynes pere did rescue his son at one point from debts related to catastrophic investment losses, but did not otherwise stake him.

After Keynes had accumulated investment capital, he did not spend it, but instead carefully nursed and tended it until, after several major investment setbacks, he finally became rich. When rich, he seems to have lived off his income, and did everything he could to become richer. Moreover, Keynes was childless. Apart from caring for his wife, he had no particular reason to want to die with a large estate.

ii. Keynes was not a vulgar Keynesian.

Keynes was also a person of refined tastes. If he were alive today, we can only imagine what he would have thought of the vulgar Keynesianism that his ideas spawned, the borrow-and-spend culture that not only abhors saving, but actually approves of getting deeper and deeper in debt each year? Would he be happy about financial companies routinely sending credit cards to college students, the same students who are already in many cases indentured to massive student loans provided directly or indirectly by the government?[HH]

By 2005, half of Americans under age 35 had unpaid credit card balances averaging $3,741, in addition to educational, car, home, or other debts.[4] One critic has referred to this as "a new form of feudalism,"[5] with young debtors as chained to their debts as serfs once were to their lord's estate. Unfortunately young people have no reason to regard this as abnormal. In many cases they have grown up in households owning more cars than drivers (1.9 vehicles per 1.75 drivers on average in America in 2008).[6] Just as often, their parents have saved nothing at all (zero average savings rate as of same date).

We will recall that Keynes planned to replace private savings with newly printed money injected into the economy via the banking system. But he seemed to assume that this newly printed money would be used either for business investment or government public works projects such as roads. Even he might have blanched at the prospect of consumers borrowing this ersatz money to finance their lifestyle during the dot-com and housing bubbles.

iii. Consumption is not the largest part of an economy.

Is consumption then the sole object of all economic activity? No. It is one of several activities, each of which must be in balance, both for the individual and for society as a whole. Even US economic statistics, which have been constructed on Keynesian principles, tend to mislead in this regard. We are told that consumer spending represents 70% of the economy. But that is only because all the business transactions—sales by one business to another as the final product is assembled—have been netted out. If not calculated in this way, production is a bigger part of the economy than consumption.

2a. Keynes: The paradoxical parable of the cake that is baked but never eaten.

> 19th century capitalists turned self-denial and thrift into a kind of religion. But it was a religion based on "bluff or deception."[7]
>
> On the one hand the laboring classes . . . could call their own very little of the cake that they and Nature and the capitalists were cooperating to produce. And on the other hand the capitalist classes were allowed to call the best part of the cake theirs and were theoretically free to consume it, on the tacit underlying condition that they consumed very little of it in practice.

The duty of "saving" became nine-tenths of virtue and the growth of the cake the object of true religion. . . . And so the cake increased; but to what end was not clearly contemplated. . . . Saving was for old age or for your children; but this was only in theory—the virtue of the cake was that it was never to be consumed, neither by you nor by your children after you.[8]

2b. Comments:

i. Applause (for the satire).

ii. Now the facts.

Living conditions for workers significantly improved throughout the 18th and 19th centuries. Moreover, the population doubled and then doubled again. Only a growing cake, made possible by saving and investment, fed all those extra mouths. As Henry Hazlitt has pointed out, many of us owe our very lives to the growing cake, because population could not have grown so rapidly without it.

A growing cake allows both owners and workers to increase personal consumption as well as saving. Assume that our incomes are growing at 3% a year, thanks to the investments we have made from our savings. If we keep spending 80% and saving 20% year after year, both the amount spent and the amount saved will double by the 25th year.

Even if our only ambition is to spend more, saving and investing still makes sense, because it will give us more and more money to spend, and we will not have to wait 25 years to feel the effect. Assume that my friend and I have an identical starting income. My friend spends 100% of it. I save 20% and as a result my income grows at 3%. Within only eight years, I will have more to spend than my friend, and after that the gap will steadily grow.

3a. Keynes: The Cult of Saving

> The morals, the politics, the literature, and the reli-
> gion of the . . . [19th century] joined in a grand con-
> spiracy for the promotion of saving. God and Mam-
> mon were reconciled. Peace on earth to men of good
> means. A rich man could, after all, enter into the
> Kingdom of Heaven—if only he saved.[9]

The "classical" economists played a pivotal role as secular priests propagating and safeguarding the dogma of saving. Yes, they said, spending was needed to make an economy work. If the baker buys fruits and vegetables from the greengrocer, the greengrocer will then have money with which to buy bread from the baker. But saving was another, much more special, form of spending. When we save, the money does not simply disappear. It is spent on expanding businesses, making them more efficient. If we work hard, produce, and save, we will enjoy a cornucopia of cheaper, better, and more abundant products. By this means, we will over-come unemployment, slump, and, in the long run, poverty.

The Cult of Saving thus

> conquered England as completely as the Holy Inqui-
> sition conquered Spain.[10]

3b. Comments:

i. Applause.

These little satirical burlesques are a Keynesian specialty. First, the greedy capitalists (think of Dickens's Scrooge paradoxically redeemed not by the spirit of Christmas, but by his own stingi-ness). Next the "classical" economists oppressing England like hooded priests of the Inquisition. It is all good theater. Some clar-ifications, however, are in order.

ii. There were no "classical" economists.

The term "classical" economist is a straw man, a caricature set up only to tear down. Economists from the 18th, 19th, and even 20th centuries cannot be lumped together as if they speak with one voice.

iii. The named economists have been misrepresented.

The named parties—David Ricardo, J. S. Mill, J. B. Say, et al—did believe in hard work, production, and saving as a reliable route to prosperity. But they did not suggest that those three principles alone would bring us to an economic utopia free of unemployment and slump. To minimize unemployment and slump, they would have said, requires, in addition to hard work, production, and saving, at the very least an unhampered price and profit system.

It is often said that Keynes refuted economists such as Ricardo, Mill, and Say. It is more accurate to say that he deliberately misrepresented them and still failed to refute them.

iv. Say was right; Keynes wrong.

Consider, for example, Keynes's alleged refutation of Say's Law. Say's Law tells us that if society works and produces, it will have the means to buy what it produces. This takes the basic idea that the greengrocer, by selling fruits and vegetables, will have the money to buy bread from the baker, and vice versa, and expands it to society as a whole. By producing, society will earn money, and that money will buy the production.[11]

What might be called Keynes's Law, in contrast to Say's, may be stated as follows. If society spends, the goods will be produced. This is also true, because production and spending are really inseparable, just two sides of the same coin. But it is nevertheless deeply misleading.

In the circular flow of production and spending, it is production that has pride of place. If we are shipwrecked on a deserted island, having money to spend will not help at all. If we do not produce, we will starve.

Even back in civilization, it is producers who have a chance to grow rich. Spenders more often than not end up poor. It is production that determines how much we can afford to spend, not the reverse.

It is true that we can spend more than we produce by borrowing. But only for a time, not indefinitely. We may also be able to increase our spending by running money off a printing press in our basement. If we are a government, we will not be jailed for this counterfeiting. But it will not make us richer in the long run, because for society as a whole the extra money will just lead to inflation of one kind or another.

Mill and Say were right; Keynes was wrong. There is no substitute for hard work, production, and saving, operating within an unhampered price and profit system. To argue otherwise is to resort to sophistry. Moreover, this is dangerous sophistry which impoverishes not only individuals, but entire societies.

4a. Keynes: The trouble with savings is that they are often not invested. Lying fallow, they reduce demand. As demand falls, so does the economy.

If societies produce and save and the savings are smoothly and fully invested, all will be well. But that is the rub—there is no certainty whatever that savings will be invested.

Perhaps the savers will want too high a rate of interest, higher than the business owners can pay.[11] Perhaps business owners or managers are lacking in the confidence or conviction required to borrow and invest. Perhaps the saver will simply decide not to lend—to hoard cash instead.

We should keep in mind that

> an act of individual saving means—so to speak—a de-
> cision not to have dinner today. But it does not neces-
> sitate a decision [either] to have dinner a week hence
> or a year hence [or to invest what is not spent].[12]

It is

"absurd"

to think that investment will be increased by one pound or one dollar for every pound or dollar that is not spent on consumption.[13]

4b. Comments:

i. Savings do not ordinarily go unused.

The picture of savers zealously skipping dinner, not to lose a
pound of flesh, but to gain a pound of money, is another burlesque. Savers do not customarily skip dinner.

What about the other assertions? Do savings often sit idle, clog-
ging up the economic system, reducing the Demand that allegedly drives economic growth? There is no reason to expect this
to happen. People generally save in order to earn money on the
savings. They do this by investing it. If savings are converted into
investments, the money will be spent on business expansion—on
new employees, new equipment, new facilities—and thus will
flow back into the economy. As it flows back into the economy,
it can be used to buy the products that investment brings us. This
in turn will bring employment, profits, and more savings. There
is no reason why this circular flow cannot continue indefinitely.

ii. Savers do not control interest rates.

Keynes responds that savers often want too high a rate of interest,
higher than business owners can pay. As we discussed in the last

chapter, this assumes a fanciful one-sided market. A free money market is two-sided, and it "solves" for the interest rate that will ensure investment of all available funds.

iii. If savers lack the confidence to invest, we must ask why.

Keynes also says that business owners or investors may lack the confidence necessary to borrow and invest. This certainly happens during an economic crisis, but there is a good reason for it then. It means that some element of the price and profit system is temporarily deranged, and savers must be very careful not to lose their savings. For example, consumer prices may be rising (inflation) or falling too fast (severe deflation), or asset prices may be collapsing.[KK]

Ironically, the most likely source of a destabilizing inflation is the same new money that Keynes wants government to print. The most likely source of severe deflation is the inflation, visible or disguised, which typically precedes it. In either case, the problem is not uninvested savings; they are just symptomatic of a larger problem. Under these circumstances, Keynesian inflationary policies will just make the problem worse.

Finally Keynes says that savers may simply decide not to invest, to hoard cash instead. Well, everyone does need a bit of idle cash. We keep a few dollar bills in our wallet for emergencies. Lacking an emergency, this cash may never be spent.

But we do not ordinarily keep cash under the proverbial mattress or in a lockbox. We invest it. If we do not invest, it is not because of some atavistic need to hoard. It is almost always because we are worried and do not want to waste our precious capital.[LL]

iv. John Stuart Mill refutes Keynes.

During the 19th century, economics in England might be said to have been dominated by John Stuart Mill (1806–1873), one of the "classical" economists criticized by Keynes. His economic textbook, *Principles of Political Economy*, was published in 1848 and reigned supreme in England and America for half a century.

Hazlitt found a Mill essay in which he specifically addresses the Keynesian idea that savings might accumulate, unused, and clog up the economic system. In this essay, Mill concludes that it is a

"palpable absurdity."[13]

Why? Because, as we already noted, the lure of a return, of profit, ensures that savings are invested and flow into the spending stream. Unlike consumer spending, investment spending helps production grow, and thus leads to more income, and more consumer spending, and more saving down the road. There is only one caveat: to make this happen, prices (including wages) must be unhampered. The profit system must be respected.

This does not mean, per Mills, that no savings, no capital, are ever "idle." We may even have "a large proportion of capital . . . idle."[14] This is because the economy is always changing. Demand is increasing here, decreasing there. Some businesses will be contracting, some expanding. There will inevitably be some idle capital and some related unemployment as a result of these changes. This is not to be regretted. It is the price of economic advance. Without these changes, dislocations, and reallocations of capital, we would still be living in caves.

Whenever we see all capital employed, almost all businesses thriving and expanding, this should serve as a warning. We are not seeing an economic advance; we are seeing a bubble. It means, as Mill said, that

some general delusion is afloat.[15]

It is not that Mill is an old fogy, that he is only happy when large numbers of people are out of work. If wages are allowed to float freely with other prices, almost everyone who wants a job should be able to find one without a long wait. But there must be at least frictional unemployment, people between jobs, because that is how an economy changes. To aim for full employment and no idle resources, as Keynes does, is to aim for a bubble, and bubbles will always blow up, bringing depression and deep unemployment in their wake. As Mill concludes,

> When the delusion vanishes, those whose commodities are relatively in excess must diminish their production or be ruined: and if during the high prices they have built mills and erected machinery, they will be likely to repent at leisure.[16]

5a. Keynes: The richer we become, the more we are menaced by unused savings.

We should not deceive ourselves that a mismatch between Saving and investment (too much savings, too little investment) is either a rare or an unlikely occurrence. On the contrary:

> There has been a chronic tendency throughout human history [for savings to exceed investment].[17]

And it has become more of a problem, not less of one, as societies have advanced.

We all know that becoming richer makes it easier to save. In the same way, a rich society tends to save more than a poor society. As the savings increase, so does the mismatch between savings and investment.

5b. Comment: If we have too much unused savings, why keep printing more money?

Keynes offers not a shred of evidence that savings have exceeded investment throughout human history. This is another of his hunches.

He is correct that rich societies, like rich individuals, save more. But it does not follow that they produce more "excess" or "unused" savings.

It is interesting that, more than half a century after Keynes death, the assertion that we are still suffering from a savings glut continues to be made with little or no substantiation. For example, Ben Bernanke, chairman of the US Federal Reserve, Alan Greenspan, chairman of the US Federal Reserve prior to Bernanke, and Paul Krugman, Nobel Prize winning economist, have all claimed that the world economy since 2002 has been plagued by "excess" savings, much of it coming from Asia.[18]

How these three would know this is hard to say, especially since the world is also awash in ersatz, government printed money, some of it supplied by Greenspan and Bernanke. This is the same substance that Keynes claimed was as "genuine" as real savings.[19] If the high savings rate in Asia really has created a savings glut, then why have the world's central banks, including Asian central banks, printed money at such a clip? Why do they not stop, so that the real savings can be used up?

6a. Keynes: The Paradox of Thrift

During an economic slump, we especially want to save more, because we fear losing our jobs. This just makes things worse, because the additional savings are unlikely to find an outlet in investment at that moment. The unused savings sit idle, the flow of money through the economy slows further and the slump deepens. What we need to understand, under these circumstances, is that the more virtuous we are, the more determinedly thrifty, the more obstinately orthodox . . . the more our incomes will have to fall. . . . Obstinacy can bring only penalty and no reward. The result is inevitable.[20]

6b. Comments:

i. There is no Paradox of Thrift.

We touched on this issue in chapter 1. The Keynesian "paradox of thrift," (along with the related "fallacy of composition," the idea that behavior advisable for an individual may be inadvisable for the larger community) was intoned by virtually all commentators during the Crash of 2008. Yes, they said, the American people had spent too much, had borrowed too much, had saved too little for many years. God lead us back to virtue, but not yet, to paraphrase St. Augustine. We must realize that too quick a return to virtue, too quick a turn away from borrowing and spending would just plunge us further into misery.

There is no paradox here; Keynes is wrong. It is prudent for families facing job loss to try to put something away. It is also prudent for a society that has overspent and overborrowed to start saving. This is true with or without an economic slump.

As we have discussed, the slump came because the government (or governments) artificially stimulated the economy by printing new money and injecting it into the economy through the financial system. This lowered interest rates and encouraged a wave of wasteful borrowing and spending by both businesses and consumers. In particular, vast sums were borrowed which could never be paid back, either because they were simply consumed, or because they were invested in poorly chosen projects.

Under these circumstances, consuming more alcohol will not cure the hangover. The bad investments of the recent past need to be liquidated, or at least marked down in price. Until this happens, savers should build their cash positions and refuse to use them. To invest at the old, unrealistic asset prices would just continue the old pattern of throwing money away.

Once liquidation has been accomplished and lower asset prices prevail, the more saving the better. These savings will bring down interest rates naturally and provide funds to rebuild the economy on the ruins of the past.

ii. Profits are the key to recovery.

Keynesian analysis tells us that what is lacking during a depression is demand. Since private savings (in this view) will lie fallow, will not be invested, the only effective demand comes from consumer or government spending. But what really drives an economy is not demand; it is production. And what really drives production is profits. If we want to restore the economy, we need to restore profits, genuine profits, not the phony profits of a bubble.

A collapse of profits tells us that the price and profit system of the market has been damaged, usually by government interventions to reduce interest rates, increase wages, increase consumption, subsidize some sectors and enforce cartels in others. It is not the savers who have wrecked the economy, it is government interventions that have penalized savers and ultimately destroyed profits.

Even Keynes must have known how important profits are. In his *Treatise on Money*, he acknowledged that

the engine which drives enterprise is . . . profit.[21]

By the time he wrote *The General Theory*, Keynes often used jargonish circumlocutions to sidestep the word profit, terms such as "the marginal efficiency of capital." But the inescapable truth is that profit is the key to prosperity. And the way to rebuild genuine profit is to allow all prices, including interest rates and currencies, to tell the truth about the economy. In an environment of free prices, hard work, production, and saving will do all that is required, just as John Stuart Mill said they would almost two hundred years ago.

7a. Keynes: there are better and worse ways to address the problem of a savings glut.

Beginning with some of the worse ways, we could hope for

> [enough] unemployment to keep us ... sufficiently ... poor ... and [our] standard of life sufficiently miserable to bring savings [down]. ...[22]

We could instead hope that

> millionaires [will stop their relentless saving and instead] find their satisfaction in [putting their savings to use by] building mighty mansions to contain their bodies when alive and pyramids to shelter them after death, or, repenting of their sins, erect cathedrals and endow monasteries. ...[23]

We could rely on the unexpected:

> [Throughout history, natural disasters such as] earthquakes, even wars ... [have] serve[d] to increase wealth [by using up savings]. ...[24]

We might petition governments, even those wholly devoted to free market ("laissez-faire") principles to

> fill old bottles with bank notes, bury them at suitable depths in disused coal mines which are then filled ... with town rubbish, and leave it to private enterprise ... to [invest in] dig[ging] the notes up again.[25]

As Keynes says, it would be

> more sensible to build houses ... but digging up bank
> notes is not so different from "gold mining" and would
> equally serve as a way to consume excessive savings.[26]

7b. Comments:

i Applause.

These suggestions are all satirical gems.

ii. Wars, natural disasters, and "make work" do not create wealth.

Wars and natural disasters can only use up wealth, they cannot increase it. Investment after World War II may have boomed to meet "pent-up" consumer demand. But that did not make us richer than we would have been without the war.

The comparison of buried paper money to gold is rather a joke on Keynes. His advice to print more and more money has, over the years, resulted in a rapidly depreciating currency. It will be recalled that the dollar, since the formation of the Federal Reserve in 1913, has lost over 95% of its purchasing power. By contrast, gold has kept its purchasing power, and become an investment refuge for those who wonder what governments, inspired by Keynes, will do next.

It could also be argued that governments have repeatedly followed Keynes's tongue-in-cheek advice to pour money down a hole in the ground, and that the amount of money wasted in this way, if properly invested, might by now have pulled the entire world out of poverty.

8a. Keynes: There are, of course, better ways to reduce unused savings.

Reducing interest rates in order to attract more borrowing, thereby reducing the glut of savings, is the best way. But there are alternatives. One may

> consume . . . more,

that is, spend more as consumers so that we save less, or

> work . . . less,

that is, reduce our income and thus our ability to save.

Keynes said that these latter two methods serve

> "just as well" as more investment.[27]

A practical way for society to consume more is to tax the rich at high rates and redistribute the wealth to those who are needy and thus sure to spend it.[28] If we keep clearly in mind that

> the growth in wealth, so far from being dependent on
> the abstinence [savings] of the rich, as is commonly
> supposed, is more likely to be impeded by it,[29]

we will then see that "death duties" (estate taxes) as well as progressive income tax rates will help society prosper.

What if the rich succeed politically in blocking these death duties and high income taxes? If so, governments can also borrow from the rich. This will soak up their excess savings. And, having borrowed the money, government can then spend it, which will get it into circulation and stimulate the economy. In this case, government becomes what might be called the spender of last resort.

8b. Comments:

i. The more you spend, the more you have.

In the passages above, Keynes makes explicit what was implicit before. He wants to see more spending and does not really care if the spending takes the form of consumption rather than investment. Consumption works "just as well." Spending is the way to wealth, saving the way to poverty.

Henry Hazlitt says about these ideas: "How marvelous is the Keynesian world! The more you spend the more you [have]. The more you eat your cake, the more cake [to eat]."[30]

ii. Estate taxes cannot make us richer.

According to Keynes, conventional views about death duties (that they reduce the invested wealth of a country) are

confused.[31]

He agrees that using death duties to reduce other taxes will lead to more consumption. But since consumption increases national income, and increased national income leads to more investment as well as consumption, death duties will actually increase investment, not reduce it.

This is so ludicrous that it hardly seems worth discussing. Consider: estates are almost always fully invested. Keynes tells us that by liquidating the investment, and spending it all, we will magically get even more investment in the end. If so, then why not liquidate all of our investments, spend everything we can get our hands on, and then confidently await the cornucopia of wealth to follow?

iii. We need workers and savers, including rich workers and savers.

Keynes's is indeed a fantasy world, one which unfortunately we all have to live in because of the dominance of his ideas among world governments. The truth is that an economy can only thrive with private savings. At the moment, the rich, precisely because they have so much, are the most reliable source of these savings. Therefore, at the moment, we need the rich both to supply the needed investment funds and to guide the investments.

Are there ways to make us less dependent on the rich? Yes. Some of them are explored in the last chapter of this author's *Are the Rich Necessary?* But, in the meantime, transferring money from the rich, the most reliable savers, to government, the inveterate spendthrift, will just impoverish everybody.

As writer, lawyer, economist, and actor Ben Stein has written, under the heading: "How to Ruin American Enterprise":

> Sneer at hard work and thrift. . . . Leave the plodding . . . worker and saver in the dust. . . . Enact a tax system that encourages class antagonism and punishes saving, while rewarding indebtedness, frivolity, and consumption. Tax the fruits of labor many times: . . . as income[,] . . . as real . . . property[,] . . . as capital gains[,] . . . again, at a staggeringly high level, at death. . . . This will deprive us of much needed capital for new investment, for innovation and our own personal aspirations.[32]

iv. Summary

Keynes told us that we suffer from excess savings. He would paradoxically solve the problem by introducing a new kind of saving (new money created by the government) that would be just as "genuine" as private savings. This new money would not cause inflation. All of this has turned out to be wrong:

▪▪ We have too little saving, at least in the US.

▪▪ Money newly printed by government is not, by any stretch of the imagination, "genuine" savings.

▪▪ The new money, introduced through the banking system in the form of very cheap credit, does create inflation.

▪▪ If the new money primarily flows into consumer goods, it produces a conventional inflation. If it primarily flows into investment assets, it produces an investment bubble like the 1920s or the recent dot-com and house bubbles.

▪▪ Either way, Keynes's print, lend, spend, and tax polices consume and destroy the private savings on which we depend for a prosperous economy.

12

What (Not) to Do
about Wall Street

1a. Keynes: Because private market participants do not know what they are doing, they lack confidence.

So far, lower interest rates are the medicine prescribed by Dr. Keynes. But this prescription will not by itself guarantee more investment in a market system. When business owners and managers consider a new investment, perhaps a new facility, borrowing costs are important, but not as important as expectations.

Investor expectations in turn depend heavily on a purely psychological factor, the state of business confidence. Unfortunately business confidence is generally weak.

The average person thinks that business owners and managers know what they are doing and, in particular, know a great deal about the future return of a factory, a mine, a product, or a service. But this is not so. All human beings, even so-called experts, are mostly in the dark about the future. Their knowledge of the future

amounts to little and sometimes to nothing,[1]

and their ability to make accurate, especially pinpoint, forecasts is usually nil.

People in general and business investors in particular cope with their ignorance of (and anxiety about) the future by falling back on a simple convention. They assume that what has happened in the recent past will continue to happen. [2]

Unfortunately this device is

arbitrary ... weak ... [and] precarious.[3]

It often fails, and failure brings with it a psychological shock.

1b. Comment: Business owners and managers do not think the way Keynes say they think.

Business is about people, not forecasts. The first requirement is to know your customers and their needs extremely well. The next step is to try to meet those needs in an effective (and also cost effective) way. It is rarely, if ever, a question of making a pinpoint forecast of the future rate of return on a plant or even a product and then comparing this forecasted rate of return with interest rates.

Keynes is correct that people very often try to drive by looking in the rear view mirror. Psychological studies suggest that this is an ingrained human trait. But good business operators consider a variety of possible future conditions or outcomes. They try to position themselves so that, even if the worst outcome arrives, they will at least avoid bankruptcy.

2a. Keynes: The role of "animal spirits."

Even if some business owners or managers guess right about the future, many will not. It is "probable" that business returns on average "disappoint,"[4] especially in relation to the "hopes" which precede them.[5] Why then do business investors keep wanting to play the "game"? Not presumably out of "cold calculation," but rather out of

animal spirits.[6]

Unfortunately "animal spirits" depend on

the nerves and hysteria and even the digestions [of the players].[7]

2b. Comment: This Is another Keynesian burlesque.

It cannot possibly be "probable" that business returns on average are disappointing. How can anyone know? No standard of success is even suggested, other than prior "hopes," and no evidence for anything.

Is business a game? Well, yes, in part. But the desire to earn a living, support oneself and one's family, build a productive enterprise, and so forth would seem to be larger motives than simply expressing one's animal spirits. If business, in the end, is merely a matter of "digestion," can the same perhaps be said about economic policy eructation from a Cambridge don?

3a. Keynes: What's wrong with the stock market, part one.

This is already a weak foundation on which to build a modern economy. But it is made even weaker by the pernicious influence of the stock market.

The stock market is not all bad. It is a way to finance companies. By offering "liquidity," the ability to buy and sell investments, such markets may also persuade the timid investor to pull money out from under the mattress and actually make an investment. Of course the liquidity is largely illusory. People cannot all get in or get out at the same time, which they typically want to do.

Then too, if money is invested in existing stocks, it will not be invested in new plant, equipment, employees, products, and services, which is what real investment is about. Much stock market investment is really sterile, not much better for society than keeping the money under a mattress.[8]

The pricing of shares on a public market is often "absurd."[9] Keynes has heard that the shares of ice companies sell at a higher price in the summer when profits are seasonally high than in winter. A rational market would know better.

If the stock market rises, this has the beneficial effect of boosting business confidence. But a fall depresses it. A fall may also depress consumer demand, because consumers who have invested will feel less rich, and even those who have not invested will fear for their jobs.[10]

3b. Comment: One fallacy and two misstatements.

As previously touched on in Note EE, it is fallacious to regard the purchase of an existing share of stock as sterile (because it does not flow directly to the company and therefore will not be used directly for business expansion). Since there is always a buyer and a seller for every market transaction, my purchase of a share transfers cash to the seller. The seller in turn may spend or invest it, but one way or another, the cash will find a place in the economy's circular flow. Moreover if more people buy a company's existing shares, the price will rise. This means that when the company issues new shares, it will have a lower cost of capital, and thus find it cheaper to expand.

Keynes's rather cavalier treatment of fact is illustrated by his reference to ice company shares. He tells us "it is said" that ice company shares sell for more in summer than in winter. Ice companies of course no longer exist, but Henry Hazlitt checked the historical record and found the statement to be false.[11]

By the way, did you notice the outlandish definition of liquidity that Keynes slipped in? According to him, a market must be able to absorb the simultaneous purchase or (conversely) simultaneous sale of all shares in order to be considered truly liquid.

4a. Keynes: What's wrong with the stock market, part two.

The worst aspect of the stock market is its

> "casino" atmosphere.[12]

The ostensible purpose of a stock market is to channel private savings into the most socially useful (and thus profitable) investments.[13] This requires a "long-term" point of view.[14] The "best brains of Wall Street," however, are completely unconcerned with the long-term. They are not even concerned with learning very much about the companies they buy.[15] Their "game," which they play with the utmost "zest" is to identify those stocks which will become popular and to buy them first.[16] Since everyone else is playing the same game, this means in effect

> anticipating what the average opinion [will] expect . . .
> the average opinion to be,

and then profiting from a correct guess.[17]

Under these circumstances, genuine long-term investing becomes "so difficult . . . as to be scarcely practicable" and anyone who attempts it will, paradoxically, seem "unconventional" and therefore "rash."[18] Even the most conservative investment committees will be uncomfortable with a long-term approach because

> worldly wisdom teaches that it is better for reputations
> to fail conventionally than to succeed unconventionally.[19]

Wall Street might seem to be merely a "spectacle," but its disfunctionality has serious consequences:

> Speculators may do no harm as bubbles on a steady
> stream of enterprise. But the position is serious when
> enterprise becomes the bubble on a whirlpool of
> speculation.[20]

Under these circumstances, capital will not only be misallocated. Average citizens will also lose faith in the system.

It is one thing to watch some people get unimaginably rich, if extremes of wealth are thought to reflect hard work, astute judgement, and the production of vital goods for society as a whole. Even then, the winners are getting far too much, whether from the point of view of justice or from the point of view of providing useful incentives. [21] But it is quite another thing if vast rewards go not to the disciplined and deserving, but only to lucky gamblers. In time, the social system will unravel, no one will want to work, and everyone will want to gamble. [22]

4b. Comments:

i. Keynes is describing a "bubble" market.

Keynes vividly portrays the stock market as a gambler's den. It articulates what many have vaguely felt. But is it accurate?

It is a reasonably accurate description of stock markets during a bubble, during periods such as the 1920s, 1990s, or the 2000s. It is during bubbles that stock buyers are most likely to focus on "anticipating . . . the average opinion" rather than on company fundamentals. For Keynes to describe out-of-control bubble markets as normal, and then condemn them, is of course more than ironic, because it is precisely the print-lend-and-spend government policies urged by Keynes that inflate these bubbles in the first place.

To the untrained eye, bubble markets are about private greed, not about government missteps. *The Economist* magazine tells us that:

When people look back on a bubble, they tend to blame the mess on crookedness, greed, and the collective insanity of others. What else but madness could explain all these overpriced Dutch tulips?[23]

But bubble markets are not just manifestations of private greed or madness. As Peter R. Fisher, former undersecretary of the US Treasury and New York Federal Reserve Bank official, explains:

Capitalism is premised on the idea that capital is a scarce commodity, and we are going to ration it with a price mechanism. When you make short term funds [available] essentially free with negative real rates [rates lower than inflation, as happened for example 2001–2004], crazy things start to happen.[MM] [24]

ii. More logical problems.

There are many oddities about Keynes's account of Wall Street excesses in *The General Theory*. For example, he disparages stock investors as speculators, yet also disparages people who hold cash (in preference to stocks) as speculators. These people are allegedly operating from a

speculative motive

because they think they

know . . . better than the market what the market will bring forth.[25]

Does this mean, then, that both the avoidance and the taking of risk make us speculators? [NN]

Another oddity: Keynes, who famously said that

In the long run we are all dead,

who recommended more spending, less saving, more concern with the present, less with the future, now tells us that short-term investing is very bad. This is indeed confusing. Which Keynes are we supposed to listen to?

By the way, we should not believe Keynes when he says that rampant short-term investing makes long-term investing

so difficult as to be scarcely practicable.[26]

This is completely illogical. In the investment world, when most people are looking solely for short-term opportunities, that makes long-term investing easier, not more difficult. Why? Because there is less competition for good long-term investment ideas.

iii. More inconsistency.

What is perhaps oddest of all about Keynes's disparagement of speculation is that he himself was such an active speculator. He took concentrated positions in stocks, commodities, and foreign exchange; was extremely active (turning over his stocks 100% a year on average); and leveraged his positions with borrowed money (frequently more than one pound borrowed for each pound of his own money).[27]

In 1920, this aggressive stance temporarily bankrupted him, but he bounced back with the help of loans from family and friends. From 1922–1929, he seems only to have been moderately successful, trailing the *Banker's Magazine* stock index in five years out of seven. He failed to anticipate trouble at the end of the 1920s and primarily because of his leverage lost 86% of his capital. He was again caught short in 1937, lost half his capital, but succeeded in recouping most of the 1937 losses by the time of his death.[28]

By 1938, speaking to the investment committee of King's College, Cambridge, he said that he no longer believed in active buying and selling, but had instead adopted a strategy of buying-and-holding a fairly small number of concentrated positions. He praised diversification among different asset classes. Most ironically of all, given his sermons against the use of gold as money, he specifically recommended the inclusion of gold mining shares in any portfolio for diversification purposes because of their lack of correlation with common stocks.[29]

5a. Keynes: The best remedy for stock market failure is for government to direct investment itself.

As we have seen, the problem of converting savings into investment has two components. The first obstacle is that interest rates tend to be chronically too high, which discourages investment, and leaves large amounts of savings unused. Government can alleviate this by printing more money and injecting it into the banking system to bring interest rates down.

But this solves only half the problem. The other problem is that

> the psychology of [private investors, both in business and on Wall Street or other stock markets, is] disobedient ... and ... uncontrollable.[30]

Operating in a cloud of ignorance, private investors tend to manic highs and morose lows. When morose they cannot be prodded to take advantage of even the most attractive interest rates.

The entire system of private investment is not

> intelligent ... [,] is not virtuous ... doesn't deliver the goods.[31]

We can only conclude that

> the duty of ordering the current volume of investment cannot safely be left in private hands.[32]

5b. Comment: We will mostly deal with this last idea in the next chapter.

For now, it is worth emphasizing that Keynes wanted government to take responsibility for the quantity, not the quality of investment. In the Keynesian system, it is always quantity that counts.

Interestingly, he did not suggest regulation as a panacea for what ailed the financial system, as many later Keynesians have done. He generally approved of Roosevelt's regulatory "reforms" of Wall Street, but did not say much about them or set forth a blueprint of his own. He clearly did not favor nationalization of the banks or of any other private companies.[33]

Although Keynes did not want government to run Wall Street day to day, he did want it to make the key decisions. He certainly did not agree with humorist P. J. O'Rourke that

> Bringing the government in to run Wall Street is like saying, "Dad burned dinner, let's get the dog to cook."[34]

13

(Do Not) Look to the State for Economic Leadership

1a. Keynes: The state should primarily focus on the volume of investment.

This means that if investment is too low to absorb all savings, and if lower interest rates do not bring investment up sufficiently, the state should make investments itself.

How will the state know that lower interest rates are not enough, that direct investment is needed? The key indicator is employment. If cheap money produces "full" employment, direct investment is not needed. If unemployment persists, then it is.

The state will not usually print the money to invest. It will get the money either by taxing wealthy individuals or by borrowing. If it borrows, this will not necessarily cause a government budget deficit; government investment may be kept off-budget or in a separate capital budget.[1]

1b. Comments:

i. We are not told exactly how to go about this.

In *Capital* and other works, Karl Marx was so busy dissecting what he called Capitalism that he failed to describe how Socialism would actually work. The operations manual had to be written by Lenin, Stalin, Mao, and others. Similarly, Keynes is remarkably sketchy about what might be called the operating details of Keynesianism.

We are not told why government will borrow the money to invest rather than print it. As mentioned previously (Note T), William Beveridge, who became a very prominent Keynesian, said that it did not matter.[2] In all probability, Keynes thought that printing such large quantities of money would be controversial.

We are also not told how to define "full" employment or "low" interest rates (although we know that the eventual target for interest rates is zero). In addition, we have to guess about how a government "investment" differs from another government expenditure. Keynes specifically refers to the construction of roads and homes, but does not seem to care, so long as money is spent.

ii. Keynesian investment/expenditure has left staggering debts and liabilities.

In the years after Keynes's death, governments spent and spent, often citing Keynes as the justification. By 2007, the year before the 2008 Financial Crash, the US government had run up an official debt of just under $9 trillion but total liabilities of $67 trillion. This was almost five times US gross domestic product (GDP) of $14 trillion. It was larger than the entire world's estimated GDP of $50 trillion, and almost as large as the estimated value of the world's real estate ($75 trillion) or the world's stock and bond markets ($100 trillion) as of that date.[3] Most of the $67 trillion owed by the US was off-budget and off-balance sheet, just as Keynes recommended.°° The Crash of 2008 then added as yet untold trillions to the total liabilities while reducing the asset values.

2a. Keynes: Government's job is not to "balance," but rather to "top off" private investment/expenditure. (The latter usually falls short of what is needed to achieve full employment.)

It is widely assumed that Keynes meant the state should "balance" what private investors are doing. Walter Lippmann described this idea of the state providing "balance" as follows:

> An uncoordinated, unplanned, disorderly individualism…inevitably produces alternating periods of boom and depression…. The state [should] undertake…to counteract the mass errors of the individualist crowd by doing the opposite of what the crowd is doing; it saves when the crowd is spending too much; it borrows when the crowd is saving too much; it economizes when the crowd is extravagant, and it spends when the crowd is afraid to spend…. [This] compensatory method is, I believe, an epoch-making invention.[4]

Did Keynes endorse this "compensatory method"? Most people think so. But the answer would seem to be no, Keynes did not endorse it, or at least did not fully endorse it. He did say that the state enters as a

balancing factor.[5]

But by this he primarily meant that the state should top off investment when it is too low.

As we know, Keynes believed that

> the right remedy for the trade cycle is not to be found
> in abolishing booms.[6]

A boom should be nursed and kept going. Most of the time, government investment would be needed at a high level. Occasionally, it might have to be reduced. But whatever level of government investment was required, interest rates should never be raised. In the very rare event that full employment was finally reached,

> we must find other means of [cooling the economy]
> than a higher rate of interest.[7]

2b. Comment: None of this is realistic.

Whatever Keynes thought of Lippmann's compensatory method, it has proven to be a complete illusion. Politicians and public officials are no more likely than anyone else to recognize an overheated economy, or if they do, to want to fix it. Keynes's method of maintaining a "quasi-boom" at all times by keeping interest rates low (and adding generous helpings of government spending as needed) is equally illusory. In either case, the only question is whether it will lead to inflation or bubble. Whether inflation or bubble, the final reckoning comes in the form of a crash.

3a. Keynes: Government will also make better investment decisions than the private sector.

It is important for the state to fill up the investment tank. Keeping it full is what matters most. But there are other reasons to welcome a larger role for the state in investment.

On the whole, Keynes appeared to sympathize with the idea that government would do a better job of investing than private markets. As we have seen, he painted a bleak portrait of private investment, handicapped (he said) by profound ignorance, uncontrollable emotion, and speculative tendencies. By contrast, as we have also seen, he thought the state able to decide matters based on

> long views, . . . the . . . general social advantage[,] . . . and . . . collective wisdom.[8]

In 1932, he criticized Harold Macmillan, later a British prime minister, for not being

> nearly bold enough with your proposals for developing the [direct] investment functions of the state.[9]

In 1936, in *The General Theory*, he said that he favored

> a somewhat comprehensive socialization of investment.[10]

In 1937, he suggested in the *London Times* that the British government set up a formal Public Office of Investment.[11] And in 1939 he enthusiastically promoted an

> amalgam of private capitalism and state socialism.[12]

These and other statements would seem to support the proposition that Keynes wanted government investment for its own sake, not just to top off private investment. He did also say that

> I see no reason to suppose that the existing [private] system seriously misemploys the factors of production which are in use.[13]

But this seems to mean that private enterprise is well equipped to run the show after the investment is made, not that private enterprise is better at choosing the investment in the first place.

3b. Comment: Government neither takes "long views" nor expresses "collective wisdom."

As we know, Keynes derived enormous fun from mocking what he considered to be sacred cows. After his death, Keynes himself became a sacred cow, surrounded by worshipful devotees, and Henry Hazlitt could not resist mocking the master in his own style:

> [Keynes has told us that] the people who have earned money are too shortsighted, hysterical, rapacious, and idiotic to be trusted to invest it themselves. The money must be seized from them by the politicians, who will invest it with almost perfect foresight and complete disinterestedness (as illustrated, for example, by the economic planners of Soviet Russia). For people who are risking their own money will of course risk it foolishly and recklessly, whereas politicians and bureaucrats who are risking *other* people's money will do so only with the greatest care and after long and profound study. Naturally the businessmen who have earned money have shown that they have no foresight; but the politicians who haven't earned the money will exhibit almost perfect foresight. The businessmen who are seeking to make cheaper and better than their competitors the goods that consumers wish, and whose success depends upon the degree to which they satisfy consumers, will of course have no concern for "the general social advantage"; but the politicians who keep themselves in power by conciliating pressure groups will of course have *only* concern for "the general social advantage." They will not dissipate the money. . . . There will never be even a hint of bribery, or corruption.

Hazlitt is fundamentally right. Politicians do not take "long views." Their eyes are firmly fixed on the next election. They are beholden to special interest groups who finance and support their campaigns. "Collective wisdom," if it is to be found anywhere, is more likely to be found in the market than in politicians or bureaucrats. Adam Smith warned us that it is

> folly and presumption ... [for any] single person, ... council or senate ... [to try] to direct [the] ... employ[ment of] capital.[14]

4a. Keynes: The state's control of the economy should not stop with interest rates, investment, taxation, and exchange rates.

In 1940, Keynes said that free prices were indispensable, but also (contrarily) that he favored setting up public boards to manage the prices of commodities.[15] In 1943, looking ahead to the postwar period, he said that

> I am ... a hopeless skeptic about [any] return to nineteenth century laissez-faire. I believe that the future lies with—(i) state trading for commodities; (ii) International cartels [government sanctioned monopolies] for necessary manufactures; and (iii) Quantitative import restrictions for nonessential manufactures. ... [These are the] instrumentalities for orderly economic life in the future.[16]

> [In general], state planning. ... intelligence and deliberation at the centre must supersede the admired disorder of the 19th century.[17]

In describing all this, Keynes acknowledged that the state would involve itself in

> many of the inner intricacies of private business.[18]

But even so, a

wide field ... of [private] activity [will be] unaffected.[19]

4b. Comment: It is not true that Keynes leaves "a wide field . . . of [private] activity unaffected."

Controlled interest rates (some of the most critical prices) are not compatible with a market system; nor are public control of investment, exchange rate controls and manipulations, commodity price controls, high taxes, government run monopolies, or trade protectionism. With all these controls in place, every field of private business activity is restricted.

5a. Keynes: State planning is not to be confused with fascism or communism.

Keynes always took pains to differentiate his ideas from those of a totalitarian system:

> We can accept the desirability and even the necessity of [economic] planning without being a Communist, a Socialist, or a Fascist.[20]

But he did not completely disparage Fascist or Communist economic management:

> Italian Fascism . . . seems to have saved Italy from chaos and to have established a modest level of material prosperity.[21]

And in his foreword to the German edition of *The General Theory* (published in Nazi Germany and not included in The Collected Works), he noted that his ideas

can be much more easily applied to the conditions of
a totalitarian state than . . . [to] the conditions of free
competition and of a considerable degree of laissez-faire,

although they had not been worked out with that in mind.[22]

As we saw in our earlier discussion of Keynes's values, he found
much that was

"detestable"

about Soviet Russia. At best he regarded Communists as a species of deranged "Methodists."[23] But what Soviet planners had
achieved by 1936 was

impressive.

They were

disinterested administrators . . . [who had put] in operation . . . the largest scale empiricism and experimen-
talism which has ever been attempted.[24]

He went further in his praise:

Let us not belittle these magnificent experiments or refuse to learn from them. . . . The Five Year Plan in Russia, The Corporative state in Italy; . . . and state planning [under] democracy in Great Britain. . . . Let us
hope that they will all be successful.[25]

It is important to recall, in assessing this, that many intelligent and
otherwise decent people in the 1930s were admirers of Fascism and
Communism. Keynes was neither. Instead, he sought what he called

new wisdom for a new age,

and did not in the least mind appearing

unorthodox, troublesome, and dangerous[26]

to conventionally minded capitalists who failed to see their own peril or to understand that a Keynesian "third" way was their only hope.

5b. Comment: Keynes did not find a "third" way between laissez-faire capitalism and fascism/communism.

He sincerely tried to do so, but did not succeed. Moreover the tack he took was illogical. One cannot rescue the price and profit system by further distorting prices and profits. This kind of crude government intervention just leads to failure. Faced with failure, government then tends to blame the market rather than itself and intervene more. More and more intervention leads to more and more failure. If the process is not interrupted, the price and profit system may completely collapse and government control ensue. This is not a "third way" but rather a recipe for the extinction of market systems.

6a. Keynes: State-run capitalism must be run by the right people.

At this point, it is necessary to ask how a self-described unorthodox thinker and rebel could put so much faith in government. Is not government, like other established social institutions, usually the embodiment of conventional wisdom?

We have previously noted Keynes's statement that

> I believe the right solution [to the economic questions of the day] will involve intellectual and scientific elements which must be above the heads of the vast mass of more or less illiterate voters. [27]

But are political leaders, even heads of government, any less economically illiterate than the voters? Did not Keynes himself in his second book (about the Versailles Peace Treaty) ridicule the leaders of Britain, France, and the United States, along with all the other old and blinkered men who have traditionally lead nations?

The answer to this conundrum is that, under Keynes's system, government will turn over the economic reins to experts.

Keynes's biographer Robert Skidelsky observed that a belief in expert opinion "runs like a leitmotiv through [his] work and is the important assumption of his political philosophy."[28]

Since Keynes was the dominant economic expert of his era, both in Britain and the US, this faith in expert opinion was, at least in part, simply faith in himself, and a manifestation of his unflagging self-confidence.

6b. Comments:

i. Keynes contradicts himself.

Although there are many passages in which Keynes extols governance by "experts," there is one in which he candidly acknowledges that

> Some of those representing themselves as such seem to me to talk much greater rubbish than an ordinary man could ever be capable of.[29]

This might seem to dispose of the matter. But there is more to be said about it.

ii. The Post-war economic record should make us doubt the rule of Keynesian experts.

We should also look at the record of the economic experts who carried Keynes's banner after his death. A good source is Robert J. Samuelson's *The Great Inflation and Its Aftermath*, a book about the inflation of the 1970s. It recounts how Keynesian economists under John F. Kennedy, Lyndon Johnson, and Richard Nixon sought to "fine-tune" the economy to achieve "full employment." (Nixon was a Republican, but famously announced that "We are all Keynesians now.")

The result was a wage-price spiral that Samuelson calls "the greatest domestic policy blunder since World War II." He adds that

> these failed policies (. . . [printing money] . . . new taxes, spending programs and regulations . . .) were not undertaken on ignorant whim. Rather, they embodied the thinking of the nation's top economists, reflecting a broad consensus among their peers. It was the scholarly respectability of these ideas . . . that recommended them to political leaders and made them easier to sell to the public.[30]

As we have seen, the status of some Keynesian ideas declined by the late 1970s. But Keynesianism remained intact. The appointment of one Keynesian, Alan Greenspan, as chairman of the US Federal Reserve by Ronald Reagan and then another, Ben Bernanke, by George W. Bush led directly to the dot-com and the housing bubbles, two more disasters on a scale with the Great Inflation of the 1970s.

iii. Experts at the US Federal Reserve grow more powerful with each failure.

The Federal Reserve Board is a case study of government by experts run amok. The agency has vast power over the economy, yet is accountable to no one. It prints the money to pay for its own operations, so Congress has no budgetary authority over it. There are no limits to the amount of debt it may create. It is not subject to government audits. President Bush's TARP Act in 2008 gave it vast new powers, and it seems likely to be given more control over financial regulation. With each policy blunder it is given more authority, and neither Congress nor the President, nor certainly the voters, have the slightest understanding of what it is actually doing.

iv. A further note on experts elsewhere in government.

Financial experts are also hard at work elsewhere in Washington. Some of them at the Office of Federal Housing Enterprise Oversight (OFHEO) developed the following formula to determine the capital requirement of government sponsored housing behemoths Fannie and Freddie:

HOW FANNIE AND FREDDIE CALCULATED RISK-BASED CAPITAL

$$LS_m^{SF} = \frac{1}{\left(1+\dfrac{DR_m}{2}\right)^{\frac{MQ}{6}}} + \frac{\left(\dfrac{MQ}{12} \times PTR_m\right)+F-MI_m}{\left(1+\dfrac{DR_m}{2}\right)^{\frac{MF}{6}}} + \frac{R-RP_m-ALCE_m}{\left(1+\dfrac{DR_m}{2}\right)^{\frac{MF+MR}{6}}}$$

Where:

LS_m SF = Net loss severity for conventional and FHA single-family loans in month m

MI_m = Mortgage insurance proceeds in month m

$ALCE_m$ = Aggregate limit credit enhancement in month m

MR = Months to recovery

F = Foreclosure costs

MQ = Months delinquent

PTR_m = Pass through rate for payments in month m

R = REO expenses

RP_m = (0.61/L TV_q) = Recovety proceeds in month m. The 0.61 is the recovery rate on defaulted loans in the benchmark loss experience as a percentage of the predicted house price using the HPI.

L TV_q = Loan to value ratio in month q (current LTV)

DR_m = Discount rate in month m

(Source: *Federal Register* and *Grant's Interest Rate Observer*, June 27, 2008, 11.)

Grant's Interest Rate Observer observed that OFHEO

made a change in the formula that bumped up the minimum risk-based capital required of Fannie to $33.1

billion from $24.6 billion. [But it also] ruled . . . that neither Fannie nor Freddie should be allowed to book a gain on the sale of a foreclosed property. So adjudicating, the regulator made hash of the formula you see [above]. Or couldn't you tell?[31]

v. And a last note about experts on Wall Street.

Meanwhile Wall Street during the bubble years was also increasingly run by financial experts who made millions and even billions by concocting complex new products, many of which blew up prior to the Crash of 2008. Ironically the products were so complex that even the heads of the Wall Street firms, even very experienced hands such as Robert Rubin, former head of Goldman Sachs and former secretary of the Treasury, seemed unable to follow what was going on, much less manage it.

7a. Keynes: Experts given responsibility for governing the economy will be more than experts.

Keynes was not satisfied that experts qua experts should be in charge. He wanted experts who also had the right values, people who might be described as platonic guardians. In a letter to Friedrich Hayek, a critic of state-run capitalism, he said that state appointed guardians of the economy had to have the right

moral position,

which would include a commitment to individual freedom. This was essential because

dangerous acts can be done safely in a community which thinks and feels rightly which would be the way to hell if they were executed by those who think and feel wrongly.[32]

Although the guardians must be exceptionally "moral," this does not necessarily refer to conventional Judaeo-Christian morality. Most economic issues by their nature are simply over the head of the average voter. It is therefore not inappropriate for economic managers to resort to sleight of hand or even mild deception in order to obtain the consent to the governed for essential actions.

In a passage in *The General Theory*, Keynes notes that the public wants

> the moon,

by which he means perennially high wages, and that to maintain high wages there must be plenty of money in circulation. The "remedy" is thus to

> persuade the public that green cheese [government printed money] is practically the same thing [as real money] and to have a green cheese factory (i.e., a central bank) under public control.[33]

7b. Comment: Who will these moral (but unconventionally moral) guardians turn out to be?

In his moral philosophy, as in his economics, Keynes was an "intuitionist." He thought that most people could directly intuit sound moral principles, although some people could intuit better than others, and they would have to lead. This approach might serve well enough in Britain, where standards of decent conduct were well established, but can only be regarded as hopelessly naïve and even dangerous for the world at large. Hitler, no doubt, thought that his own intuitions were best, and that he therefore had the right to lead.

To say, as Keynes did, that expert guardians are subject to their own morality, and thus might dispense with much of conventional morality, seems even more dangerous. It is one thing to lead a Bohemian life, or to scoff at conventional morality, as Keynes did. But why mix this all up with Platonic ideals of guardianship?

In thinking about this, we must also remember that Keynes did not merely wish for his experts to rule a nation. He wanted them, at least in monetary policy, to rule the world through the device of a global central bank, an idea that we will discuss further in chapter 19.

14

Government for Sale

(A Digression to Discuss "Soft" US Political Corruption in the Context of the Housing Bubble and the Drug and Auto Industries)

I N THE PRIOR chapter, we considered Keynes's claim that government could do a better job of investing than private enterprise. We evaluated this in terms of the potential threat that it posed for the economy. We have not yet considered what is arguably more important: the threat posed to our democratic institutions by allowing government to become completely mixed up with the world of money and business.

Historian Doris Kearns Goodwin observed that a degree of financial corruption has always existed in American government, but that it grew exponentially after the Civil War.[1] Why? Because business and government became so closely involved with each other. Sometimes it was the "hard" corruption of outright bribery. More often, it was the "soft" corruption of selling laws, tax breaks, rules, and decisions for campaign contributions, election-eering help, jobs, or other favors.

Government's job is to guard and protect us. But who will pro-tect us from the guardians themselves, once they become cor-rupted? There is no certain recourse against a corrupt government.

In Russia today, a holding company, Basic Element, run by the financial oligarch Oleg Deripaska, owes $650 million to Alfa Bank, led by fellow oligarch Mikhail Fridman. Fridman presses Deripaska for repayment. Deripaska speaks to the Russian presi-dent, Dimitry Medvedev. The president calls in Fridman and the loan is magically deferred.[2]

Russia, having abandoned Communism, has embraced age-old principles of mercantilism. The state does not own the private sector as it once did. But there are really no boundaries between private and public. When businessmen need political favors, they know whom to call. When politicians need money, they also know whom to call. The crony capitalists and politicians are clever; they keep most of it concealed behind closed doors.

The world's most developed countries have not reached this point—yet. But day by day they are edging closer to the Russian model. The United States is a case in point.

In 2008, before the rapid expansion of the federal government by the Bush and Obama administrations, government (both fed-eral and state) represented about a third of the economy. The nonprofit sector represented roughly another 10%. This implied that a (bare) majority of the economy was comprised of private, for-profit concerns, the so-called private sector. But taking into account companies that are directly or indirectly controlled by government, perhaps as much as two-thirds of the economy is really in the government sphere.

The term Government Sponsored Enterprise (GSE) is gen-erally used to describe private businesses that have been started by government and that continue to enjoy government support. The pre-eminent examples over the years have been the mortgage giants Fannie Mae and Freddie Mac. It seems appropriate, however, to apply the term GSE more broadly to describe a large number of private firms, all of which either sell to government (defense), are highly regulated, subsidized, price supported, and cartelized by government (health care, drugs, housing, and banking and finance), or are dominated by government in a wide variety of ways (law, education, agriculture, autos, broadcasting, utilities, etc.).

The common theme that runs through all these broadly defined GSEs, apart from their dependence on government, is the large amounts of money they give to politicians of both parties and the large amount they spend on lobbying. In 2008, for example, individuals and political action committees (PACs) connected to the finance, insurance, and real estate industries gave $463 million to politicians, with 51% going to Democrats and 49% to Republicans.[3] That same year, then candidate Obama received more money from this source than any other except for trial lawyers. His take from donors in finance ($37.6 million) far exceeded what the Republican candidate, John McCain, got.[4] This flow of money is extremely important to politicians.

The flow of money is not usually tied to a specific favor. But sometimes the connection is unmistakable. For example, in 2007 Congress threatened to end the tax loophole allowing private investment partnership managers to escape taxation at earned income rates. Senator Charles Schumer (D-NY) immediately took steps to protect the loophole. His Democratic Senatorial Campaign Committee subsequently collected almost $5 million from such funds for the 2008 election, double what the Republican committee got.[5]

Campaign contributions are the main thing that politicians want from Wall Street firms and other GSEs. But there are other financial ties including funds from related foundations and jobs for friends or for the politicians themselves. For example, Rahm Emanuel, between stints in the Clinton White House, in Congress, and then in the Obama White House as Chief of Staff, went to Wall Street. Making use of his government contacts, he earned $18 million in only two and a half years, according to his government disclosure forms.[6]

It is especially ironic that Wall Street is regarded by most people as the epicenter of market capitalism. It is, in reality, the epicenter of government-sponsored enterprise. Where Wall Street stops and Washington begins and vice versa is impossible to say. The current symbiosis was not caused, as many suppose, by the Crash of 2008. Rather the Crash of 2008 was caused by the long-standing Wall Street–Washington symbiosis.

In the balance of this chapter, we will examine three GSE case studies, each of which illustrate different aspects of the problem. The first case study will focus on the housing bubble, which involves the Federal Reserve, Congress, the Bush administration, and the real estate and finance industries. The second will focus on the drug industry and how it interacts with Washington. The third will very briefly look at automobile industry troubles. Although this chapter mainly focuses on government/industry ties, we should not forget the vast sums of money flowing to Washington from labor unions and trial lawyers and other special interests as well as from broadly defined GSE industries.

Case Study One: The US Housing Bubble

Conventional wisdom blames the housing bubble on Wall Street greed. This is only a half-truth. When government serves free drinks by printing money, driving interest rates down, and overspending, Wall Street tends to get drunk. This is very convenient for government because, when the hangover comes, the average person will blame the drunk, not the bartender. This happened each time a bubble popped, at the end of the 1920s, the end of the 1990s, and the end of the recent housing bubble.

Throughout the housing bubble, the government sought to provide cheap mortgages by driving interest rates down, generally with the help of other central banks. When the Fed Funds Rate was held below the rate of inflation for three years, this was virtually giving money away to those with the clout and the collateral to get it. These initial borrowers then made the money available to other borrowers, especially to consumers for housing loans.

The US government had already made mortgage interest tax deductible and eliminated most capital gains taxes on homes. It also provided loan guarantees through the Federal Housing Administration (FHA) and its own cheap mortgages both through the Federal Home Loan Banks and the private/public entities Fannie Mae and Freddie Mac. The government's Department of Housing and Urban Development did its part by mandating that Fannie and Freddie invest what became 50% of assets in lower-end mortgages, including, if necessary, unqualified mortgages, the ones that later blew up.[7]

By the end of 2007, government-sponsored mortgages accounted for 81% of all the mortgage loans made in the US.[8] During 2008, Fannie Mae developed the Home Saver program. This enabled defaulting homeowners to borrow additional money to cover the arrears in their mortgage payments. Although ostensibly designed to help struggling homeowners, the new loans meant that none of the original loans had to be considered in default. More importantly, none of them had to be written off. Many of the new Home Saver loans were written off almost immediately, nearly half a billion worth, but this sum was small compared to the original loans that could be kept on the books for a while longer. In this and other creative ways, Fannie executives kicked the can (of mortgage defaults) down the road a bit further into the future.[9]

Official government propaganda kept touting home ownership as the American dream. No one paid attention to studies showing that countries and regions with the highest home ownership also had the highest unemployment rate. Why? Because home ownership makes it difficult for workers to move to where the jobs are, especially to where the best jobs for their particular skills are.[10] This was finally noticed after the housing crash.

Democratic politicians especially liked Fannie and Freddie. They exempted both from state and local taxes and some Securities and Exchange Commission (SEC) requirements and also gave them implied government backing for their bonds. They fought off Bush administration efforts to regulate them more, even after it became apparent that both firms had issued false accounting statements. They also saw nothing wrong with Fannie and Freddie borrowing $60 for each $1 of capital, much more leverage then even Wall Street used.

Representative Barney Frank, chair of the US House Financial Services Committee, said that fears of a looming crisis were "exaggerated." His counterpart in the Senate, Christopher Dodd, chair of the Banking Committee, agreed.[11] As late as July 2008, Dodd said that: "[Fannie and Freddie] are fundamentally sound and strong. There is no reason for the reaction we're getting."[12] Before the end of that year, both companies had collapsed and been refinanced by the government. Earlier, Frank was worried that any attempt to rein in Fannie and Freddie would make housing less "affordable," presumably for people of modest means. He did not explain what Fannie and Freddie government-supported loans of as large as $625,000 had to do with affordability, or how soaring home values made homes more affordable.

By 2006, cheap credit had doubled the price of the average house in less than ten years.[13] By then, the housing bubble had spread around the world and become the largest and most universal bubble in economic history. The 1920s bubble in the US led to a total debt to gross domestic product ratio of 185% in 1928. The housing bubble led to a total US debt to GDP ratio of 357% by 2008.[14]

What nobody mentioned throughout the debate about Fannie and Freddie was how convenient their supposedly private but actually public status was for politicians. As private companies, they could make campaign contributions through their employees and their PACs (Political Action Committees). Their "foundations" could also provide "soft" funding for a host of political purposes. As *Forbes Magazine* publisher Steve Forbes noted in August 2008:

> The two most mammoth political powerhouses in America today are Fannie Mae and Freddie Mac. Their lobbying muscle makes Arnold Schwarzenegger look like a 90-pound weakling. Directly and indirectly they employ legions of ex-pols to help them [and their friends] on the Hill. They hand out largesse of one sort or another to any pol who matters and is willing to take it. Fannie Mae's "charitable" operations have field people in virtually every congressional district.
>
> These monsters are fiercely resistant to any change affecting their ability to tap Uncle Sam's ATM at will while privatizing profits and socializing losses.[15]

Fannie's nonpolitical money even went to Acorn, the group charged in 2008 with voter fraud.[16] Altogether, excluding "charitable" gifts, Fannie spent $170 million on lobbying from 1998–2007 and $19.3 million on campaign contributions from 1990. The largest sum during the 2006–2008 electoral cycle went to

Senate Banking Committee Chair Dodd, and the second largest to then Senator Obama.[17]

Senator Dodd was also the second largest recipient of funds from a political action committee (PAC) organized by Countrywide Financial, a leading subprime mortgage lender, as well as recipient of two mortgages from Countrywide's VIP program that waived points and other fees. Later Dodd stated that he did not realize he was getting special treatment and refinanced the loans elsewhere. The largest recipient of funds from the Countrywide PAC was then Senator Obama.[18]

As the Crash of 2008 unfolded, the government did not of course just bail out Fannie and Freddie. It bailed out banks and investment banks as well. In early October 2008, the government told nine major banks and investment banks that they must sell the government an ownership stake in their companies even if they did not need the money, just to show that the government stood behind the banks.[19]

In a stroke, banks like Citigroup, JP Morgan Chase, Bank of America, Wells Fargo, Bank of New York, and State Street became full-fledged GSEs, little different than traditional GSEs like Fannie and Freddie. So did investment banks like Goldman Sachs and Morgan Stanley. Shortly thereafter, Barney Frank received $9,500 from Wells Fargo's and Goldman Sachs's PACs,[20] presumably just a beginning. With tighter controls over the old GSEs and many new ones, the flow of money to Washington would inevitably break all records.

Not surprisingly, Democratic Party leaders selected eleven newly elected Democratic members of the house who had won their races by narrow margins and assigned them to the Financial Services Committee. In this way, they could be sure to raise plenty of money. The money alone might discourage Republican challengers. In this way, control of Congress helps to cement future control of Congress.

During the fall of 2008, leading investment banks such as Goldman Sachs and Morgan Stanley legally became banks. This meant that these firms, essentially giant hedge funds, could enjoy permanent access to newly printed government money offered at the lowest possible rates, rates that shortly fell to just above zero. This was deeply ironic. At a time when many sound companies on "Main Street" were struggling to obtain loans at high rates, the leading Wall Street speculators could borrow directly from the government at bargain rates.

At that very moment, the recent head of Goldman Sachs, Hank Paulson, now secretary of the Treasury, was running the government's Wall Street rescue operation with Ben Bernanke, chairman of the US Federal Reserve. Paulson's firm directly received $10 billion of TARP bailout money[21] in addition to cheap money from the Fed's loan window. But that was not all.

The largest single chunk of TARP money, $173 billion, went to American International Group (AIG), a giant insurer. When the company ran into trouble, Paulson selected Edward Liddy, previously a director of Goldman Sachs, to run it.[22] Because AIG owed money to others, much of the bailout flowed through to other firms whose names the government refused to disclose, possibly because some of these firms were foreign. Some of the names leaked, however, and it turned out that almost $13 billion of the AIG bailout money had also gone to Goldman Sachs.[23]

AIG, by the way, had been a major source of campaign donations. The number two recipient of these funds for 2003–2008 had been Senator Dodd. The number one recipient had been then Senator Obama.[24]

During the fall of 2008, Secretary Paulson also arranged for Bank of America, a recipient of TARP money, to rescue Merrill Lynch, the giant investment firm. The head of Bank of America later testified that Paulson had directed him to complete the transaction and also asked him not to disclose how bad Merrill's losses were, which may have been illegal. The then head of Merrill Lynch was a former head of Goldman Sachs and thus a former colleague of Paulson's.

When the Obama administration came in, Timothy Geithner, the president of the New York Federal Reserve, the operating arm of the US Federal Reserve, took Paulson's job. A former chief economist of Goldman Sachs, William Dudley, then took Geithner's New York Fed job. Shortly thereafter, the chairman of the New York Fed, Stephen Freidman, another former Goldman Sachs head and also former chief economic advisor to President George W. Bush, decided to resign because he wanted to be more active at Goldman.[25]

The cozy Wall Street-Washington club described above has many departments. One of them is the leading private securities rating services—Standard and Poor's, Moody's, and Fitch. These firms played an important role in blowing up the housing bubble by giving safe ratings to mortgage securities that turned out to be anything but safe.

How did these firms come to hold so much power in the securities market? The answer: government laws and regulations forbid the purchase (by insurance companies, banks, money market funds, et al) of securities not rated by these select firms. In other words, the government has created a protected cartel of raters. Since the cartel was immune from competition, it was easy for Wall Street to win approval for dubious securities, especially since the flood of such securities was generating so much fee income for the raters.

All bubbles eventually pop. The housing bubble was no exception. But why did it pop when it did? A major precipitating factor was an obscure accounting rule applied to banks (but not insurance companies) in 2007 called "mark-to-market." This rule change (FASB 157) forced many banks to write down the value of their assets, thereby creating either insolvency or worries about insolvency, which in turn triggered federal bailouts.

There was a Keystone Cops element about this. Mark-to-market was accurately described by some critics as mark-to-make-believe. When real market prices are not available, often the case with bank assets, the rule essentially makes them up. Auditors implementing the rule operated in an atmosphere of fear created by the federal Sarbanes Oxley Act, and also looked nervously over their shoulder at the threat of lawsuits from trial lawyers. They were naturally more inclined to play it safe by writing down assets, sometimes to zero, even when cash flows from the investments were still entirely positive.

Even Fannie Mae, the most egregiously overleveraged financial firm, never actually ran out of money, the commonsense definition of bankruptcy. The government, acting through the Securities and Exchange Commissions, could have called a "mark-to-market" time out. It could have temporarily or permanently suspended mark-to-market while requiring the same information to be provided as footnotes to accounting statements.

Why did both the Bush and Obama administrations choose to let what *Forbes Magazine* publisher Steve Forbes called "accounting asininity" continue unchecked? Perhaps because Fed Chairman Ben Bernanke strongly opposed even a temporary suspension.[26] Perhaps because European governments, partial architects of the rule through the Basle Accords, did not want to admit error. The rule was finally revised, but not until April of 2009.

This was not the only instance of misjudgment on Bernanke's part. It was one of a cascading avalanche of such errors. Both as a governor, and then as chairman of the Federal Reserve, Bernanke had been generally responsible for financing the bubble with cheap debt. He clung to the idea that so long as consumer price increases were restrained, there was no reason to worry about an asset bubble. As the signs of trouble steadily gathered, he said that

■■ "US households have been managing their personal finances well" (June 13, 2006).
■■ "We do not expect significant spillovers from the subprime [mortgage] market to the rest of the economy or to the financial system" (March 28, 2007).[27]

He also made one last crucial error, when he drastically cut the Fed Funds rate again in early September of 2007.

By this time, no one could claim that consumer price increases were restrained. Even the government's doctored index showed them advancing at 5% a year. Bernanke cut rates anyway, and his action had the completely unintended consequence of setting off a race out of the dollar and into commodities such as oil. The price of a barrel of oil quickly doubled, which helped to panic consumers and slow business.

In more Keystone Cops fashion, Senator Joe Lieberman blamed the oil price rise, not on Bernanke's actions, but rather on speculators. He threatened to enact legislation banning large institutional investors from investing in commodities altogether.[28] By the time he spoke, commodity prices had already peaked and were about to free-fall during the Crash.

Bernanke had hoped that his rate cut would help bring down mortgage rates. Instead mortgage rates kept climbing. Meanwhile Wall Street firms responded by taking one last, long gulp of Bernanke's cheap money—only to find very shortly that more leverage at very short maturities was the last thing they needed in an imploding economy. And it was not just Wall Street. Ship owners ordered more ships, businesses added to inventory, all just at the wrong time, all prompted by the Fed's rate cut.

By October 2008, President Bush was spreading panic by saying on television that a failure to pass his TARP (Troubled Assets
Relief Program) bill would leave the economy in ruin. Retail sales
began to fall dramatically right after the President spoke.[29] So did
Republican election prospects.

Seven hundred billion dollars in TARP money was sold as a
program to buy troubled mortgages from banks. After passage,
the treasury secretary agreed (privately, not publicly) that the
plan made little sense. There being no market for the mortgages,
there was no way to price them. Even if there had been a market,
buying them at real market values would not help the banks. Later
Tim Geithner, Obama's new secretary of the Treasury, revived the
idea anyway, in the form of a giveaway to Wall Street.

Consider what was happening here. After endless government
interference, the price system had broken down in the mortgage
field. The most important task was to establish real market prices
(not phony "mark-to-market" prices) for mortgages.

The main reason that the mortgage price system had broken
down was because of cheap government loan money and loan
guarantees. So what does Secretary of the Treasury Geithner
decide to do? He decides to offer still more guaranteed government loans, in this case loans intended to convince Wall Street
firms to buy the bad mortgages. Result:

- More taxpayer money dumped into Wall Street pockets.
- Complete frustration of the market price discovery
  process.

What if Geithner's plan failed? What if Wall Street refused to
buy the bad mortgages from the banks or the banks refused to sell
them despite the government price subsidies? In that case, said
Federal Deposit Insurance Corporation (FDIC) Chairman Sheila
Bair, the banks would "need to be told" by the government to sell
the mortgages whether they wanted to or not at the government

engineered price.[30] That of course would make it even more impossible to discover true market prices for the mortgages, the one step that would really help end the crisis.

The banks originally targeted for President Bush's TARP funds were those considered "too big to fail." In most cases, these banks had grown to giant size with government encouragement. Each time a smaller bank is in danger of failing, the usual government response is to try to merge it into one of the banking behemoths. In practice, the TARP funds became a honey pot that firms in a great variety of congressional districts tried to get at through their members of Congress.

Not all the TARP funds were even used for the financial crisis. In order to win passage, it included special provisions for Puerto Rican rum producers, auto race tracks, companies operating in American Samoa (one of which, Starkist, was based in Speaker of the House Nancy Pelosi's district), tax benefits for various parties, even a requirement that medical insurance companies cover mental health.[31]

Buried deep in the fine print, the Act also vastly expanded the power of the Federal Reserve by allowing it to pay interest on member bank deposits. This was a critically important change in the monetary system, one that would allow the Fed to print much more money. Did members of Congress even know about this provision of the bill? It is doubtful. If they did, they probably had no conception of its purpose or importance.

The housing bubble illustrates how government errors may paradoxically increase government control over large swaths of the economy. Yet in the long run, it is not at all clear who will control whom. Will government keep the upper hand in a government-Wall Street "partnership"? Or will Wall Street eventually take control of government, using its vast powers to restrict competition and create sustainable monopoly pricing?

This is not an idle question. To see how a regulated industry co-opts the regulator and uses the power of government for its own purposes, we need only turn to our next case study.

Case Study Two: The Drug Industry

The drug industry at one time was called the patent medicine industry, and this is still the more revealing name.

Drug companies devote themselves to inventing non-natural molecules for use in medicine. Why non-natural? Because molecules previously occurring in nature cannot, as a rule, be patented. It is essential to develop a patentable medicine, because only a medicine protected by a government patent can hope to recoup the enormous cost (up to $1 billion) of taking a new drug through the government's drug approval process.

Getting a new drug through the US Food and Drug Administration (FDA) is not just expensive. It also requires having the right people on your side. Drug companies know that they must hire former FDA employees to assist with the process. They also hire leading experts as consultants, experts who will probably be called on by the FDA to serve on screening panels. Direct payments must also be made to support the FDA's budget.

Although the costs are astronomical, the financial payoff from FDA approval is even bigger. Only FDA-approved drugs can be prescribed within government programs such as Medicare. Doctors may prescribe unapproved substances outside of Medicare, Medicaid, or the Veteran's Administration but by doing so risk losing their license to practice.

The FDA will also discourage, and often ban, substances that might compete with approved drugs. When antidepression drugs (based on extending the life of a hormone, serotonin, inside the body) were approved, the Agency promptly banned a natural substance, L-Tryptophan, that increased serotonin, even though the natural substance was much cheaper and had long been available. Many years later, after the antidepression drugs were well established, Tryptophan was finally allowed back, but under restrictions that made it more expensive.

In effect, then, drug companies are not really private companies competing in an open market. They are also government-sponsored enterprises (GSEs) not unlike Fannie Mae or Freddie Mac, and (now) the big Wall Street banks and firms. It should not be surprising therefore that drug companies, like Fannie and Freddie, spend millions on political lobbying and campaign contributions. Many politicians rely on these campaign contributions and thus have a vested interest in maintaining the drug cartel, even though needlessly high drug costs contribute to soaring medical costs.

The government's share of these soaring medical costs is, in part, financed by borrowing from China and other countries. Too much of the borrowed money is spent making old people miserable in the discomfort of hospitals prior to their deaths. In too many cases, the medical care actually causes the death. In fact, medical errors and unintended consequences of treatment may be the leading cause of death in the US.[32]

In the US, businesses pay for a great deal of medical care. Consequently, monopoly-driven drug prices also reduce business profits, which in turn leads to fewer raises for existing employees, less hiring, and ultimately to higher unemployment. Higher business costs also lead to fewer export sales, which increases the US trade deficit, and so on it goes, with one undesirable and unintended consequence after another.

The bottom line here is that drug companies, ostensibly regulated by the government, have come to dominate and even control the regulators. The result is a semisocialized drug cartel, enforced by government, whose pricing power is wreaking economic havoc. This is an inherently unstable situation. One possibility is that government will reassert itself through price controls.

Does the drug industry story shed further light on what happened in Wall Street after the housing bubble? It might. In the immediate aftermath of the Crash of 2008, it seemed that government was taking control of Wall Street. But money, power, and control have been flowing back and forth between Wall Street and Washington for years. There is always traffic in both directions. In the short run, Washington is reasserting itself. In the long run, as previously noted, Wall Street may turn a tighter relationship to its own advantage.

Case Study Three: The Automobile Industry

Polls consistently showed the bailout of General Motors and Chrysler by the Bush and Obama Administrations to be unpopular with American voters.

Nor can a failing industry contribute large amounts of campaign funds. This is clearly not like finance or drugs, two of the cash cows of American politics.

Why then did the bailouts take place? First, because the employees of these two companies largely live in six Midwestern presidential "swing" states. These are states that typically decide a presidential election. Second, because the United Auto Workers, like other major unions, is an important source of campaign funds and campaign assistance to the Democratic Party.

Ironically, it is wage and benefit concessions to the United Auto Workers over the years that left General Motors and Chrysler unable to compete. Payments to retired workers in particular added thousands of dollars to the cost of each car, expense that Toyota and other competitors did not have to bear. This presented the American companies with what seemed to be an irresolvable conundrum. The only way to escape the burdens of the past was to declare bankruptcy. But a long drawn out bankruptcy process would destroy customer confidence in the value of warranties, the availability of servicing, and related to these, the resale value of the car.

What the Obama administration did in response to these challenges was extraordinary. It provided billions in bailout funds. It fired the chief executive of General Motors and selected his successor. It put the full faith and credit of the government behind auto warranties, an unprecedented step. But that was only the beginning.

The administration knew that the stockholders of the two companies had already lost everything. The remaining financial stakeholders were the secured creditors and the unsecured creditors. Among the unsecured creditors (those without a direct claim on the company's assets) was the United Auto Workers. According to law, the secured creditors should be paid first, then the unsecured creditors equally. These are well-established property rights enshrined in bankruptcy law and ultimately guaranteed by the US Constitution. The Obama administration nevertheless developed a plan which, by ignoring these rights, was arguably illegal.

The specifics of the Obama plan called for the secured creditors of Chrysler to receive about 28% of their money back. The major unsecured creditor, the United Auto Workers, would receive a $4.6 billion note equivalent to 43% of its total claim and 55% of the company. Some of the secured lenders were big banks being kept alive by the federal government, and they agreed to the terms. How could they not do what government told them to do? When the other secured lenders initially balked, they were publicly scolded by President Obama and labeled "speculators."[33]

After even more pressure was applied, all the secured lenders reluctantly accepted the government plan.

The plan for General Motors was similar. In this case, unsecured debt holders other than the United Auto Workers would be offered 10% of the company shares, worth no more than 5% of their investment even if the company recovered. The union by contrast would receive $10.2 billion in cash, equivalent to half its claim, and 39% of the company. If the union received the same deal as the other unsecured creditors, it would have had no cash and only about 8% of the company shares.

A group representing some of the creditors at one point in the negotiations pointed out that "[This] amounts to using taxpayers' money to show political favoritism of one creditor over another."[34] Law school teachers objected that it amounted to a "sub rosa" reorganization prohibited by law, that it violated property rights, and that it represented a very dangerous precedent.[35] Columnist Lawrence Kudlow said that "political decisions are replacing the rule of law."[36]

———— ◆ ————

As more and more industries drift or cascade into the government-sponsored sector of the economy, we need to stop and ask ourselves: what is this doing to American democracy? Our economy may survive; economies are resilient. But will our political life, our democracy, survive? Do we like the new world that we are creating and leaving our children?[PP]

This new world is not just about politicians, their financial needs, and the businesses whose cash flows they increasingly control. It is also about new men and women, specialists and operatives who live and thrive in the Wall Street–Washington and wider GSE world.

Consider the career of John Podesta. He worked as a Capitol Hill staffer before forming a lobbying firm, Podesta Associates Inc., with his brother Tony in 1988. He then joined the Clinton White House and rose to become chief of staff.

At the end of the Clinton Administration, Podesta returned to lobbying, but a few years later in 2003 founded the Center for American Progress in Washington, which quickly became the pre-eminent Democratic Party think tank. The Center does not reveal its funders, but is believed to be supported by mega hedge fund investor George Soros among others. When Barack Obama was elected president, Podesta was asked to co-chair the presidential transition team.

Meanwhile the Podesta lobbying firm flourishes. Tony Podesta and his wife Heather are considered among the most powerful Capitol Hill lobbyists; they have garnered many new clients since the start of the Obama administration. The firm's clients include a defense contractor, a drug company, a giant financial firm, and so forth.

The Podestas have brought it all together: power, money, and intellectual firepower. This is truly a Keynesian world, although not, one thinks, what Keynes himself expected from greater government control of the economy.

15

In an Economic Crisis, Printing, Lending, Borrowing, and Spending Just Sow the Seeds of the Next Crisis

1a. Keynes: It is sometimes alleged that economic crises, recessions, and depressions serve a useful purpose. This is false.

Keynes is aware that booms bring some

misdirected investment[1]

and that slumps may help to

get rid of a lot of deadwood.[2]

But even misdirected investment is better than no investment at all.[3]

It is a

serious error

to think that slumps are in some sense necessary to economic progress, either because of their purgative role, or because they moderate speculation and reckless risk-taking by introducing an element of fear. On the contrary, as we have seen, we should

abolish slumps[4]

and instead seek to maintain a perpetual

quasi-boom.[5]

1b. Comments:

i. The attempt to abolish economic contractions is mistaken. There are times when we need them.

We touched very briefly on this subject in our earlier discussion of interest rates (chapter 10, section 4, b, iv). But we now need to delve more deeply into it. Are recessions unnecessary? Can we abolish them entirely? No. We have already paid a heavy price for trying to do so.

Alan Greenspan, chairman of the US Federal Reserve, agreed with Keynes that recessions should be eliminated and resolved to do so. When a mild recession came anyway after the collapse of the dot-com bubble in 2000, the minutes of the Federal Reserve reveal that he deliberately sought to persuade the consumer to borrow more. The argument seemed to be that any deeper or longer recession in a country so encumbered by debt would lead to large-scale debtor bankruptcy. To deal with this problem of too much debt, much of it bad, even more debt had to be created.

If the Fed had allowed a real recession to follow the dot-com madness, the investment mistakes of the 1990s might have been fully liquidated. Assets would have passed from weaker to stronger hands through fire-sale prices and been redeployed along more rational lines. Bad debt would have been written off and the decks cleared for future growth, much as had happened after the collapse of the Great Inflation in the early 1980s. Instead, total debt in the US just ballooned (from 2.8 times gross domestic product in 2000 to 3.7 times by the end of 2008).[6] Bad debt was piled on bad debt and poor investment on poor investment.

A real recession in 2000 and 2001 would have been painful. It would nevertheless have spared the US the much greater pain that came with the Crash of 2008. Following the Crash of 2008, first the Bush and then the Obama administration again sought to stop the pain by rescuing, and if possible reviving, the failed paradigm of borrow and misspend.

Each tried to prevent debt liquidation, to hold up business asset prices, to prevent assets from passing from weak to strong hands. As in Japan following the bubble of the 1980s, the result was to freeze the economy in a nether world, neither dead nor alive, to create "zombie" banks and companies, to prevent needed liquidations and adjustments. To the degree that any of this succeeded, the likely result was at best yet another postponement of pain with a greater and even harsher reckoning to come in the end.

ii. Bubbles are synonymous with misdirected investment.

Keynes was also wrong to think that booms bring some "misdirected investment." When the boom is artificially created by printing money (usually with government deficit spending thrown in), when money is virtually free, almost any investment may look good. Eventually the party ends and much of the prior investment turns out to be a waste of money.

Nor is it true, as Keynes said, that even misdirected investment is better than no investment at all. Under the Keynesian system, much of the misdirected investment is financed by debt. After the investments prove worthless, the debt bill remains, and someone—debtor, lender, or, in the event of a public bailout, taxpayer—will be poorer.

iii. Must we then just resign ourselves to frequent and deep slumps? No.

There is a credible argument that so long as people make misjudgments, there will be slumps. But it is quite possible that the really deep slumps could be avoided, especially if we do not indulge in the inflationary policies recommended by Keynes, policies which, perversely, create rather than cure slumps.

A genuine effort to avoid deep slumps would require a total overhaul of government policy. It would require government to reverse its long-standing policy of trying to "stimulate" lending by continually shrinking the required reserves of banks and other lending institutions. It would, at the same time, require government to stop its reckless money printing, borrowing, and spending.

The German economist Wilhelm Röpke said that "The more stabilization, the less stability."[7] He meant by this that Keynesian policies destabilize the economy, but also that the false promise of stabilization leads people to reckless behavior. The Austrian economist Friedrich Hayek added that "The more we try to provide full security by interfering with the market system, the greater the insecurity becomes."[8]

iv. In the final analysis, bankruptcy (including large-scale bankruptcy) is and always will be an essential element of the market system.

Apart from free prices, the most essential part of the market system extolled by Röpke and Hayek is the carrot of profit and the stick of loss or bankruptcy. Bankruptcy serves two essential ends. It makes people think through risks carefully. And, just as importantly, it liquidates the misjudgements of the past and redirects assets to more competent hands. As Röpke has said, "Our economic system (in the final analysis) is regulated by bankruptcy."[9]

Keynesian economist Paul Krugman has ridiculed the idea that recession is a "necessary punishment" for the errors of the boom.[10] But it is not a "punishment." It is a way to remove the debris of economics misjudgements and begin anew.

Distinguished Keynesian economist Robert Solow goes even further than Krugman in mischaracterizing what recessions and bankruptcies are meant to do. He states, "[To say] that a recession weeds out inefficient firms and practices . . . is a little like saying that a plague . . . cleans up the gene pool."[11] Can Solow really mean this? Are we supposed to regard Wall Street banks using debt leverage (debt up to 30x equity) as plague victims?

To eliminate bankruptcy, especially the large-scale bankruptcy of economic crisis, is to render the market system incapable of doing its job. Keynes said, repeatedly, that he wanted to save the market system. But he seemed to lack any real understanding of what he said he wanted to save.

2a. Keynes: An incipient financial crash, an economic slump, or first one and then the other, require prompt and decisive government intervention.

Either or both of these events tell us that we have made

> a colossal muddle,

that we have

> blundered in the control of a delicate machine,[12]

and that repairs are urgently needed. Bold, strong, corrective action should be administered at the first sign of trouble. It should be as

> radical[13]

as necessary.

In early 1932, more than two years into what became the Great Depression, Keynes warned that

a collapse of this kind feeds on itself,

and complained that

It is very much more difficult to solve the problem today than it would have been a year ago. . . . The . . . authorities of the world have lacked the courage or conviction at each stage of the decline to apply the available remedies in sufficiently drastic doses.[14]

Keynes went on to state that a point of no return might be reached, where the system would lose its

capacity for a rebound.[15]

2b. Comments:

i. Keynes did not, in fact, prescribe what later became the full Keynesian program at the onset of the Great Depression.

His initial reaction to the 1929 Crash was that it might be a blessing in disguise. He thought the Crash had been caused by too high interest rates. In the immediate wake of the crisis, monetary authorities in the US and Britain would have to bring interest rates down and keep them there, and this might all turn out for the best.

He noted that:

Money in America has already become very cheap indeed.

Consequently, there is

Daylight . . . ahead. . . . The longer look . . . [is] decidedly encouraging. . . . I do not doubt . . . cheap money['s] . . . remedial efficacy. The world always underestimates the influence of dear money as a depressing influence and cheap money as a reviving one. . . .[16]

By 1932, however, Keynes had developed doubts about the efficacy of cheap money alone. He argued in an *Atlantic Monthly* article, as he later did in *The General Theory*, that business owners and managers might pass up even the lowest interest rates out of sheer fright, thus thwarting the low interest rate policy. As a result, he now recommended that the state step in and start spending on its own.[17]

Given his earlier statements, it was disingenuous for Keynes to criticize governments in 1932 for

Lack[ing] . . . the courage or conviction at each stage of the decline to apply the available remedies in sufficiently drastic doses.[18]

His own advice about the required remedies and doses had been changing as events unfolded.

ii. Keynesian remedies are still untested.

It is also important to emphasize that the full Keynesian program of cheap money and large-scale government spending (along with occasional add-ons such as protectionism) remains to this day merely a hypothesis. Each time it has been applied, whether by the Roosevelt administration during the Depression, the Japanese government after the bubble of the late 1980s, or the second Bush administration (working with the Greenspan Fed) after the dot-com bubble, it has not produced the hoped for results. There are indeed good reasons to think that it has caused the very problems it was meant to prevent or cure.

iii. The record of the Great Depression.

Consider the following facts. The Great Depression lasted longer than any previous American slump. But for World War II, it might have continued even longer. Massive monetary inflation succeeded in ending the deflation, but unemployment remained stubbornly high. Even the addition of deficit spending failed to bring unemployment below 14%.

Keynesians of course have their response. In America in the 1930s, they say, Roosevelt's efforts to end deflation and control interest rates had been effective, but the deficit spending had been half-hearted. If the New Deal had spent more and spent it sooner, the Depression would not have lingered until the War. When the War came, it provided the truly massive spending stimulus that had been needed all along.

Note, however, that by 1937 Keynes himself no longer advocated more stimulus through deficit spending, at least not in Britain.[19] Nor is it correct to interpret World War II as a giant stimulus program. The massive spending of World War II would have led to horrendous inflation but for wage and price controls. Wage and price controls in turn only work under conditions of total war, when economic activities can be channeled into the relatively straightforward business of war production, and when the entire work force is willing to accept consumption limits and otherwise cooperate with the government. As President Nixon discovered in the early 1970s, wage and price controls do not work either in peacetime or under conditions of a limited war such as Vietnam.

Keynesians often point to the secondary depression of 1937 in order to press their claim that stronger doses of stimulus would have ended the Depression sooner. The argument runs along these lines. Roosevelt had initially been afraid to unbalance his budget, but did so in his first term. Deficit spending hit $2.8 billion in 1935, $4.4 billion in 1936. This produced a recovery. Then, during the second term, an excess of caution led to a reduction in the deficit to $2.8 billion in 1937 and $1.2 billion in 1938. This fall in deficit spending precipitated the sharp downturn that began in late 1937.

Does this make sense? Perhaps not. First, it seems a stretch to say that the economy had recovered prior to the 1937 slump, since employment remained at such a high level. Second, not withstanding the deficit spending, Roosevelt's fiscal policy mix included very high income taxes on the better-off and excise taxes on everyone. President Hoover had raised income taxes in 1932 (to a top bracket of 60%) in addition to raising and extending excise or sales taxes. Roosevelt compounded these mistakes. It is not unreasonable to blame either the high taxes or even the high budget deficit of 1936 for the slump that followed in late 1937.

Moreover, there were other important factors that might explain the late 1937 slump. The administration's new corporate profits tax was a major blow to business confidence. So was the Wagner Act which strengthened the position of employed, unionized workers at the expense of unemployed workers.[99] So was the relentless trust-busting (threats to break up companies) of the second term. The corporate profits tax alone was sufficient to explain the free-fall in employment, since profits are by far the best lead indicator of employment.

iv. The record of Japan's "Lost Decades."

Like the Great Depression, the period following the Japanese bubble of the 1980s is often cited as a testing ground for Keynesian policy. The full Keynesian program of driving interest rates down, bailing out banks, and borrowing to spend was applied. Government deficit spending increased public debt levels from

55% of gross domestic product in 1990 to over 160% in 2007.[20] What is most notable about this period is that Keynesian "pump priming" failed. The economy never really recovered.

By the 2008 Crash, the Japanese economy was again in free-fall, and it was doubtful how much more government debt could be piled on, since aging Japanese consumers were no longer able to save and lend as they had done in the past. Surprising as it seemed to long-time observers, Japan's saving rate by the end of 2008 had actually fallen below that of America, partly because America's had rebounded in response to its economic crisis.

This did not, however, prevent Japanese politicians from borrowing and spending. Each round of "stimulus" was succeeded by another. The government even proposed borrowing to buy common stocks as yet another recovery measure.

Just as Keynesian apologists have their explanation for the economic failure of the New Deal, they have similar explanations for what happened in Japan after the bubble. Yes, they say, Japan applied Keynesian remedies, but not soon enough, and not boldly enough. In particular, this argument goes, the banks should have been rescued and refinanced early in the process, not belatedly in 1998. Public works spending may not quite have done the job, but it was better than nothing.

Keynesian Paul Krugman agreed with Barack Obama that "bold" government action was needed to save America during the Crash of 2008. He proposed, again, the full suite of Keynesian remedies. When he got to public works spending, he paused to offer a word of explanation:

> Some readers may object that providing a fiscal stimulus through public works spending is what Japan did in the 1990s—and it is. Even in Japan, however, public spending probably prevented a weak economy from plunging into an actual depression. There are, moreover,

reasons to believe that stimulus through public spending would work better in the United States.[21]

Contrary to Krugman, there are also important reasons to expect
stimulus spending to work less well in the US than in Japan. At
least the Japanese borrowed from themselves, not massively from
the Chinese. We should also note Krugman's use of the qualifier
"probably" when he asserts that public works spared Japan a full
depression. This word "probably" is also a favorite of Keynes's. It
signals that we are getting an unsupported intuition, a hunch.

v. Counterfactuals.

The logic of why Keynes's hunches are wrong we will mostly
reserve for chapter 16. But there are some "counterfactuals" worth
mentioning here. Take the depression of 1921. It was a sudden
and deep depression, but also very brief, lasting hardly more than
a year. In this instance, Keynesian remedies were not applied. The
Federal Reserve had come into being in 1913, but had not yet
learned how to manipulate the economy—that came later in the
1920s. The president and Congress did nothing, and the economy repaired itself in record time.

There had been earlier American depressions as well, although
none nearly as long as the Great Depression. The longest was
the depression of 1873–1879. This slump had followed a bubble
blown up by the printing of paper money during and after the
Civil War. When sound money (in the form of a gold standard)
returned in 1879, the depression ended.[RR]

Another counterfactual might be the South Asian financial crisis of the late 1990s. In this case, Keynesian remedies were not
implemented, because the governments affected did not have the
financial resources needed to implement them. Insolvent banks
were shut down, failing companies failed. To everyone's surprise, it worked. The economies recovered and went on to greater

strength. A letter writer to the *Economist* magazine contrasts the advice that the US gave South Asia in the late 1990s and the advice the US gave itself a decade later:

> Having been in Asia during the financial crisis a decade ago, I am struck by the similarities . . . [to the American and British Crash of 2008]. . . . The only ingredient . . . missing [is] . . . the American trade representative demanding that weak banks go bust. Whatever happened to "let the markets decide," which in 1998 was sold as economic truth to Asian countries? Is the medicine . . . so liberally handed out to South Korea, Thailand, etc. too bitter for the doctor?[22]

It is useful to keep all this in mind. We should be skeptical about the Keynesian program for handling crashes and slumps, not simply accept it on faith as so many do. Keeping this in mind, we will now start, in the next sections, to drill down deeper into the Keynesian program in order to scrutinize further each of its individual components.

3a. Keynes: The state must be particularly vigilant about spotting an incipient financial crash and promptly move to prevent it.

The script for preventing a financial crash was written long ago. We need to follow it.

In 1873, Walter Bagehot, famed editor of the *Economist* magazine, published a book called *Lombard Street*. This book argued that the Bank of England, then a private institution although with semi-official status, should stand ready to act as the "lender of last resort." If the public is nervous and starts withdrawing funds from a bank, that bank should be able to replace those funds by borrowing from the Bank of England.

Of course there were rules. The borrowing bank must still be solvent, it must give the Bank of England sound securities as collateral for the loan, and it must pay a stiff interest rate. The sound collateral meant that, no matter what happened, the Bank of England would not lose money.

Here is where Bagehot became controversial: he said that the Bank of England should stand ready to make as many of these loans as necessary to reassure the public and stop bank runs. It should stand ready to make these loans even if it had already made as many loans as its own reserves, under then current banking law, allowed. In other words, the Bank of England should do whatever it took to stop a bank run, even if it had to abandon sound banking procedure or even, technically, violate the law.

Bagehot's ideas were not without critics. One, Thomas Hankey, thought that a "lender of last resort" system would lead banks to take on riskier loans, or otherwise behave recklessly, because they would expect to be bailed out, even if at a penalty interest rate.[23]

Bagehot's ideas triumphed over those of his friend Hankey. Keynes also sided with Bagehot, but worried that his ideas may be applied too late or timidly. The way to stop a financial crisis is for the government to step in decisively. If unlimited funds are made available to threatened financial institutions, a downward spiraling mass panic can be stopped. Individuals, confident of the government's support, will no longer rush to protect themselves in ways that quickly backfire by bringing down the system and guaranteeing a bad outcome for all.

3b. Comments:

i. It was Hankey, not Bagehot, who was right about bailouts.

The promise to bail out banks and other lending institutions eventually leads to reckless lending. The need for central banks to furnish, on short notice, an unlimited amount of cash also leads to the printing of money. Once a central bank has gotten into the habit of printing money, inflation is sure to follow, either an inflation of consumer prices or of assets. This in turn leads to a financial crisis, followed by another inflation in a vicious circle played out over time.

ii. Why banks are always the weak link.

The financial system is, without question, the weak link in the market system. But it need not be so. The problem is that banks, as presently set up, are always technically insolvent. They are technically insolvent from the day they open. Why? Because they accept deposits, many of which must be paid back on demand, but then lend money without usually having a comparable right to get it back on demand. The result: on any given day, depositors can "break" the bank by demanding all their money back at once.

This is one of the reasons why "mark-to-market" accounting for banks makes little sense. A literal and rigorous application of it would bankrupt any bank even in normal times. When times are tough, it guarantees that the entire banking system will fail. During the Great Depression, about two thirds of US banks survived. If "mark-to-market" had existed, few would have survived.

Today we take the riskiness, and resulting instability, of the banking system for granted. But it did not have to be this way. In earlier centuries, banks acted as storage depots for gold and silver, analogous to grain storage companies today. No grain storage company is allowed to lend out customers' grain in the hope that it will always have enough grain on hand to meet customer demands for withdrawals. The grain stays in the storage bin until called for, and if it is used, it is always with the customer's consent.

When bankers began to treat gold and silver storage differently, to lend it out for profit without the owner's direct consent for the loan, there were lawsuits. The outcome of the lawsuits was uncertain, but over time the right to lend money on completely different principles than other commodities was established.

In retrospect, these judicial decisions opened Pandora's Box. They not only put banks in constant peril of a bank run, of a panicked demand for the return of funds by all customers at the same time; they also allowed banks to create new money through the simple act of making loans.* As a result, the amount of money in the economy became completely unpredictable. This is truly a lunatic system.

iii. What to do about banks.

The most obvious reform would be to increase the reserve requirement. The ideal reserve would be 100%. Banks would then charge for storage, for processing checks and other transactions, and for acting as our loan agent. In the event of a loan, the term of the loan could not be longer than the term of the deposit.†

Most bankers would oppose the concept of 100% reserves. They know they can make much more money in most years with lower reserves. What they do not fully comprehend is that banking, as presently structured, is not truly profitable. The gains of many years are eventually forfeited in a crisis that wipes out the existing shareholders. New shareholders may do well for another generation, only to be wiped out in turn. Any move toward higher reserves would help to establish banking on a sounder footing.

The greatest obstacle to sound banking is government. The US Federal Reserve was established in 1913, in part, to reduce bank reserves. Over the years, it has lowered reserve requirements repeatedly, always seeking in this and other ways to create more

---

* See Note SS.

† For more on 100% reserve banking, see Note TT.

money and pour it into the economy through the banking sys-
tem.ᵁᵁ In the eyes of politicians, more money is almost always
better. It will help the economy look better in the short run, and
that will help incumbents get reelected. The idea that the government (in the form of the Federal Reserve) guards us from inflation makes no sense. The record tells us otherwise. The Fed is the
source, not the cure, for inflation.

4a. Keynes: Bagehot needs updating.

Bagehot's approach, if applied, with vigor, is generally correct, but
still needs further refinement. In particular, interest rates need to
be lower, lending standards lower, and the overall scale of government assistance higher.

Bagehot wanted the "lender of last resort" to lend at rates high
enough to impose a penalty. Keynes, on the other hand, wanted
low interest rates to prevail throughout the financial system at all
times, both in regular loans and, presumably, in emergency loans
as well. Nor should the "lender of last resort" be so choosy about
who is helped.

As we have noted, Keynes also recognized that if interest rates
are already low when the crisis strikes, there is only so much that
cheap credit can do. In addition, no matter how cheap the credit
is, people may be too frightened to borrow. In this case,

> direct state intervention is needed.[24]

This intervention may take the form of subsidized long-term
loans to industry (at very low rates) or direct subsidies to industry.[25] In addition, the state should prepare plans to expand and
accelerate its own direct investment program, and put the plan
into effect at the first sign of need.[26]

4b. Comments:

i. Bagehot's system was already unstable. Keynes just makes it even more unstable.

At least under Bagehot, banks that got into trouble through bad loans of their own had to put up good collateral for any rescue loans from the Bank of England. They also had to pay a penalty rate of interest, one high enough to discourage over-reliance on the rescue service. If a troubled bank either lacked good collateral or could not pay a penalty rate, it failed and was promptly liquidated by creditors.

Hankey was right: Bagehot's system encouraged a degree of recklessness. Worse, it encouraged a central bank to become reckless itself. But it was the picture of sobriety and sanity compared to Keynes's system.

ii. Ben Bernanke's version of Bagehot.

We have already discussed Bernanke's performance as governor and then chairman of the Federal Reserve in chapter 14, ("Housing Bubble"). But a few more words are in order. During the Crash of 2008, the US Federal Reserve adopted a full-fledged Keynesian stance. Keynesian remedies had been adopted before, but never on such a vast scale. In fourteen months, (January 2007–February 2009), $1.2 trillion new dollars were conjured out of "thin air" and injected into the economy, with at least $2 trillion more promised.

These new dollars could in turn be multiplied into many, many more new dollars within the banking system.[55] No one could be sure how many dollars. But whatever happened, the total impact on an economy of $14 trillion would be profound.

Nor was this all. In addition, there were various other Fed commitments totaling another $4.5 trillion. By 2009, the total Fed program had thus reached $7.5 trillion.

Almost as startling as the scale of the Bernanke program was its secrecy. No one—not even Congress—was told where or to whom the money went. Some of it may have been used to bail out foreign as well as US banks. No one knows or perhaps ever will know.

iii. What would all this new mystery money mean?

Alan Meltzer, the respected historian of the Federal Reserve, argued that the flood of new Fed money would eventually produce a consumer price inflation "higher than . . . in the 1970s."[27] Many other observers agreed, including mega investor Warren Buffett.[28] We must also keep in mind that the Fed's actions augmented other US government bailout expenditures and guarantees approximating $5.5 trillion. The grand total of $13 trillion as of early 2009 represented $131,000 for every tax filer in America and $42,000 per person.[29]

iv. The Fed violated Bagehot's rules in other ways.

As previously noted, the Fed rescued, not just banks, but investment banks, the most leveraged speculators of the bubble years. It made loans at vanishingly low rates to these same speculators at a time when many very good companies outside the Fed's protection had to pay sky-high rates. It accepted very poor collateral. It rescued insolvent as well as solvent financial firms without a clear or consistent plan.

v. Can the Fed reverse itself? Perhaps not.

If the Fed had an "exit strategy," a way to extinguish all the new dollars it was creating, it did not reveal it. Fed backers just assumed that what had been done could be undone. If an attempt were made to undo it, there would be a firestorm of protest among politicians on Capitol Hill. Moreover, the American economy had become so leveraged and vulnerable that even an interruption of dollar/liquidity/credit growth, much less a reduction, might easily prove too much of a shock for the system to take.

vi. Is the Fed itself insolvent? Perhaps.

The US Federal Reserve itself is a highly leveraged institution. Its operating arm, the Federal Reserve Bank of New York, has an assets to capital ratio of 100 to 1.[30] If the new collateral it accepted during the crisis were "marked-to-market," one wonders whether it would be insolvent itself.

Of course, a central bank can always just print more money to cover losses. This might or might not be legal under existing law, but who would know, and if they did know, who would care? The Fed may have already exceeded its legal mandate by taking the steps it did in 2008. Former Federal Reserve Chairman Paul Volcker said that it was a close question.[31]

vii. Credit should not be confused with speculation.

The Fed's actions during the 2008 Crash, together with those of the Treasury, did not initially get credit flowing again. One observer, journalist Christopher Caldwell, senior editor of the politically conservative *Weekly Standard*, offered this very Keynesian explanation:

> To be blunt, credit is successfully reestablished when financial elites [on Wall Street] say, "When." Credit is close to a synonym for the mood of the ruling class. To say an economy is based on credit is to say it is based on animal mysteries. Glamour, prestige, élan, sprezzatura, cutting a figure . . . that is what the economy is made of.[32]

Caldwell's "animal mysteries" is of course a direct echo of Keynes's "animal spirits." But this is not what an economy should be made of. It is rather what a Keynesian economy is made of, one that has fallen into a regular pattern of bubbling speculation alternating with bust.

5a. Keynes: Can a country spend its way into recovery? Yes.

Keynes wrote an article in 1934 for the popular American magazine *Redbook* entitled

"Can America Spend Its Way Into Recovery?"

and opened the article with

Why, obviously![33]

The article continued: The very behavior which would make

a man poor

could make

a nation wealthy.[34]

Yes, the extra government spending needed during a slump will exceed tax revenues, no matter how high tax rates are, because taxes fall during an economic contraction. There would necessarily be a government budget deficit and a need to borrow. But the nation's debt would usually be to its own citizens.

Moreover, tax rates should never have to be increased to pay the new debt. The money borrowed and spent will revive the economy. A revived economy requires less government spending on the "dole" (unemployment insurance) and generates a stream of new tax revenue. Together, the savings and the new taxes will more than cover the debt service. So, in sum, government spending of borrowed money under conditions of less than full employment is (what economists after Keynes came to call) a free lunch.[35]

5b. Comments:

i. If the case for spending our way to recovery is so obvious, why does Keynes not make it?

In this article and elsewhere, Keynes provided only indirect and often contradictory arguments in support of his proposition and no evidence for it whatever. No one since has supplied the missing arguments or evidence. As we have seen, the historical record of the Great Depression and the Japanese Lost Decades is not particularly encouraging. Christina Romer, President Obama's chairman of the Council of Economic Advisors, also looked at post-war American recessions and found little evidence that fiscal stimulus had helped end them.[36]

As John Cochrane, University of Chicago Business School professor, has concluded, "I've been looking through graduate course outlines and textbooks, and I can find nowhere in the last 50 years that anybody in economics has said that [deficit spending as a] fiscal stimulus is a good idea. What are we doing giving [such] advice . . . [when] there's nothing [in what] . . . we teach our graduate students that says fiscal stimulus works?" [37]

ii. The "fiscal stimulus" bandwagon.

Not surprisingly, world governments (and their economists) do not speak openly about "deficit spending." They prefer to use euphemisms such as "fiscal policy" or "fiscal stimulus." During the 2008 Crash, economist Lawrence Kudlow noted that

> At the G-20 meeting in Washington [a meeting of wealthy nations], . . . all one heard was "global fiscal stimulus." . . . It won't work. It never has. Hundreds of academic studies over the past 25 years show clearly that countries [whose governments] spend more grow less.[38]

The Economist magazine noted that Germany alone seemed to be reluctant to increase its budget deficit for "stimulus" purposes. Why? Because "spending packages enacted to fight slumps in the 1970s produced little but new debt. Since then the prevailing wisdom has been that they do not work."[39]

Of course, in the end Germany decided to follow the pack by adopting some "stimulus," albeit less than others.

iii. China props up its economy.

A leading voice in favor of global "stimulus" was that of China. This was not unexpected. China's brand of capitalism is broadly mercantilist (without the protectionism); Keynesian ideas fit perfectly within this framework; and, apart from the United States, no other country had done more to blow up the global bubble of 2002–2008.

China's government committed itself after the 2008 Crash to a $585 billion stimulus package, bigger than Europe's $542 billion and much bigger in relation to the size of the economy. The head of the central bank praised his own country's ability to "act boldly and expeditiously without having to go through a lengthy or even painful approval process" and also warned about the "complacency" of other countries.[40]

iv. Obama speaks, but the words are Keynes's.

The leading stimulus program in dollar terms came from America. President Bush made a $152 billion down payment in February 2008, and President Obama followed up with $787 billion in early 2009. The second bill represented 6% of gross domestic product (GDP), only topped by China at 15%.[41]

Bush had been a reluctant and even somewhat apologetic Keynesian; Obama expressed no such doubts. Obama even sounded like Keynes:

The failure to act, and act now, will turn a crisis into a catastrophe. . . . [Without stimulus] at some point we may not be able to reverse [the] . . . crisis.[42]

This was identical to Keynes's statement that a contracting economy, left to its own devices, could lose the

capacity for a rebound.[43]

(Of course, Keynes offered neither logic nor evidence for this proposition, and as we shall see in the next chapter, it has largely been abandoned by Keynesian economists. But no matter, it lives on and guides the American and other governments today.)

Obama habitually referred to government "investments" whenever he spoke of government spending, just at Keynes did. He said that his opponents preferred to "do nothing," just as Keynes did.[44] He spoke of the need to increase "demand," just as Keynes did. One doubts, however, that Obama was using the term "demand" in just the way that Keynes did.

v. Keynes on "demand."

Keynes's use of the term "effective demand" is extremely confused. It is not defined as an economy's overall buying or buying power, the definition that Obama probably had in mind. It is instead defined as thew total income which businesses "expect to receive" (note the word expect).[45] Keynes then takes this nebulous expectation, labels it D (for demand), and states that

$$N = F (D),$$

which means that N, employment, is a function, F, of D, expected demand.[46]

Translated from mathematics, this means that employment is determined by expected demand. Note that it does not say that these variables are connected or somehow influence each other. It says that expected demand directly causes employment.

In reality, of course, expectations are not a measurable quantity and thus have no place in an equation. Nor is it possible for a purely subjective expectation to determine or cause anything, or for the functional relationship to be verified in any way. Although Keynes cannot verify such a claim, he can at least furnish reasons for thinking that is might be true, but does not bother. He simply assumes it. No logical explanation is offered, no statistical or other evidence. We just have Keynes's word for it, and the same is true for all of Keynes's other "functions."

vi. Obama overstates the case.

We certainly cannot blame President Obama for Keynes's confused definition of "demand" or misuse of math. But perhaps we can hold the President accountable for exaggerating the support for "stimulus" among economists. Some examples of what the president has said:

> There is no disagreement that we need . . . to jump-start the economy;[47]
>
> No one doubts that some form of big stimulus is urgently needed;[48]
>
> Most economists, almost unanimously . . . [support the idea of] government . . . introducing some additional demand into the economy.

He claimed all this even though 100 leading economists wrote him a letter explicitly stating their disagreement.[49] In general, Obama dismissed his critics' "worn out old ideas" without explaining why his Keynesian ideas from three quarters of a century ago should be regarded as new.[50]

vii. Obama's Stimulus Act.

As noted in chapter 14, President Bush had spread panic in October of 2008 by going on television to say that the consequences of not passing his bank bailout bill would be dire. President Obama did exactly the same thing in order to sell his stimulus bill. At the time, Obama promised that the bill would be free of Congressional earmarks ("pork" for individual members of Congress) and later, after the bill passed, boasted that he had kept it clean. But he had not.

Speaker of the House Nancy Pelosi got a special wetlands provision for her district. Senate Majority Leader Harry Reid (D-Nevada) got what could be billions for a high-speed rail connection from Los Angeles to Las Vegas. The House bill had nothing at all for high-speed transit. The Senate bill had $2 billion. The Congressional committee that was charged with reconciling $0 and $2 billion "compromised" at $8 billion.[51] This must have been a Congressional first and reflected Senator Reid's power.

In addition to the stealth earmarks, the bill had lots of nongermane spending such as $246 million in targeted tax breaks for Hollywood and $198 million for aging Filipino World War II veterans, many not living in the US.[52] One of the nongermane provisions required that all medical records be computerized and made available to the government and other private parties with no opt-out for privacy. The data would be used by the government to evaluate both the effectiveness and cost-effectiveness of medical procedures, which would facilitate government control over medicine.

This provision, like others, had nothing to do with economic stimulus. It was buried within the huge economic stimulus bill precisely to avoid an open debate about its merits.

The initial stimulus bill that emerged from the House of Representatives had 40% of its spending targeted for 2011 and later, when the crisis would supposedly have passed. Critics thought this odd. They forgot that 2012 would be a Congressional election year, something that the House drafters clearly had in mind. Three Senate Republicans voting for the bill reduced the "out" spending to about 25%.[vv]

Congressional Democratic leaders promised that the Stimulus Act would create almost four million jobs. Of course these figures were more or less pulled out of thin air. But even if true, the cost would be over $200,000 per job,[53] four times what it costs to create an average job in the private economy. And of course the quality of the jobs, and how long they would last after the government's money were spent—well, time would tell.

viii. Why should we expect stimulus to work?

Putting aside Keynes's peculiar definition of demand and even more peculiar math, does stimulus spending actually increase demand (in the conventional sense of economic buying power)? Will it thereby reduce unemployment? It depends, in part, on where the money comes from. If it comes from taxing the rich, we must heed what (the pre-*General Theory*) Keynes himself said:

> [Should] ... taxation ... [be] made to fall ... [not] over the whole community ... but ... solely on [rich] ... employers then we must not be surprised if the level of employment and output is below what it should be.[54]

If government spending is financed by borrowing from the rich, one must ask how the rich might have used the money otherwise. If the money is borrowed from foreign governments, will it be invested in a way that generates a reliable stream of income from which to repay the debt? Otherwise, when we pay it back, we will be reducing future demand. (We may also be financing, according to humorist P. J. O'Rourke, "Chinese nuclear submarines ... popping up in San Francisco Bay to get some decent Szechuan take-out.")[55] If the spending is simply financed by printing money, a likely outcome will be short-term employment gains followed later by inflation and economic destruction.

Is this really a way to restore economic growth? Not according to Jason Furman, an economist who was candidate Obama's campaign Economic Policy Director and subsequently Deputy Director of the White House National Economic Council. In January 2008, Furman wrote that stimulus was "a less effective option." As he said then, "the key to economic growth is higher saving and investment to increase the capital stock and thus the productive capacity of the economy."[56]

ix. Is deficit spending a "free lunch"?

Keynes offered deficit spending as an example of what economists today call a "free lunch." It is "free" because the resulting economic growth should provide all the tax money and more needed to service and eventually retire the debt. This is completely fanciful. Only ask the Japanese government, whose debt to gross domestic product ratio has almost tripled since the collapse of their late 1980s bubble and the beginning of Keynesian therapy.

x. Can stimulus be shut off?

The Victorian novelists warned that debt is addictive. It is no different with government debt. Easy to start, it is hard to stop. Economist Wilhelm Röpke warned about this shortly after Keynes's death, that deficit spending might start for alleged economic policy reasons, but then continue as payoffs for political pressure groups. The post-war record in the US, Europe, and Japan bears this out.

Some leading Dutch economists have called for binding, "irreversible" commitments by governments to repay deficits, but even if that were desirable, everyone knows that government commitments are never binding.[57] The problem was anticipated over two hundred years ago by the economist James Mill, father of John Stuart Mill:

> Should the disposition of government to spend become heated by an opinion that it is right to spend, and should this be still farther inflamed by [popular support], no bounds would then be set. . . . Such a delusion . . . [would produce] the most baneful consequences.[58]

Czech Prime Minister Mirek Topolanek (then serving as European Union President) dared speak the truth when he said in March 2009 that deficit spending for stimulus is "the road to hell."[59]

6a. Keynes: There is no shortage of useful projects for government to spend money on.

Any spending under dire economic circumstances is better than no spending. The main thing is to

get the money spent.[60]

It will always be hard to get the

dead-heads[61]

to agree that any project is legitimate, but in truth such projects abound.

Roads are a good choice and Keynes liked a proposal he had heard to build a "broad boulevard" along the south side of the Thames in London. He also liked housing projects and asked why the whole of South London should not be torn down and replaced with

far better buildings.[62]

In general, as noted in chapter 4, he always liked schemes that combined art and commerce to produce something both beautiful and useful.

6b. Comments:

i. Stimulus spending to be effective has to go right out the door. But useful projects cannot be rushed.

Economist George Reisman has pointed out that Keynes set the bar rather low for useful public spending projects. Since "pyramid-building" and digging up "old bottles . . . fill[ed] with bank notes" buried in coal mines by the Treasury "may serve to increase wealth,"[63] almost any other project selected by the government will look good by comparison.[64]

That was Keynes's essential position: spend on anything. Any spending, if done quickly enough, is better than no spending. Keynes really had to take this position because he realized that the better projects take time, a great deal of time, and the whole point of "stimulus" during a slump is get it into the economy quickly. Unfortunately the examples of public works projects that Keynes gave, apart from pyramids, do not pass his own urgency test.

Take Keynes's endorsement of a proposal (he said he had heard about) for a broad, new boulevard on the south side of the Thames in London. A project of such scale and complexity would take years to plan, much less execute. Keynes would have responded that the planning should be done in advance, during good economic times, so that the project could be ready. But just taking the needed land from private owners would itself take a long time, and undoubtedly face legal challenges.

In 2008, President Obama talked about public spending on alternative energy research and construction to reduce American dependence on foreign oil, much of it controlled by hostile regimes. This was a very popular idea, but it was also the kind of project that would take many years to implement properly. If pursued too rapidly, there is even a risk of locking into place inferior standards or technologies, because there would not be adequate time to develop better ones. As a general rule, the more rushed government "investment" is, the more likely that it will be misspent, put into politicians' pet projects, or flow to favored interest groups or constituencies.

ii. Only a fraction of stimulus spending actually "stimulates."

For US government capital projects in general, only one fourth of the money on average is spent in the same year the money is appropriated by Congress.[65] When the money is spent, much of it goes to payroll. These payrolls will be higher than in the private sector because of government rules requiring the use of union labor, or in the absence of union labor, paying at the highest union labor rates.

Workers who receive this extra government money will not spend it all. During an economic slump, they will try to pay down credit card and other debt or if possible save some of it. Even if they do spend the money, it may be on cheaper imported goods. So, for every dollar spent by the government, only a fraction of it may boost the domestic economy, and much of the boost may come in out years when the economic crisis should have passed and when the extra "demand" may actually do more harm than good.

iii. Is it better to stimulate with tax cuts?

If stimulus cannot be speeded up without sacrificing the quality of the projects selected, why not stimulate the economy with tax cuts rather than government spending? This proposal, favored by so-called Supply-siders and most Republicans, does get the money out fast. But, reply Keynesians and most Democrats, what if it is all saved or used to retire debt?

Although Supply-siders and Keynesians, Republicans and Democrats, differ on this and other important points, note that both endorse government deficit spending. Both also endorse the idea of government printing money in order to manipulate the supply of money and the level of interest rates. On balance, the similarities outweigh the differences, and Supply-side Republicans may properly be regarded as apostate Keynesians. At least in economics, it is reasonable to argue that there are not two political parties in America, but rather one party with two branches.

7a. Keynes: The impact of government spending during a slump is magnified by the "investment or employment multiplier."

The Keynesian multiplier springs from the initial observation that a newly employed person will start to spend money. This spending will in turn help employ others. Employment leads to further employment, just as unemployment leads to further unemployment. If an economy is near full employment, the spending of one more newly employed person will not matter much. If unemployment is widespread, each increment of new employment and new spending will matter more.

Keynes gives an example in which 5,200,000 persons are employed. 100,000 new jobs are created by a government public works program. These new jobs then lead to more new jobs until total employment rises to 6,400,000 which is 1,200,000 more jobs. In this instance, the employment multiplier is 12.[66] Although the actual multiplier will vary, it should be

at least three or four times[67]

on public works expenditure. The concept of the multiplier is critical because it refutes the criticism that public works programs will never be large enough to make much of a difference in a developed economy. As Keynes says,

> Public works even of doubtful utility may pay for themselves over and over again at a time of severe unemployment, if only from the diminished cost of relief expenditure.[68]

7b. Comments:

i. Misuse of math.

Keynes's multiplier is perhaps his best-known concept, although it was actually developed by his student (and later trustee) Richard Kahn. It is a textbook example of the misuse of math to make what is uncertain appear certain.

The idea that a given amount of investment will have a greater impact on an economy at the bottom of the cycle than at the top makes sense. Wesley C. Mitchell proposed this in his 1913 book, *Business Cycles*. Nothing about this, however, is predictable, mechanical, or adaptable to a mathematical equation.

Nor should we expect any "multiplication" if basic economic relationships are askew. If, for example, many businesses are going bankrupt because wages are too high in relation to prices, or if the economy is choked with bad debt, we should not expect "multiplication." If (and only if) conditions are right at the bottom of the cycle, then the first wave of new investment should lead to further investment and eventual recovery. Given the complexity and complete uncertainty surrounding the variables, economist Benjamin Anderson thought that even Mitchell's original multiplier concept was "unfruitful."[69]

Keynes ignored all this. He took Kahn's mathematical equation (previously called the "employment multiplier") and re-christened it the "investment multiplier." He did this even though his multiplier was about spending, not investment. Presumably investment sounded better to the public then spending, so why be concerned about accuracy of terminology?

ii. Quantifying the unquantifiable.

How did Keynes then go about quantifying the unquantifiable? First, he made an assumption about how much people would spend and how much they would save from their income, expressed as percentages. This was called the "marginal propensity to consume." Keynes mostly picked the percentages out of the air, but he did stop to look at some US statistics from Simon Kuznets, some of which he accepted, some of which he dismissed as

> improbable[70]

without offering much explanation.

Having arbitrarily determined the marginal propensity to consume, he then said that the MPC is

> of considerable importance because it tells us how the next increment of output will have to be divided between consumption and [saving].[71]

Note the words "have to be." As Henry Hazlitt has remarked, these words suggest that an assumption of Keynes's has somehow been elevated to an iron law determining how people will actually behave. Keynes even refers to it as a

> fundamental psychological law.[72]

To make a long story short, we finally arrive at a conclusion that if the marginal propensity to consume is 90%, then the multiplier will be 10. This means that a government stimulus check will first go to a group of workers who will spend 90% of it. This second round of spending will then go to another group of workers who will also spend 90%, and so on, until the spending chain finally exhausts itself for reasons that Keynes did not explain clearly. The net result will be that an original sum Y spent by the government will eventually lead to 10(Y) of spending.

iii. Better check the fine print.

All of this implicitly assumes that the 10% which is not spent is put under some kind of mattress. It is inconvenient to think that this money might instead be invested, and the invested funds also spent, because if 100% of funds are spent, the mathematical multiplier self-destructs by becoming infinite. Even Keynes would have had to agree that an infinite multiplier was "improbable," to use one of his favorite words.[ww]

iv. Is there any evidence for Keynes's version of the multiplier?

Whether the Keynesian multiplier actually exists continues to be debated by economists. Economist George Reisman dismisses it as "totally fallacious."[73] Even economists Paul Samuelson and William Nordhaus, Keynesian authors of a best-selling economics textbook, admitted that "no proof has yet been presented that the [Keynesian] multiplier will be greater than 1,"[74] although they thought that it should be.

Economists who try to derive multiplier results from actual statistical data usually arrive at much lower multipliers than the minimum of "three or four times" predicted by Keynes. Some Keynesians, looking back, have estimated that the 1930s multiplier was not far above 1.[75]

There is also considerable debate about whether tax cuts might produce a higher multiplier than government spending. This matters because the alleged existence of the multiplier has been used to support government stimulus spending. If multiplication exists, but if tax cuts multiply better, then the case for government stimulus spending falls apart.

Christina Romer, head of The Council of Economic Advisors under President Obama, studied tax cuts from 1947 to 2005 and found that a cut equivalent to 1% of gross domestic product stimulated three times as much GDP growth, but only if the tax cut was permanent, not temporary.[76] This fits the "rational expectations" view that, in order to be effective, stimulus spending would have to persuade producers and consumers to start spending their own money, and that temporary measures will not convince them to do so.

Economist Mark Zandi has estimated the multiplier on government food stamps or unemployment benefits, both items likely to be spent immediately, not saved, at 1.73x and 1.63x respectively.[77] Christina Romer has also published work suggesting a 1.57x multiplier for stimulus spending.[78] But noted economist Gary Becker responded that the evidence for Romer's conclusion was so thin as to be nonexistent. He and fellow economist Kevin Murphy guessed that a stimulus spending multiplier would be less than 1.[79]

v. Deficit spending for "stimulus" is not a rational policy.

In conclusion, Keynes's claim that deficit spending for stimulus purposes would pay for itself just from

the diminished cost of relief expenditure[80]

looks, in retrospect, like wildly wishful thinking. The rest of his claim, that even

public works of doubtful utility[81]

would pay for themselves thanks to the multiplier, looks no more believable.

This characteristically Keynesian emphasis on quantity, not quality of investment, and not even investment, just spending, all financed by debt, is a formula for waste. It is the kind of thinking that led the US to borrow in order to build overlavish or unneeded homes during the housing bubble. Even worse, it led to borrowing money from China in order to buy cheap Chinese consumer goods that, long before the debts were paid, would end up in a landfill. Wasteful spending can only lead eventually to poverty, not to wealth.

We will give the last word to John Cochrane, professor at the University of Chicago Business School whom we previously quoted:

> The idea that [government] spending can spur the economy was discredited decades ago. . . . It is very comforting in times of stress to go back to the fairy tales we heard as children but it doesn't make them less false.[82]

16

Markets Do Self-Correct

1a. Keynes: Economic contractions do not cure themselves.

It is an especially grave mistake to think that a malfunctioning economic machine can be left alone. Economies are not, as the "classical" economists thought,

> self-adjusting.[1]

They do not fix themselves.[2] On the contrary, without government intervention, markets are more likely to cycle down and establish a new

> "equilibrium" [at a] sub-normal [level of] employment [and remain there] in a chronic condition.[3]

1b. Comment: Even Keynesians acknowledge that Keynes is wrong.

This is one of Keynes's most famous ideas: that markets are not naturally self-correcting, that the 25% unemployment rate reached in the US during the Great Depression might have simply stayed there, stuck indefinitely, without government intervention. As we saw in the last chapter, President Obama echoed Keynes in 2009 when he said that an economy might fall too far to recover.

There is a great deal that can be said about this, and we will explore it throughout this chapter. For now, suffice it to say that the concept of a depression equilibrium is self-contradictory just on its own terms. Keynes also contradicted it himself in other passages. And Keynes's most ardent followers soon abandoned it.

The notion of equilibrium during depression is self-contradictory because of the way that equilibrium is defined in economics. An equilibrium occurs when all parts of an economy are meshing perfectly. This cannot be true when unemployment is at 25%. Keynes presumably meant that markets, left to their own devices, either cannot or will not initiate actions necessary to correct the problem. But Keynes himself admitted that they might.[4]

Franco Modigliani, Paul Samuelson, James Tobin, and Don Patinkin were some of the most prominent Keynesians of the post-war era. In a 1944 paper, written even before Keynes's death, Modigliani showed that Keynes's primary assumption about unemployment (that it was caused by lack of investment which in turn reflected too high interest rates) was usually wrong. As Modigliani wrote:

> It is true that a reduced level of employment and a reduced level of investment go together, but this is not, in general, the result of causal relationship. It is true instead that the low level of investment and unemployment are both the effect of the same cause, namely [an imbalance within the economy between wages and prices].[5]

Since wages are just one of many prices, this meant that unemployment is caused by an imbalance of prices. Since the primary function of markets is to bring prices into balance, it makes no sense to say that markets cannot correct unemployment. As fellow Keynesian Don Patinkin said in 1948 about Modigliani's and other's works, "It should now be definitely recognized that [the concept of an unemployment equilibrium] is an indefensible position."[6]

2a. Keynes: The "classical" case for flexible wages.

"Classical" economists thought that economies were self-adjusting and therefore advised governments confronted with a slump to: Do Nothing. But (as Keynes saw it) Do Nothing really meant: Drive Wages Down.

These two positions—Do Nothing and Drive Wages Down—were not necessarily inconsistent. "Classical" economists thought that markets suffering from a slump would drive wages down on their own. Action by government to achieve this was neither necessary nor desirable.

What was the rationale for such a policy? Did not working people suffer enough during slumps from job loss? Why would it be desirable to drive wages down? The "classical" response (the response Keynes was taught in his youth) runs as follows:

During a slump, people buy less. This reduces business revenues. Because revenues fall first, before expenses, profits fall. Business owners then lay off employees to reduce costs and restore profitability. If, instead, wages fall, profitability can be restored without layoffs.

This is especially necessary if prices start falling throughout the economy. If people buy so much less that almost all prices start to fall, business revenues will be especially hard hit. Not only will fewer widgets be sold, but each individual widget will sell for less. Under these circumstances, if wages do not fall with prices, businesses will certainly face bankruptcy. On the other hand, if both prices and wages fall together, workers should be no worse off. Although wages are lower, the consumer products workers buy will also cost less. It will be a wash.

Keynes agreed that lowering wages along with prices during a depression could save jobs. But, even so, he strongly objected to lowering wages, for a variety of different reasons.

2b. Comments:

i. Keynes's account of flexible wages is not complete.

As we have previously noted, there is no such thing as one homogenous group of "classical" economists. If we look to John Stuart Mill as the leading 19th century economist in the English speaking world, he would have said that lower wages were not a cure-all for unemployment. To achieve maximum employment, he would have said, requires that all prices be in the right balance, as determined by market supply and demand. But it is especially important for wages to be at the right level.

ii. Nor is Keynes's argument against flexible wages direct.

As Henry Hazlitt points out, Keynes does not challenge the logic of flexible wages

> head-on by any coherent and clear-cut argument. [It is difficult to] . . . deny what has become in the last two centuries the most strongly established principle in economics—to wit, that if the price of any commodity or service is kept too high (i.e., above the point of equilibrium) some of that commodity or service will remain unsold. This is true of eggs, cheese, cotton, Cadillacs, or labor. When wage-rates are too high there will be unemployment. Reducing the myriad wage-rates to

their respective equilibrium points may not in itself be a *sufficient* step to the restoration of full employment (for there are other possible disequilibriums to be considered), but it is an absolutely *necessary* step.

This is the elementary and inescapable truth that Keynes, with an incredible display of sophistry, irrelevance, and complicated obfuscation, tries to refute.[7]

3a. Keynes: A flexible wage policy takes too long and causes too much social damage.

Even if ultimately successful, a policy of Drive Wages Down takes too long to cure unemployment during a slump.

In 1930, Keynes wrote that

> the correct answer [to deep unemployment] along austere lines is as follows: A reduction of money wages by 10 percent will ease unemployment in five year's time. In the meanwhile you must grin and bear it.

> If you can't grin and bear it, and are prepared to have some abandonment of laissez-faire [i.e., let the government take charge of the economy in different ways], then you can hope to get straight sooner. You will also be richer ... five years hence. You may, moreover, have avoided a social catastrophe.[8]

3b. Comments:

i. Keynes's caricature has it backwards.

The historical record flatly contradicts Keynes. It suggests that if you want to get through a depression quickly, the best way is to let the price system sort itself out. Economists like John Stuart Mill were correct. If prices fall, wages need to fall. If they do, jobs will be protected and workers will not lose purchasing power.

ii. Flexible wages helped cure the 1921 Depression.

The US depression of 1921 recorded the sharpest price break ever known, sharper even than in the Great Depression. Wholesale prices fell 38% on average from 1920 to 1922. Hourly wages also fell, by 11% on average.[9]

Workers who lost their jobs suffered dreadfully. Those who kept their jobs may have gained on average, because prices fell more than wages, which meant that workers' wages bought more then before.[xx] In real (price-adjusted) terms, average hourly wages rose. Still, because nominal wages were allowed to fall freely, a profitable relationship between prices and wages was reestablished in a very short time, not much more than a year. As mentioned in chapter 15, no lasting damage was done, and both prices and wages quickly began to recover to earlier levels.

iii. Why recovery was less complete in Britain.

The recovery was more complete in the US than in Britain, where unemployment remained a problem for much of the 1920s. The usual explanation is that British industry as a whole was antiquated. Its plant was old, its technology behind the times. But the real problem lay in wage rates.

Lower wage rates in Britain would have boosted profits enough to pay for new plant and technology. This in turn would have led to lower cost products, more exports, and renewed hiring. Instead, generous unemployment compensation and strong unions kept wages up, but also kept millions unemployed.

iv. Inflexible and ultimately rising wages lengthened and deepened the Great Depression.

The 1929 US Crash brought another wave of falling prices. By 1933, prices were down 23%.[10] First Hoover and then Roosevelt did everything they could to keep wages from falling along with prices. They thought, erroneously, that falling wages would damage the economy.

The National Recovery Act virtually outlawed wage reductions and also brought other price controls. In one famous incident, a New Jersey immigrant worker, Jacob Maged, was jailed for three months in 1934 on a charge of pressing a suit for 35¢ instead of the prescribed 40¢. The Wagner Act greatly strengthened labor unions (union membership soon tripled) and also introduced minimum wages and overtime.

Not surprisingly, wages actually rose during the depression by 24% in nominal terms 1931–1939 and by 32% in real terms (adjusted for consumer prices). Economists Harold L. Cole and Lee E. Ohanian, of the University of Pennsylvania and UCLA respectively, estimate that in the late 1930s manufacturing wages were 20% above trend for the century as a whole.[11] The result was a three-tier employment system. There were the millions of unemployed who had effectively been cast to the wolves, employed workers who may have made more rather than less through hard times, and unionized workers who had both job security and big wage gains.

v. The price system was thwarted in other ways.

Throughout the Roosevelt administration, interest rates were extremely low. Liquidity was plentiful. This was supplemented by public works spending. But the price system was continually thwarted in large and small ways. Herbert Hoover even put an excise tax on checks, thereby discouraging people from writing checks at a time when the banks were at risk. Roosevelt expanded these consumer excise taxes throughout the economy, even though they fell especially hard on the poor. As we have already noted, Roosevelt's greatest folly was the corporate profits tax enacted in 1936. It was only removed over the president's strong protest in 1938, following the unemployment spike that began in 1937.

vi. Profits are the key.

To understand why the Great Depression lasted so long, one need only read Wesley Mitchell's *Business Cycles* (1913), previously referred to in chapter 15. Mitchell explains that it is business profits (and the prospect of profits) that drive the economy. If profits are up, and prospects are good, the economy and employment rise. When the opposite is true, employment falls.

Wages are only part of the profit equation, but they are a very important part. In particular, if prices fall, wages must be flexible enough to fall with them, so that profits and jobs may be preserved. If the price and profit system is completely thwarted, with wages and public spending only mobile on the upside and interest rates only mobile on the downside, the predictable result will be mass joblessness, a form of joblessness that has been engineered by government policy errors, but in a way that few if any workers would ever be able to understand.

4a. Keynes: Flexible wages in a slump also threaten business revenues.

Even if one has the patience for market solutions, there are reasons to doubt that lower wages will solve unemployment. We must keep clearly in mind that

one man's expenditure is another man's income.[12]

A business owner will readily see

> the obvious great advantages to . . . a reduction of the wages he has to pay.[13]

But will not see

> so clearly the disadvantages he will suffer if the money incomes of his customers are reduced.[14]

If consumer spending falls with wages, we could find ourselves in a situation where both spending and wages fall in a vicious downward spiral. According to Keynes, there is no theoretical reason why wages might not just fall and fall

> without limit,[15]

since a free market ("laissez-faire") system is not

> self-adjusting.[16]

4b. Comments:

i. The Idea of collapsing wages is nonsense.

Keynes, as usual, simply tells us. He does not bother to explain, much less support. He not only states that wages, once they start falling, might fall "without limit." He underscores "without limit" by saying that wages might even fall to

> zero.[17]

The idea that workers will work for free is patently ridiculous. But we need not dwell on it. A little further in this chapter, we shall deal with Keynes's contradictory claim that, in the real world, wages will not fall at all, because workers will not accept wage cuts. If so, then we can presumably disregard the worry that wage cuts will prove uncontrollable and race toward zero.

ii. The idea of collapsing business revenues (from falling wages) is also nonsense.

What about the accompanying claim, that wage cuts will backfire by reducing workers' buying power, which in turn will reduce business revenue? As Henry Hazlitt noted,[18] Keynes is confusing wage rates with wages earned. If prices fall without wage cuts, businesses will frantically lay off workers in an effort to avoid bankruptcy. Under these circumstances, aggregate worker income will plummet.

If wage rates are allowed to fall with prices, profits are protected, workers are not laid off, and aggregate worker income may be much higher than it would have been with the layoffs. As we have just seen, so long as prices fall faster than wages, real (price-adjusted) worker income may actually rise.

5a. Keynes: Although falling wages are not good medicine for a slump, it does not follow that rising wages would help.

Prior to the Great Depression of the 1930s, a popular argument held that capitalism chronically falls into crisis because workers are not paid enough. Because they are not paid enough, they cannot afford to buy enough of the goods they are making. The result is a tendency for production to outstrip consumption. In economic jargon, there is an under-consumption gap.

Rich business owners partly close the underconsumption gap by spending extravagantly, but are too few to close it completely. The result is that the economic system sputters. From time to time it stops altogether. Famed newspaper columnist Walter Lippmann seemed to think that something along these lines had been responsible for the Great Depression:

> The heart of the problem . . . [has been] . . . an insufficiency of consumer . . . purchasing power.[19]

Presidents Hoover and Roosevelt probably did not accept the underconsumption theory, at least not in full, but as we have seen, they did believe that falling wages would be disastrous for an economy. Keynes agreed that wage cuts were inadvisable, but did not endorse wage increases either. In his view, rising wages were a positive insofar as they increased consumer purchasing power, but a negative insofar as they increased labor costs. As he said, increasing labor costs would lead to a less

> "optimistic tone"[20]

among business people.

Keynes concluded that

> the net result of two opposing influences [from rising wages] is to cancel out.[21]

The best policy was therefore neither to cut nor to increase wages in a depression, but rather to leave them where they started.

5b. Comments:

i. What the consumer purchasing power theory misses.

There are several reasons why the consumer purchasing power theory is wrong. It is true that the greengrocer's employee's wages become the baker's income when the greengrocer's employee buys bread. It is true, but also incomplete.

All business costs represent someone else's income, not just wages. If a car manufacturer buys tires, those tires represent income for the tire workers, and for the rubber plantation workers as well. Since all business costs represent someone's wages, the logic of the consumer purchasing power theory would have us raise all costs, not just wages. To do so would, of course, be folly. It would bankrupt all businesses.

The consumer purchasing power theory also assumes that the excessive profits going to capitalists are not all spent. The assumption is that, try as they may, greedy capitalists cannot spend all of their swollen incomes. This too is misleading. Business profits not spent on consumer goods are invested, which means they will flow into additional business spending, including on new employee hires.

The consumer purchasing power theory is still taught in some elementary schools as a primary cause of the Great Depression. As we have seen, Keynes only flirted with it, by harping on the danger that wage reductions would reduce consumption and thus business revenue.

ii. Keynes's idea that wage reductions both reduce consumption and reduce business costs, producing "a wash," is complete nonsense.

As we have seen, wage reductions that accompany price reductions do not necessarily reduce consumption. Wages are falling in this instance precisely in order to protect jobs and protect worker's consumption. Consequently, the idea of "a wash" makes no sense. Not surprisingly, Keynes offers no support for it. The bottom line is that wage cuts (in the particular context of falling prices) are helpful, although they may not be the only remedy needed.

To see this in personal terms, imagine that you work for a small business. The boss calls the staff together and announces that revenues are falling because of a crashing economy. "We can either lay off a third of you or reduce wages all around," the boss explains.

Some of you respond bluntly, "Let's run down profits first." The boss replies, "We are already as close to break even as we dare go. If we get too close to break even, and miscalculate, we will run out of cash and have to close down, because no bank will lend to us now."

What would you prefer under these circumstances? Take a chance on layoffs and hope that someone else gets dropped? Or accept an all-around cut in wages? It is exactly the kind of question that many businesses faced after the Crash of 2008, just as in earlier business contractions.

iii. It should be self-evident that one cannot fix a problem of unbalanced prices by freezing them.

Keynes said that rising wages might lead to a less "optimistic tone" among business people, which would not be helpful. But elsewhere[22] he says that falling wages may also threaten business optimism. The logical inference is that Keynes wants wages to be frozen, neither rising nor falling. Since a depression means that the price system is not working properly, freezing prices is the worst possible thing to do.

6a. Keynes: Uniform wage cuts would make more sense.

A better case could be made for wage cuts if they could be mandated across the board for all workers.

Keynes noted that

> Except in a socialized community where wage-policy
> is settled by decree, there is no means of securing uni-
> form wage reductions for every class of labor. . . . It is
> only in a highly authoritarian society, where sudden,
> substantially all-around changes could be decreed that
> a flexible wage policy could function with success. One
> can imagine it in operation in [then Fascist] Italy, [then
> Fascist] Germany or [then Communist] Russia, but
> not in France, the United States or Great Britain. . . .
> [Wage reductions that are not across the board can]
> only be brought about by a series of gradual, irregular
> changes, justifiable on no criterion of social justice or
> economic expediency.[23]

6b. Comment: Uniform wage cuts make no sense at all in a free price system.

In this case, Keynes's love of paradoxical pronouncement has got the better of him. He is telling us that an authoritarian regime is flexible while a market regime is not, which even for him is oxymoronic.

The passage quoted also demonstrates that Keynes, the student of markets, has not the slightest notion of how markets work. Economist Friedrich Hayek pointed out that markets are a discovery system. They discover what is scarce, what is available; they communicate it through prices. Individual factors are then organized through the profit system which continually interacts with prices.

If an economy is stumbling, and unemployment is high, it means that some prices are far out of balance with others. Wages, for example, may be too high in relation to prices, because prices have fallen at the onset of an economic slump. But if so, the problem is not all wages or all prices.

Some companies, some industries may be doing well; others may be in desperate straits. What is needed is an adjustment of particular wages and particular prices within and between companies, within and between industries, within and between sectors. These adjustments are not a one-time event. They must be ongoing, as each change leads to another in a vast feedback loop.

In some cases, the wages or other prices should rise. In other cases, they should fall. No single across-the-board adjustment will work. It will just make things worse. It is as if Keynes thought of the economy as a kind of water tank to be filled or drained until the right level is reached. Such crude plumbing will not adjust or coordinate anything. It will just make a mess.

7a. Keynes: From a practical standpoint, wages cannot be cut anyway.

Whatever the theoretical arguments for or against reducing wages in a depression, it is a completely impractical idea.

In the 19th century, workers accepted wage cuts in order to keep their jobs during a slump. Today this is no longer true. Partly because of the power of labor unions, partly because of unemployment insurance, partly because of a change in expectations, layoffs are the only practical way to reduce labor costs.

7b. Comment: The idea that wages cannot be cut is not generally true, although it may be true in some unionized industries or companies.

To the degree that workers participate in profit sharing or bonus plans, they are currently accepting variable pay without demur. Admittedly, profit sharing plans are not so common, but bonus plans are. (Ironically political attacks in 2009 on bonuses paid by government-assisted banks led those banks to cut back on bonuses and raise less flexible base pay. Result: the compensation system in government-assisted industries became less flexible, making the companies more vulnerable to downturns and more likely to fail.)

What do workers themselves really prefer? Will they, given a choice between a possible layoff or a certain wage cut, choose the latter? It is hard to say. Unemployment benefits are a factor. In some European countries, these extend for up to five years, although the trend has been to cut them back.

Unionization is another, rather complicated factor. Unionized workers in the US as a group are estimated by the Bureau of Labor Statistics to earn 30% more than their nonunionized counterparts. As a rule, their wages are also harder to reduce. For example, as General Motors approached bankruptcy in the US, direct wage cuts were never seriously discussed, much less implemented. Apparently the United Auto Workers still preferred massive job loss to wage cuts.

Part of the reason that unionized workers in the US earn 30% more on average is that unionization is high among government workers. Governments, being free from profit pressures, often pay more. In addition, governments often trade higher pay for union electoral support.

It is widely accepted by economists that although union wage gains in a particular company or industry may come at the expense of business profits, this is not true for the economy as a whole. For the economy as a whole, union labor gains come at the expense of other workers.*

It is not clear whether Keynes meant that wages could not be cut, even during a slump, because of unions. Nor is his general attitude toward unions clear, or, for that matter, his attitude toward what he called the working class. He said in *The General Theory* that unemployment in the 1930s could not be blamed on labor's

obstina[cy] or truculen[ce].[24]

But that rather begged the question, since these moral qualities were not really at issue. Some years before, Keynes characterized unions as

once the oppressed, now the tyrants.[25]

8a. Keynes: Wage reductions, even if practicable, would not be fair.

Market forces cannot be relied upon to allocate society's wealth in a just way. The market's

_____

* See Note QQ.

juggernaut ... settle[s the issue] by economic pressure.

The right way to go about it is to fix wages based on

> what is "fair" and "reasonable" ... having regard to all
> the circumstances ... between classes.[26]

8b. Comment: Fair in whose judgement?

If not the market, who then will decide on wage levels? Keynes's economic experts? Did not Soviet planning experts demonstrate the impossibility of setting prices and wages outside a market system? It does seem that Keynesianism is more Marxist than Keynes acknowledges, and in the long run, just as impractical and dystopian.

9a. Keynes: A flexible money policy can in any case replace flexible wages.

Fortunately, it is not necessary to reduce wages (to offset falling prices) during a depression in order to prevent business bankruptcies. There is a better way.

Let us remember: the starting problem is not that wages are high. It is, rather, that prices have fallen. The primary lesson to be drawn from this is that prices should never be allowed to fall in the first place. Deflation is poison for an economy. It threatens not only debtors, but everyone.

If preventative measures have failed, and prices are falling, the fall should be promptly arrested. The previous price level should be restored. Once this has been done, wages will not have to be cut and neither profits nor employment will be threatened by unstable prices.

So far so good. But how will prices be prevented from falling, or if they have fallen, restored to the previous level? The answer is simple: government should engineer enough inflation to counteract deflationary forces and thus either maintain or restore previous prices. There are different ways to accomplish this, but the easiest way is for the government to inject new money into the economy.

To see how this might work, we will return to our earlier example of two shipwrecked people living on an isolated tropical island. Their "economy" consists of two knives and two dollars rescued from their lost ship. Under these circumstances, we might expect that each knife would be "worth" $1.

Next assume that two more dollars wash ashore inside a bottle. As a result of this money infusion, each knife is now "worth" $2. In the same way, government can pull prices up by printing a large amount of new money and injecting it into the economy through any number of channels (lending it through banks, giving it as cash grants, or spending it through the government's budget).

Keynes sums this up by stating that

> having regard to human nature and our institutions, it can only be a foolish person who would prefer a flexible wage policy to a flexible money policy.[27]

Keynes thought that the primary purpose of a "flexible money policy" would be to combat deflation, but that it would have other uses as well. In particular, it could be used to manage labor demands. If, during normal times, labor productivity was increasing at 2%, but unions insisted on a 4% wage increase, a 2% inflation would ensure that labor's real (inflation-adjusted) raise was not 4%, but rather 2%. As Keynes saw it, workers were mainly concerned with the nominal level of wages, not the real (inflation adjusted) level.[28]

For all of these reasons then, but especially to control hyperdeflation, Keynes called for a policy of

> price raising—which one can call inflation for short— throughout the world.[29]

9b. Comments:

i. A flexible money policy leads to perpetual inflation.

The impact on the world of Keynes's flexible money policy has been truly profound. It is the way that virtually all modern governments (or government central banks) run their affairs. They are determined at all cost to avoid falling prices (deflation), and they will print any amount of new money to avoid it. Since a productive economy naturally produces goods at lower and lower costs and prices, this means that central banks are inflating all the time, not just during depressions.ᵁ

Nor do central banks stop there. They begin to worry: If we create just enough inflation to arrest what would otherwise be a tendency for prices to fall modestly each year, we will keep overall consumer prices flat. But this would mean falling prices for many firms and, in general, keep us too close to deflation, too close for comfort. So, at least in the late 20th and early 21st centuries, established central bank policy has been to print enough new currency to ensure that inflation will never fall below 1-2% a year. If the natural tendency of prices is to fall 3%, this then produces a chronic inflation, year in and year out, of 4–5%.

ii. Inflation is bad medicine. It will make the patient sicker and sicker.

We have already seen that when an economy is sick, it does not need a single adjustment of all wages or all prices. That will just make things worse. It needs constant adjustment of particular wages and prices, with appropriate readjustment and coordination through the market's feedback loop.

Inflation, it is true, does not affect all wages or all prices equally. In the most common case, the government prints money, the banks lend it out, the money enters the economy wherever the borrowers are. From there the money begins to change hands and move hither, thither, and yon in a completely haphazard and unpredictable way. Industries where costs already exceed prices may never see a penny of it. Industries already enjoying fat profits may get almost all the new demand and enjoy even fatter profits.

Inflation does not help adjust all the innumerable wages and prices that need to be adjusted, in response to market demand, in order to arrive at profitability. Instead, it overwhelms and confuses the system. Prices are supposed to tell business owners and investors what the underlying realities are, so they can make sensible decisions. As inflation distorts prices, it becomes impossible to make sensible decisions.

iii. The stealthier inflation is, the more treacherous.

When inflation is stealthy, as it is during a bubble, it is especially confusing. When the dot-com bubble burst, it was natural to pour scorn on people who wasted billions on internet follies. When the housing bubble burst, it was equally natural to blame the people who overbuilt and overmortgaged. Looking back, we wonder why corporate chief executives, presumably the most sophisticated market players, took on so much debt. And we completely forget that those who resisted the debt craze were pilloried, called incompetent, and threatened with the loss of their companies to corporate raiders who would "put the assets to work."

Under these particularly disturbing circumstances of stealth inflation, it is not business owners and investors who are the chief villains. It is the inflaters, the central banks and governments, who have set the whole deadly process in motion.

iv. Inflation brings not only more unemployment, but sub-optimal employment.

Inflation is not a cure for unemployment. It is a principal cause of it. It causes not only unemployment, but what economist W. H. Hutt called "sub-optimal" employment.

When millions of people are channeled into housing jobs that will shortly disappear, that is clearly "sub-optimal." When the crash comes, housing related layoffs become unavoidable, because the jobs were never really there in the first place. What happens next, in other industries, depends on wage flexibility.

If wages are flexible, then fewer layoffs will follow in industries other than housing. The more layoffs there are, the greater likelihood that people will find only sub-optimal jobs, that is, jobs which do not employ their real skills, if they can find jobs at all. Both deep unemployment and sub-optimal employment are human tragedies. Both can be avoided if the price system is allowed to do its work of adjustment without interference, work that will bring the economy back into conformance with reality.

The younger Keynes was himself a harsh critic of inflationary policies. As we have seen, he warned that inflation turns an economy into a

> gamble and a lottery. . . . It engages all the hidden forces of economic law on the side of destruction, and does it in a manner which not one man in a million can diagnose.[30]

17

Yes to Economic Globalization

1a. Keynes: Gold is a "barbarous relic."[1]

In his second book, Keynes described the wonders and pleasures of the first real global economy, the one that flourished in his youth before the beginning of World War I. It was a golden age, both metaphorically and materially, since its monetary system rested firmly on a foundation of gold.

> What an extraordinary episode in the economic progress of man that age was which came to an end in August, 1914! The inhabitant of London could order by telephone, sipping his morning tea in bed, the various products of the whole earth, in such quantity as he might see fit, and reasonably expect their early delivery upon his doorstep. . . . He could secure forthwith, if he wished it, cheap and comfortable means of transit to any country or climate without passport or other formality, could dispatch his servant to the neighboring office of a bank for such supply of the precious metals as might

seem convenient, and could then proceed abroad to foreign quarters, without knowledge of their religion, language, or customs, bearing coined wealth upon his person, and would consider himself greatly aggrieved and much surprised at the least interference.[2]

The classic gold standard of this first global economy meant that the world shared one money. The dollar might represent one fraction of an ounce of gold, the British pound another fraction, the French franc another, but it was all really just the same thing, gold. A few countries relied on silver, but the United States rejected bimetallism (using both metals), so world money became gold.

Despite the advantages of having one world money, Keynes considered the gold standard to be unduly restrictive. It gives a national government little or no control over its own money supply. When interest rates are too high, which, according to Keynes, they tend chronically to be, additional money cannot be printed in order to bring interest rates down.

Keynes thought that our belief in gold is also irrational. He said that its

> prestige [depends on] . . . color, [even] smell. . . . Dr. Freud related that there are peculiar reasons deep in our subconscious why gold in particular should satisfy strong instincts.[3]

Our primitive relationship with gold has, over the years, been encrusted with rationalizations and evolved into an elaborate yet

> outworn dogma.

The challenge for contemporary society is to pierce the veil of ancient superstition in order to fashion

> a more scientific [exchange] standard.[4]

1b. Comments:

i. Far from being a "barbarous relic," gold is an insurance policy against Keynesian economic policies.

Gold has not officially counted as money since 1972. But people all over the world still buy it as a money substitute, a physical store of value. Why? Because governments keep printing more and more paper money, thereby debasing its value.

As we have noted, the dollar has lost almost all of its purchasing power since the creation of the US Federal Reserve in 1913. Only a few pennies then would buy as much as a dollar today. And it is the same for other leading world currencies, some of which became totally worthless at times. Gold by contrast has held its value.

In some respects, it is very disadvantageous to own gold. If we hold dollars, pounds, euros, or yen, we can invest our cash and earn some interest on it. If we hold gold, we get no current income, and have to pay for storage and protection to boot. Yet people still want to own gold precisely because they fear, and have good reasons to fear, what will happen to the purchasing power ofdollars, pounds, euros, and yen over time.

During the time that Ben Bernanke served on the US Federal Reserve Board, first as governor, then as chairman, the price of gold soared.[vv] This was no accident. As we have noted, Bernanke is a committed Keynesian, and the Fed under his watch both encouraged other central banks to print more of their currencies and, especially after 2007, printed much more of its own.

In the same passage where Keynes teases us that we are falling for gold's "color" and even "smell," he acknowledges the argument that gold

provides a reasonably stable standard of value.

Also that, because

> governing authorities lack wisdom . . . a managed currency will, sooner or later, come to grief.[5]

Whatever the merit of these arguments right after World War I, they are stronger still today, precisely because world governments are following Keynes's advice to debase their currencies.

ii. The classic gold standard of the 19th century had many advantages.

So far, we have discussed why the "barbarous relic" still maintains its appeal as an investment holding. But we should also take a moment to recall some of the virtues of the classic international gold standard, the standard that prevailed when gold and money were synonymous. Most history books say that the gold standard was abandoned in the 1930s and again in the 1970s, but these were pseudo gold standards. The real gold standard did not survive the beginning of World War I.

In retrospect, the greatest virtue of the classic gold standard was its discipline, the very feature that Keynes denigrated as "unscientific." Governments of all countries, large or small, had to play by the rules or suffer the consequences. If a country imported much more than it exported, gold would leave the country in payment for the imports. Since gold was money, the money supply would fall. This would usually make money more expensive to borrow (raise interest rates), which would slow the economy. A slowing economy would in turn reduce the demand for imports, which would bring exports and imports back into balance.

Having a single world currency, gold, also made international commerce more convenient. Sellers of goods did not have to worry, as they do today, about the unpredictable ups and downs of different currency values. Nor were business owners located in small or poor countries handicapped by the obscurity, unpredictability, or lack of marketability of their home currencies.

Gold was especially useful in managing global trade. But it also helped to maintain order inside a national economy. If a nation's banks made too many loans, that would expand the money supply, which would reduce interest rates. Gold would then leave the country seeking higher interest rates elsewhere. This would reduce the money supply, raise interest rates, and thus restore a rough equilibrium. The gold standard did not solve the underlying instability of a fractional reserve banking system able to create money out of thin air, but it did rein it in and make it less dangerous.

iii. Some of the most frequently citied disadvantages of a gold standard are actually advantages.

In *The General Theory* and elsewhere, Keynes consistently misrepresents the classic gold standard. For example, he presents it as a ruthless international scramble for gold, with victory going to the country with the most bars in its vaults.[6] This is a hopeless caricature, one that echoes Mercantilist economic thinkers of the 16th century whose ideas have long been discredited.

In a gold-based economy, people will want to own some gold, because it is money. But they will also want to own homes, businesses, personal possessions, and other commodities. When gold is exchanged for goods, there is no winner or loser. So long as both sides receive what they want, both sides win.

Keynes also complained that the scarcity of gold made money scarce.[7] But, as Henry Hazlitt pointed out:

> If precious metals had been abundant, they would not have been precious. If abundance of the monetary metal is what is needed, then the logical remedy would be a copper standard, or, still better, an iron standard.[8]

If money is not naturally scarce, then individuals (or more likely governments) will create more and more of it, and in the process destabilize the economy with inflations and bubbles.

It is not even true, as many people think, that the money supply needs to grow as the economy grows. As mentioned in chapters 15 and 16, if money is stable and we produce more goods, the only result will be modestly lower prices each year. Modestly lower prices help everyone, but especially the very poor, whose limited incomes will go further.

2a. Keynes: A "gold exchange standard" is better than a classic "gold standard," but not much better.

The classic gold standard was abandoned at the onset of World War I in 1914. It was succeeded in the mid 1920s by a very diluted version called the "gold exchange standard." The "gold exchange standard" gave governments much more control over money, but Keynes still felt that it was a

shackle[9]

and greeted its abandonment during the Great Depression as

the breaking of our gold fetters . . . and [a] blessed event.[10]

Efforts to establish a new global monetary and trade system during the Depression failed, primarily because President Roosevelt sent a letter torpedoing the idea at the London Conference of 1933. Many people felt that the Great Depression was thereby deepened and prolonged, but Keynes responded that

President Roosevelt is magnificently right.[11]

At this juncture, Keynes was operating more or less as an economic nationalist who wanted as much freedom of action as possible for Britain.

By the end of World War II, Keynes agreed that a new global monetary and trade system was needed. The system that emerged, named "Bretton Woods" for the New Hampshire resort where it was formally adopted, was another gold exchange standard. Keynes reluctantly went along with this because the Americans wanted a gold link. A quarter century later, the US also found gold to be a "shackle" and cast it off in favor of an unrestrained paper money system.

2b. Comment: A gold exchange standard is worse, not better, than a real gold standard. Floating rates that do not float are not any better.

Since the "gold standard" is often blamed for the Great Depression, it is important to emphasize that the gold exchange standard of the 1920s was not a real gold standard. If there had been a real gold standard, it would have helped restrain the excessive money printing and borrowing of the 1920s (all applauded by Keynes) that led directly to the bubble, the Crash, and the Depression.

Keynes quite agreed with the proposition that the "gold exchange standard" of the 1920s and early 1930s was not a real gold standard. He said in 1923:

> [The classic gold standard] is dead as mutton. . . . The
> United States has pretended to maintain a gold standard.
> In fact, it has established a [global] dollar standard.[12]

The Bretton Woods Agreement that Keynes helped craft was another dollar-dominated, gold-linked system. But it represented a significant advance over the anarchy and autarchy of the Depression years, and led to large increases in global trade and investment.

The chief flaw in the Bretton Woods system was the "reserve" currency status of the US dollar. A "reserve" country provides its own currency for global transactions. In return, it has the privilege of being able to borrow abroad in its own money. Unfortunately, this brings with it a built-in conflict of interest. A country that is allowed to borrow abroad without limit in its own currency can hardly be expected to set responsible money supply or interest rate targets. It only took a few decades for the US to print enough dollars to plunge the whole world into inflation. This led to the collapse of the Bretton Woods system in 1971.

Thereafter world trade depended on floating rates that did not actually float, but were instead controlled ever more closely by governments. The US remained in the reserve currency role, but without any constraints at all. The currency printing presses then ran faster, which reflected Keynes's ideas of "unshackling" government, and led directly, first to inflation and bust, later to bubble and bust.

3a. Keynes: What is actually needed is a single world monetary authority run on scientific lines.

Since Keynes opposed both the classic gold standard and pseudo gold standards, the question arises: what did he prefer? He had at different times said both negative and positive things about the concept of floating rates.[13] But what he actually preferred, and tried unsuccessfully to establish within the Bretton Woods system, was a supranational agency authorized to create its own paper money:

> We have reached a stage in the evolution of money when a "managed" currency is inevitable, but ... [this is best entrusted] to a single authority ... with [the] plenary wisdom [and] scientific management ... [of] a supernational authority.[14]

Robert Mundell, the Columbia University economist who founded what came to be called Supply-side economics, later agreed with Keynes that a single world money system (other than gold) would be desirable:

> Ideally the [global] economy ought to have one money, with one central bank, perhaps. [In the meantime], a system of truly fixed exchange rates would simulate a world money.[15]

3b. Comments:

i. Central banks are political institutions.

The single greatest challenge for a monetary system is to insulate it as far as possible from politics. Good economics is about the long-term and the greater good. Politics, whether we like it or not, is about the next election and the voter groups or special interest groups necessary for victory.

Central bankers, again whether we like it or not, are politicians. They are not, and never will be, the virtuous and all-knowing economic scientists of Keynes's utopian dreams. Even when central bankers are not being politicians, they rely on tools and models whose inputs are so subjective that they seem almost pitifully unscientific.

By and large, the modern concept of central banking has been a failure, as evidenced by the inflations, bubbles, and busts. To concentrate all authority in one global central bank will just make it worse. The unelected officials running it would wield massive power. But they would be also politicians, subject to the whims and pressures of all world governments. The inevitable result would be worldwide inflation on an unprecedented scale.

ii. Governance by unelected experts threatens democracy around the world.

In thinking about Keynes's idea of a global central bank run by experts, there are some additional issues to consider. As we have discussed earlier, it is difficult enough for democracies to keep a rein on their experts. In the US, the Federal Reserve operates without the need to go to Congress for funds and without Congressional audits. It is essentially accountable to no one. A world central bank would either be ruled chaotically by all the governments of the world, making all sorts of murky deals, or it would be ruled by no one and assume extraordinary and despotic powers.

The German economist Wilhelm Röpke warned in the 1950s and 1960s that "[The idea of] international organization goes by many an attractive name, such as 'Europe,' 'supernational sovereignty,' [or] 'international harmonization.'"[16] But it is really a device for removing power from democratically elected officials and placing it in the hands of anonymous experts and bureaucrats.

This process has by now proceeded very far in Europe. There the economy, and much of private life, is controlled by bureaucrats in Brussels who, as a body, The European Commission, are self-perpetuating and accountable to no one. The only real check on their authority is another body of experts, those running the judicial system.

The rulings of The European Commission are not, however, restricted to Europe alone. Through the search for "international harmonization," their ideas, and especially their restrictions, spread to other bureaucracies around the world.

Keynes was a democrat, in the broad sense of the word. He was not a fascist. But this drift away from democratic governance toward governance by unelected and often self-perpetuating experts is an important part of his legacy.

4a. Keynes on free trade.

The first global economy, the one that ended with World War I, depended on the classic gold standard, but also on a strong commitment to international trade. In Britain's case, a commitment to international trade meant a commitment to free trade.

Keynes was all over the map about free trade, and he acknowledged as much. He agreed that free trade encouraged nations to specialize, and that a high degree of specialization could make us all much richer. As a young economist, he regarded departures from the free trade doctrine as an

> imbecility and ... outrage.[17]

In 1923, he wrote that

> We must hold to Free Trade, in it widest interpretation, as an inflexible dogma.[18]

And also,

> If there is one thing that Protection cannot do, it is to cure Unemployment.... The claim to cure Unemployment involves the Protectionist fallacy in its grossest and crudest form.[19]

Keynes himself cited this last passage in *The General Theory* to show how far his ideas had changed by 1936.

What changed Keynes's mind was the Great Depression and the protectionist tide that followed its onset. The United States passed the infamous Smoot–Hawley Tariff Act (raising trade barriers) in 1930. A thousand American economists condemned it at the time. Most economists condemn it today for at least deepening and possibly even precipitating the Depression. (It might have helped precipitate the Depression because hearings on the bill were underway before the Crash of 1929).

America was already the greatest economy in the world. Its actions mattered enormously. But America also had a strong tradition of protectionism, at least since the Civil War. Britain, on the other hand, was by far the leading practitioner and defender of free trade. How would it respond to the Smoot-Hawley tariffs?

It was a close thing. Some commentators believe that Keynes's about face on free trade, his endorsement of protectionism in the early 1930s,[20] turned the tide.[21] Whether or not this is accurate, Britain did abandon free trade in 1932 in favor of Imperial Preference (free trade within the Empire). This meant that world trade suffered yet another major blow, and the Depression deepened.

By 1936, in *The General Theory*, Keynes was reappraising 16th and 17th century Mercantilist doctrine, which had been protectionist, and finding in it an

element of scientific truth,[22]

but also insisting on

the ... real and substantial ... advantages of the international division of labor ... [albeit] advantages [that have previously been] overstressed.[23]

On the question of globalization, it seems that Keynes generally approved of a global economy, even though, from time to time, he endorsed economic nationalism, protectionism, capital controls,[24] and so on. In the end, he certainly wanted a single world monetary authority, presumably with free trade, so long as someone like himself could run it.

4b. Comments:

i. The bad bird half apologizes.

Keynes described himself as

> a bad bird [who says] one thing one day [about free
> trade] and something else the next.[25]

He half apologized, saying that protectionism was

> crude,

that it might be dropped if

> a comprehensive scheme of national planning[26] could
> be put in its place.

   Although willing to criticize himself, Keynes was not about to
tolerate criticism from others. He dismissed critics as

> free trade fundamentalists,[27]

and, in a letter to the *Times*, said that their concerns represented

> pure intellectual error.[28]

Since Keynes re-adopted free trade toward the very end of his life,
the intellectual error seems to have been his.[29]

ii. Misrepresentations and non sequiturs.

During the middle 1930s, when Keynes was most deeply protectionist, he not only renounced free trade. He also increasingly misrepresented it. The basic idea of free trade is that a
country should concentrate on what it does best and then trade
with others for what it does not produce. Just as specialization
makes us more productive within a country, a global division of
labor will also make us much more productive and prosperous.

This is a system of competition between firms but of coopera-
tion between countries.

Keynes completely distorted all this, and even suggested that
international trade is a primary source of global conflict and
war.[30] In order to minimize global conflict, he said,

> Let goods be homespun . . . and above all let finance
> be primarily national.[31]

At the same time, Keynes tells us that economic nationalism will
somehow actually lead to more

> international trade.[32]

Exactly how a policy of limiting ourselves to "homespungoods"
will expand international trade we are not told.

iii. Something new, something useful, or just something old
and long since discredited?

Keynes's praise for 16th and 17th century protectionists known
as Mercantilists comes toward the end of *The General Theory*. It
is not just protectionism that, per Keynes, the Mercantilists got
right. They also wanted government to intervene in order to drive
down interest rates and to spend money on public works.

There is an unintended irony here. In the preface to *The General Theory*, Keynes says that critics will accuse him of

> saying nothing new.[33]

But in his revival of the long disparaged Mercantilists, he seems to
reach the same conclusion, that at least in his policy recommendations he is indeed:

> saying nothing new.[zz]

Part Four

More on Keynes

18

How Keynesian Was Keynes?

T HERE ARE VALID reasons to ask this odd question.
It is not just that Keynes said so many different things
to different people or changed his mind so often. Nor is
it the widespread belief among Keynes's fellow economists that
his economic arguments were marshaled as needed, and changed
as needed, to make his policy recommendations sound plausible.[1]
In addition, there are specific reasons to wonder whether Keynes
changed his mind about the policy recommendations contained
in *The General Theory*.

As early as 1937, Keynes said in a letter to his disciple Joan Robinson that

> I am gradually getting myself into an outside position
> towards the book, and am feeling my way to new lines
> of exposition.[2]

So, as usual, *The General Theory* was not meant to be the last
word. But then the war came along and turned Keynes's attention
from unemployment and related issues treated in *The General*

Theory toward those of war finance and the construction of a post-war monetary and trade system. If Keynes had second thoughts about *The General Theory*, he had little time or opportunity to write them down.

During World War II, most Keynesians assumed, based on the master's ideas, that large-scale unemployment would resume at the end of the war. They focused on how to prevent it. But an American economist, David McCord Wright, wrote to Keynes expressing concern about the potential for post-war inflation rather than unemployment, and Keynes wrote back that he agreed.[3]

Another American economist, John H. Williams, wrote an article in the *American Economic Review* in which he recounted a conversation with Keynes "a few months before his death" in 1946:

> He complained that the easy money policy was being pushed too far, both in England and here, and emphasized interest as an element of income, and its basic importance in the structure and functioning of private capitalism. He was amused by my remark that it was time to write another book because the all-out easy money policy was being preached in his name, and replied that he did think he ought to keep one jump ahead. [4]

This conversation would seem to be a repudiation of the drive down interest rates doctrine or at least a repudiation of the drive interest rates down to zero and thereby eliminate an offensive feature of capitalism doctrine.

Shortly thereafter the Austrian economist Friedrich Hayek had a similar conversation with Keynes:

> He [said he] was seriously alarmed by the agitation for [money and] credit expansion by some of his closest associates. He went so far as to assure me that if his theories, which [he said] had been badly needed in

the deflation of the 1930s, should ever produce dangerous effects he would rapidly change public opinion in the right direction. A few weeks later he was dead and could not do it.[5]

These are, of course, only anecdotal accounts, and not from Keynes's close friends and colleagues. Was Keynes really having second thoughts about *The General Theory*? The only evidence we have from Keynes's own hand is his last article, published following his death in the *Economic Journal* which he had long edited. Entitled "The Balance of Payments of the United Sates" (No. 185, 1946), it mostly discusses the named subject. But then, unexpectedly, a few pages veer off into a qualified defense of "classical" economics:

> I find myself moved, not for the first time, to remind contemporary economists that the classical teaching embodied some permanent truths of great significance.... Admittedly, if the classical medicine is to work, it is essential that import tariffs and export subsidies should not progressively offset its influence.

Keynes then seems to reverse direction:

> I must not be misunderstood. I do not suppose that the classical medicine will work by itself or that we can depend on it. We need quicker and less painful aids of which exchange variation [government exchange controls and currency management] and overall import control are the most important.

Exchange and import controls are further described as "expedients," which suggests that they are not meant to be permanent. Even so, this passage represents a nearly incoherent attempt, as Henry Hazlitt says, to reconcile the irreconcilable. We need the classical medicine, but not yet, or not fully. To get this right, we will have to ask Keynes at each step of the way, but of course he was already dead.

This was also the article in which Keynes condemned opposition to the emerging post-war monetary and trade system as

> modernist stuff, gone wrong and turned sour and silly . . .
> circulating in our system, also incongruously mixed, it
> seems, with age-old poisons.

It is hard to say what the "modernist stuff" might refer to, other than Keynes's own teaching. Perhaps he thought that he had been misunderstood, or had gone too far in *The General Theory*, and would have to set his disciples right, as he suggested in the conversations with Williams and Hayek. Or perhaps not. One can only guess. *The General Theory* remains Keynes's last book and personal testament.

19

Keynes Speaking

KEYNES WAS A virtuoso of the spoken word. He could out-talk and out-debate anyone, and he knew it.

Bertrand Russell, fellow Cambridge professor, world famous philosopher and mathematician, and by common agreement one of the keenest minds of the 20th century, knew Keynes intimately. He said of their relationship, "When I disagreed with him, I felt I took my life in my hands and I seldom emerged without feeling something of a fool."[1]

Contemporaries described Keynes as brilliant, quick-witted, ingenious, clever, dazzling, expansive, dramatic, lively, vivid, ironic, witty. He was a master both of exposition and of repartee. He could shift mood and mode of expression with lightning speed. Moreover, he always seemed to be "on," able to draw upon deep stores of nervous energy. As the art historian Kenneth Clark observed, "He never dimmed his headlights."[2]

Keynes might in turn seduce, charm, assist, instruct, guide, dissemble, mislead, attack, or insult, depending on topic, circumstance, the play of personality, or simply whim. When he was seductive, he could be irresistible. The words he used to describe World War I British Prime Minister Lloyd George might equally be applied to himself:

> [He had an] unerring, almost medium-like sensibility to everyone immediately around him. . . . [He could be seen] watching the company with six or seven senses not available to ordinary men, judging character, motive, and subconscious impulse, perceiving what each was thinking, and even what each was going to say next.[3]

Keynes described Lloyd George's brain and tongue as a

> swift and glittering blade,[4]

and, like Lloyd George, Keynes could also cut, wound, and impale. Kingsley Martin, editor of *The New Statesman and Nation*, which Keynes co-owned with others, described his proprietor in an obituary notice as

> the most formidable of antagonists, ruthless and sometimes unscrupulous in argument. . . . His wit was shattering and his capacity for rudeness was unequalled.[5]

Michael Holroyd (biographer of Keynes's friend Lytton Stratchey) observed that Keynes dismissed opponents as idiots.[6] Other favorite Keynesian epithets were "barmy," "crazy," and "lunatic."[7] During a public exchange with fellow economist Friedrich Hayek, Keynes stormed that Hayek was

> put[ting] . . . propositions . . . in my mouth[8]

and fired back that Hayek's book, *Prices and Production*,

> seems to me to be one of the most frightful muddles I have ever read, with scarcely a sound proposition. . . .

It is an extraordinary example of how, starting with a mistake, a remorseless logician can end up in Bedlam.[9]

Keynes could also be coldly dismissive, belittling, or simply petulant about others' work. About Philip Wicksteed's *The Common Sense of Political Economy*, referred to in Note A of this book, he said that

> One could make a splendid book by the application of scissors and paste, and the reduction of its 700 pages to 200.[10]

On one occasion in the British Treasury during World War II, he reduced James Meade, a younger pro-Keynesian economist who later won the Nobel Prize, to tears.[11]

During the 1930s and 1940s, fewer and fewer economists seemed willing to tangle with Keynes. They knew he represented Cambridge University, a world center of economics, that he was world famous, that he edited and controlled the *Economic Journal*, the leading professional organ for economics in Britain, and that he had a reputation for invincibility in verbal combat. Under these circumstances, any economist mindful of his career in Britain or even in the US thought twice about taking on such a formidable and intimidating figure.

Outside the ranks of economists, Keynes had ardent admirers and sharp detractors. People were rarely neutral about him. The admirers included many powerful people, because Keynes was an inveterate "networker." Lord Macmillan, chair of the British government's 1930 Committee on Finance and Industry, told Keynes, after listening to him for six and a half hours straight one day, that "We hardly notice the lapse of time when you are speaking."[12]

Dean Acheson, American secretary of state, said in his memoir that Keynes's "many-faceted and highly polished mind sparkled and danced with light."[13] Sir Richard "Otto" Clarke, a

British Treasury Department colleague of Keynes, agreed that "The extraordinary thing about him was his intellectual attraction and zing—always fresh and interesting and original and provocative."[14]

Economist Lionel Robbins was fond of Keynes, despite having suffered some frontal personal attacks over the years. He described him opening monetary negotiations in Washington near the end of World War II:

> Keynes was in his most lucid and persuasive mood; and the effect was irresistible. At such moments, I often find myself thinking that Keynes must be one of the most remarkable men that have ever lived—the quick logic, the birdlike swoop of intuition, the vivid fancy, the wide vision, above all the incomparable sense of the fitness of words, all combine to make something several degrees beyond the limit of ordinary human achievement.[15]

As noted, however, not everyone was an admirer. Henry Morgenthau, US secretary of the Treasury, wrote in his diary that "[Keynes is] one of the fellows that just knows all the answers."[16] Fred Vinson, Morgenthau's successor and later Chief Justice of the Supreme Court, also failed to appreciate Keynes's style. When the two were together at Bretton Woods in New Hampshire to complete work on a new global monetary system, Keynes playfully referred to the Sleeping Beauty Ballet by expressing, in an after dinner toast, the hope that no malicious fairy, no Carabosse, would spoil their work. Vinson privately quipped that "I don't mind being called malicious, but I do mind being called a fairy."[17]

Keynes had an especially rocky relationship with Harry Dexter White, the US Treasury representative who, more than any other individual, fashioned the post-war monetary system (and who later turned out to be a Soviet sympathizer and sometime informant). James Meade described the interaction of the two "prima donnas":[18]

> Keynes and White sit next to each other . . . without
> any agenda . . . they go for each other in a strident duet
> of discord which after a crescendo of abuse on either
> side leads up to a chaotic adjournment."[19]

White had the upper hand, because he represented the dominant power, and the treaty ultimately reflected his thinking more than Keynes's. But Keynes still dominated the debate, as he always did. This initially frustrated White, then made him anxious and physically sick, and finally led him to send his deputy to the meetings.[20]

Keynes's masterful biographer Robert Skidelsky suggests that his subject's "true greatness" lay in rhetoric . . . using that word in the classic sense of the 'art of persuasion.'"[21] This seems just, especially when applied to Keynes speaking, and especially when applied to Keynes speaking extemporaneously.

Keynes was of course more than a speaker. He was a writer as well, and here the record is mixed, as we shall discuss in the next chapter.

20

Keynes Writing

IT WAS KEYNES'S second book, *The Economic Consequences of the Peace* (1920), that made him world famous and launched his career as a public intellectual. His thesis, that the victors of World War I had sowed the seeds of future conflict by treating Germany harshly, remains debatable. Historian Paul Johnson calls it "one of the most destructive books of the [twentieth] century,"[1] because it encouraged acquiescence in German military revival.

Whatever one thinks of the thesis, the style is clear, sparkling, clever, and witty, although a bit mannered for modern tastes. Keynes never wrote so well again, perhaps because his schedule was always jam-packed and he simply lacked the time to concentrate. Another book almost as good, *Essays in Persuasion*, repackaged material from *The Economic Consequences of the Peace* along with shorter pieces originally written for periodicals or newspapers or as pamphlets.

We have already mentioned (in chapter 4) Keynes's excellent but highly technical *Treatise on Probability* (1921). The two volume

Treatise on Money (1930) was meant to be a magnum opus, but fell short even in Keynes's view. He wrote his mother that

> artistically it is a failure—I have changed my mind too much during the course of [writing] it.[2]

Biographer Robert Skidelsky notes the "dreadfully convoluted sentences" and "dismal algebra" in part of volume one, although he feels that some of the "sparkle" returns in volume two.[3]

In his preface to *The General Theory* (1936), Keynes tells us that the book is for professional economists. He must nevertheless have entertained hopes for a wider audience, because he kept the price down to the then unheard of sum of five shillings ($1.50 in the US).[4] With the exception of a few sparkling (and widely quoted) passages, most of the writing is worse than the *Treatise*'s, and the algebra just as dismal and irrelevant.

Paul Samuelson, professor of economics at MIT after World War II and author of a best-selling economics textbook, was one of Keynes's most ardent American disciples. Here is what he has to say about his beloved *General Theory*:

> It is a badly written book, poorly organized. . . . It is arrogant, bad-tempered, polemical, and not overly generous in its acknowledgements. It abounds in mare's nests and confusion. . . . [It is] an obscure book so that would-be anti-Keynesians must assume their position largely on credit unless they are willing to put in a great deal of work and run the risk of seduction . . . [by this] work of genius.[5]

In reading this, one recalls Keynes's infatuation with paradox. Samuelson, the ardent disciple, is telling us that the master's book is good because it is bad.

We do not, however, have to take Samuelson's word about the bad writing, poor organization, and general confusion of

The General Theory. Following publication in 1936, many leading economists pointed to the same problems, although some of
them hesitated to criticize or quarrel with Keynes and thus chose
their words carefully. Frank H. Knight, a leading American economist, complained that it was "inordinately difficult to tell what
the author means. . . . The direct contention of the work [also]
seems to me quite unsubstantiated."[6]

Joseph Schumpeter, the most famous economist of the mid-
twentieth century after Keynes, noted Keynes's "technique of
skirting problems by artificial definitions which, tied up with
highly specialized assumptions, produce paradoxical-looking tau-
tologies. . . ."[7] British economist Hubert Henderson privately
stated that: "I have allowed myself to be inhibited for many
years . . . by a desire not to quarrel in public with Maynard . . . .
But . . . I regard Maynard's books as a farrago of confused sophis-
tication."[8] French economist Étienne Mantoux added that the
whole thing simply appeared to be "rationalization of a policy . . .
long known to be . . . dear to him.[9]

In *The General Theory* itself, Keynes has a good word to say
about clarity, consistency, and logic.[10] He is quick to pounce
on what he considers the errors of others. But he then leads us
down a rabbit hole of convolution, needless and misleading jargon, mis-statement, confusion, contradiction, unfactuality, and
general illogic.

It is not that Keynes is entirely opaque. It is quite feasible to follow him down the hole and make out what he seems to be saying.
Having done so, it is not difficult to extract and order his ideas in
more intelligible form.

This has been our task up to this point. We have sought to present Keynes, not in the murky way that he presents himself, but as
clearly as possible. It seemed important to do this, first to reveal
what Keynes himself really said, and then to muster arguments

against it. In the remainder of this chapter, however, we will very briefly explore the rabbit hole itself, and in particular some of the rhetorical devices and obfuscations that Keynes employed in order to defend the indefensible and generally support his paradoxical policy recommendations.

Device One: Obscurity

A typical sentence from *The General Theory*:

> We have full employment when output has risen to a level at which the marginal return from a representative unit of the factors of production has fallen to the minimum figure at which a quantity of the factors sufficient to produce this output is available.[11]

This means, in essence, that we have not reached full employment until all factors of production are fully employed. We will recall that, per Keynes, only at this point do we have to worry about inflation.

Keynes took exception when other economists wrote in this convoluted way. For example, in a 1931 letter to the editor of *The New Statesman and Nation*, he charged Lionel Robbins with the same sin, even though Robbins was, on the whole, a very clear writer:

> Professor Robbins wants "increased elasticity of local wage costs" . . . which means in plain English, I suppose, a reduction of average wages.[12]

Given this stab at Robbins, can we at least assume that Keynes will avoid the term "elasticity" in *The General Theory*? No, not at all, he uses (and misuses) it repeatedly.

Device Two: Misuse of Technical Language

In the example above, Lionel Robbins was at least using standard economist's jargon. Keynes liked to make up his own jargon, or worse, use standard jargon in a non standard way. This led to a scolding by economist Frank H. Knight in the review of *The General Theory* that we have already cited: "Familiar terms and modes of expression seem to be shunned on principle."[13]

The only legitimate reason to use technical language is to make a sentence clearer, if not to the average reader, at least to the professional reader. Keynes habitually uses technical language to confuse, and as we shall shortly see, this may have been a deliberate strategy.

Device Three: Shifting Definitions

Keynes tells us in *The General Theory* that economists have not clearly defined the jargonish term "marginal efficiency of capital" (which roughly means return on capital).[14] He then proceeds throughout the book to use the term in many different ways, at least seven by Henry Hazlitt's count.[15] Another slippery word in *The General Theory* is wages, which can mean an hourly rate or total employee pay or something else. Keynes does not seem to notice the difference, which leads him into serious logical errors.

Once again, Keynes criticized the same lapse in others. In a book review early in his career, he took an author to task for

> us[ing] the [same] expression some thirty times in some apparently eight different senses.[16]

Device Four: Misuse of Common Terms

In some cases, Keynes stretches the meaning of a commonly used word beyond recognition without explicitly redefining it. For example, he tells us that for every commodity there is an implicit rate of interest, a wheat rate of interest, a copper rate of interest, a steel plant rate of interest, and so on. This confuses commodity options and futures pricing with interest rates, a clear case of mixing apples and bananas. We have already seen in chapter 16 that Keynes uses the word equilibrium to describe what is actually disequilibrium.

Device Five: Reversing Cause and Effect

We will mostly treat this subject in Part Five, when we return to the substance of Keynesian economics. But it is part of the style as well. Keynes says that entrepreneurs calculate how much revenue they will earn from x employees. But they do not. They calculate how many employees they can afford from x revenue.[17] Keynes says that prices are low if production is low. In actuality, it is the reverse: production is low if prices are low.[18] Keynes seems to like these reversals, perhaps because they dress up the ordinary with a gloss of novelty, even of profundity. But it is really no more than a parlor trick, and just piles error on error.

Device Six: False Determinism

Keynesian economist Alvin H. Hansen, whose book *A Guide to Keynes*, attempted to de-mystify the master, tells us that "Keynes's most notable contribution was his consumption function."[19] As may be recalled from chapter 15, the so-called marginal propensity to consume (consumption function) tells us that people tend to save more as their income rises. Stated as such, it is a commonplace, certainly nothing new. But Keynes calls it a "fundamental psychological law,"[20] which it certainly is not. We can neither predict with certainty that people will always save more as their income rises, nor can we work out a forecastable schedule of increased saving, as Keynes assumed.

In the Keynesian model, the marginal propensity to consume is also treated as an independent variable. (It is supposed to determine other variables, not be determined by them.) This is clearly false. As Benjamin Anderson, economist and early Keynes critic, pointed out, "The so-called independent Keynesian variables (1. The marginal propensity to consume, 2. The schedule of the marginal efficiency of capital, and, 3. The rate of interest) are all influenced by each other. They are interdependent, not independent. Keynes even forgets himself and admits at one point that #2 is influenced by #1."[21]

Device Seven: Slipping Back and Forth between Mutually Inconsistent Categories

We have already seen this in Keynes's use of words, for example when he uses the word "wages" to mean either a wage rate or total wages. He is also prone to move back and forth between physical commodities and services and money prices for commodities and services, another case of mixing up apples and bananas.^AAA

Device Eight: Unsupported Assertion

In the entirety of *The General Theory*, there are only two references to statistical studies,[22] one of which Keynes partly dismisses as improbable:

> Mr. Kuznet's method must surely lead to too low an estimate.[23]

Even when he discusses a subject that especially lends itself to statistical analysis, such as a suggested relationship between agricultural harvests and the business cycle,[24] he simply takes a position without bothering to search for relevant data.

Device Nine: Misstatement

We saw an example of this in chapter 11, which discusses Keynes's mischaracterization of corporate sinking funds. How could Keynes make such an elementary error? Probably because he had said the same thing many times when speaking on his feet, and, being busy, did not take sufficient time to check his written work.

Sometimes Keynes seems too busy even to think. He says that if a lender lends money to a business owner, this doubles the risk of a business owner using his own money, which doubled risk is reflected in the interest rate.[25] This makes no sense, as Henry Hazlitt notes.[26] Risk is not doubled when a lender enters the picture. The lender and the business owner share what is still the same risk of failure.

Device Ten: Macro or Aggregative Economics

Keynes is usually credited with "inventing" macroeconomics, which looks at economy-wide flows rather than the micro-economics of specific firms or industries. This is not entirely accurate. Other economists adopted an economy-wide perspective, although they often extrapolated from the firm or industry to the economy as a whole, which Keynes wrongly criticized. Ironically, Keynes attacked Say's Law (see chapter 11) which is, itself, an example of macroeconomics. It is certainly fair to say that Keynes developed his own type of macroeconomics, which his followers developed into the macroeconomics of today. It is also true that a macroeconomic viewpoint makes it easier for a skilled casuist to mislead and confuse, and that Keynes fully exploited this opening.

Device Eleven: Misuse of Math

In chapter 15, we saw how Keynes wrote $N = F(D)$, which means that employment, denoted N, is a function of demand. Demand however is defined as expected sales, not actual sales. We noted that expectations are not a measurable quantity and thus do not belong in an equation.

Much of Keynes's math is like this. As Henry Hazlitt has pointed out,

> A mathematical statement, to be scientifically useful, must, like a verbal statement, at least be *verifiable*, even when it is not verified. If I say, for example (and am not merely joking), that John's love of Alice varies in an exact and determinable relationship with Mary's love of John, I ought to be able to prove that this is so. I do not prove my statement—in fact, I do not make it a whit more plausible or "scientific"—if I write, solemnly,
>
> let X equal Mary's love of John,
>
> and Y equal John's love of Alice,
>
> then $Y = f(X)$
>
> —and go on triumphantly from there. Yet this is the kind of assertion constantly being made by mathematical economists, and especially by Keynes.[27]

Given the Alice In Wonderland quality of *The General Theory*,[BBB] it should not surprise us that Keynes interrupts his own misuse of math to tell us that he (apparently) agrees with Hazlitt:

> To say that Queen Victoria was a better queen but not a happier woman than Queen Elizabeth [is] a proposition not without meaning and not without interest, but unsuitable as material for the differential calculus. Our precision will be a mock precision if we try to use such partly vague and nonquantitative concepts as the basis of a quantitative analysis.[28]

He also warns of

> symbolic pseudo-mathematical methods . . . of economic analysis.[29]

After some of his own algebra he adds that:

> I do not myself attach much value to manipulations of this kind.[30]

It is quite typical of Keynes now to attack, now to disarm, now to shout, now to whisper, now to qualify his mathematical claims, now to ignore, even blatantly ignore, the same qualifications. On occasion, Keynes was even capable of a crude bluff. Writing a private letter to Montagu Norman, Governor of the Bank of England, he said that his theories (the same theories that would later appear in *The General Theory*) were a

> mathematical certainty, [not] open to dispute.[31]

Keynes certainly knew better. Some of his disciples did not. Economist Wilhelm Röpke noted in 1952 that

> The [Keynesian] revolutionaries [take a stance of] . . . vehement self-assertion and barely veiled contempt, such as are habitual to the "enlightened" in dealing with those who remain in the dark. They seem to regard themselves as all the more superior in that they can point with obvious pride to the difficulty of their literature and to the use of mathematics, which lifts the "new economics" almost to the lofty heights of physics.[32]

One could go on, almost indefinitely, citing Keynes's obscurities, convolutions, inconsistencies, factual or logical lapses, and so on, but it is time to ask the obvious question: why did he write *The General Theory* this way? Keynes could be orderly, organized, consistent, relevant, clear, complete, and factual, in addition to being playful and witty, when he wanted to be. This is apparent from the earlier books and many of the shorter pieces. There are some snippets from *The General Theory* that also reflect these characteristics. So why is most of *The General Theory* so different?

There are many possible answers. Historian Paul Johnson has said, unrelated to Keynes, that "In financial matters, the object of complexity is all too often to conceal the truth, to deceive." [33] The French economist Étienne Mantoux, reviewing *The General Theory* shortly after publication, quoted an earlier English economist, Samuel Bailey, from 1825: "An author's reputation for the profundity of his ideas often gains by a small admixture of the unintelligible." [34]

This may be part of the explanation, that Keynes intended to deceive or impress. But we must bear in mind that Keynes was a salesman. He was trying to sell a particular type of economic policy, and he was prepared to utilize any rhetorical device, from crystal clarity and wit all the way to complete unintelligibility, in order to make the sale.

Why would unintelligibility help to make the sale? Not just because it can be used to impress. Equally important, it can be used to intimidate. As we saw in the last chapter, Keynes (the speaker) often made people feel, as his very intelligent friend Bob Brand said, like "the bottom boy in the class." [35]

In this author's opinion, Keynes developed obscurity as one of his speaking styles. He obscured, confused, and scrambled the mental "chessboard," because he felt confident that he could always keep the position of the "chess pieces" in mind, and combine them as he saw fit for an attack in any direction, whereas his opponents could not. This is a very impressive skill indeed, especially when one is speaking extemporaneously. No wonder that Sir Josiah Stamp, a very respected economist who often partnered with Keynes on BBC broadcasts, said on the air that "I can never answer you when you are [verbally] theorizing."[36]

Whether this was a deliberate style on Keynes's part, or just a habit, we cannot know. But it was natural for him to fall into the same scrambling, intimidating style when writing *The General Theory*. The problem is that it does not work as well in print as in conversation or debate. When confined to print, it can be examined, examined minutely, and all the myriad flaws, the errors of fact or reasoning, the rhetorical tricks, the pseudo originality, may be revealed.

A few prominent economists, notably Ludwig von Mises, Friedrich Hayek, Wilhelm Röpke, Jacques Rueff, and Henry Hazlitt, among others, saw through it completely. Others perceived that something was wrong, but hesitated to say so out of fear of Keynes's position and powers of retaliation. Regrettably, no major economist published an immediate book-length refutation, so that the influence of *The General Theory* spread and spread, notwithstanding its all too apparent flaws.

Today many people—economists, financiers, investors, business owners, and managers—say that Keynes is their intellectual hero. Have they actually read *The General Theory*? Read more than the few clear and witty passages so widely quoted? Read it cover to cover? Read it from the perspective of mature years, not just while in school?

Part Five

Conclusion

21

Upside-Down Economics: What Keynes Would Have You Believe

IN CHAPTER 1, we suggested that Keynesian economics defied commonsense.

Keynes, as usual, seemed both to agree and disagree. On page 349 of *The General Theory*, he extolled commonsense and pilloried "orthodox" economists for lacking it. Perhaps he forgot that on page 16 he had argued for an economics transcending simple observation and logic, the elements of commonsense, and had pilloried orthodox economists for being too simple.

Whatever Keynes may have thought about commonsense, he was not a commonsense economist. As we have seen, his stock in trade was to take a commonsense proposition, for example that savers are more likely to get rich than spenders, turn it on its head, present it as a profound new insight, enjoy the gasps of astonishment, and await the torrent of admiring applause. This is not, however, an example of non-Euclidian geometry or the higher physics. It is an example of the higher sophistry.

Thousands of years ago, the ancient Roman philosopher Seneca warned about silver-tongued persuaders who will talk us into believing almost anything. He observed that "Once you let [this] sort of person . . . into your home, . . . you will have someone regulating . . . the way you use your jaws as you eat, and in fact going just as far as your patience and credulity [permit]."[1] We did of course let Keynes into our global economic policy home, and our credulity has been stretched ever since. Consider, for example, a few samples from the complete inventory of Keynesian or Keynesian-inspired paradoxes, partial paradoxes, and challenges to economic commonsense:

I. Keynesian Debt Paradoxes

A. If too much bad debt is the problem, for example during the Crash of 2008, the solution is to add more debt.

B. An economy depends on the players' confidence. If confidence has been shaken by too much bad debt, restore confidence by adding more.

C. If the public has wasted money on unwise borrowing and spending, help them to borrow and spend more.

D. If government control of short-term interest rates has driven down rates and encouraged too much bad debt, nationalize all interest rates and drive them down too. (This is essentially what the US Federal Reserve promised to do on March 18, 2009.)

E. After printing enough new money to drive down all interest rates in order to encourage more borrowing, add some new legal controls on borrowing so that no one borrows too much.

F. If the public seems to be opposing the idea of borrowing and spending more, their elected representatives in government can do it for them.

G. Better yet, let government develop and announce a target for the amount of total borrowing we want each year. (This is a proposal from Keynesian economists George Akerlof and Robert Shiller.)[2] In general, we should always start with the amount we want to borrow, not with what the borrowed money will be used for.

H. The more indebted an economy is, the more important it is to increase borrowing. Alan Greenspan, former chairman of the US Federal Reserve, argued this point in a 2006 interview.[3] President-elect Obama agreed in 2008: "[If the government does not intervene by printing money, borrowing, and lending], we . . . risk falling into a deflationary spiral that could increase our massive debt even further."[4]

I. If interest rates are approaching zero, they can still be driven down a lot lower. How? The US Federal Reserve (or any other central bank) should hold the nominal rate at near zero, but also create some "significant" consumer price inflation. This way, real (inflation-adjusted) interest rates will be way below zero. Just think: −4% rates? −6% rates? Nobody will be able to resist borrowing at those kind of rates! (This is a proposal from distinguished Keynesian-inspired economist Gregory Mankiw. He does not specify what the "significant" inflation target should be. Others have suggested as much as −6%.)[5]

J. Do not be confused by thinking of government in traditional terms as a taker and borrower. Government is actually the chief lender.

II. Keynesian Spending-and-Saving Paradoxes

A. Spending is the way to wealth. The more we spend, the more we have. Stated as Keynes's Law: If society spends, goods will be produced. This refutes Say's Law: If society works and produces, it will have the means to buy what is produced.

B. Each dollar of government expenditure magically multiplies itself as it moves through the economy. Partly as a result, government deficit spending pays for itself through lower unemployment payments and increased revenues. Government debt burdens do not increase over time.

   (Reminder: Tell that to either the US or Japan, but especially the latter.)

C. We do not need to save in order to invest.

   (Reminder: This assumes that government will print the money to be invested.)

D. New money printed by the government is a form of savings "just as genuine" as traditional savings. But unlike traditional savings, it does not cause slumps. On the contrary, it prevents and cures slumps. When too much money is sloshing around the economy in the form of traditional savings, government corrects the problem by printing new money (savings) and injecting it into the economy. (For examples of this paradoxical argument, see Paul Klugman, "Revenge of The [Savings] Glut," *New York Times*, March 1, 2009 and Alan Greenspan, "The Fed Didn't Cause the Housing Bubble," *Wall Street Journal*, March 11, 2009.)

E. Saving on a personal level may be prudent, even virtuous. But on the national level, it is an antisocial act. So long as government prints new money, we do not want more personal savings. Or if we do, not now.

F. Another solution to the problem of too much savings is simply to work less. In this case, working less is the responsible thing to do.

(Reminder: Please do as Keynes says, not as he does, since he worked hard and saved diligently.)

G. If our puritan upbringing does not allow us to work less, "make work" will serve just as well. Or we can hope for a natural disaster or even a war to soak up savings.

III. Some Keynesian Style Paradoxes from President Obama

A. Borrowing and spending is actually saving and investing! The President said that his first budget, which sharply racheted up borrowing and spending, "leads to broad economic growth by moving from an era of borrow and spend to one where we save and invest." (This budget is called "A New Era of Responsibility." It represents a step away from the culture of "instant gratification," "excessive debt," and "passing . . . [a] growing debt . . . on to our children." Stepped up spending and borrowing will "increase aggregate demand." This will "rebuild [the] economy, [not] on the same pile of sand, [but] . . . on a rock.")[6]

B. "Deficits . . . helped cause . . . this crisis, [but bigger deficits will help solve it]."[7]

C. Government spending programs not deemed affordable prior to a slump become affordable during a slump.

D. In order to reduce government spending on health care, it is necessary to increase that spending.

E. More government spending is a reliable way to increase economic demand, but it will not increase demand (and thereby raise prices) in health care.

IV. More Money Printing Paradoxes (In Addition to Those Already Covered under Debt)

A. Governments should not just drive down interest rates during a crisis. As Keynes emphasized, they should keep interest rates down at all times.

   (Reminder: Flooding the economy with new money eventually leads to consumer price inflation. Consumer price inflation generally leads to higher not lower interest rates. Alternatively, the new money may flow into investment assets, in which case it produces asset inflation. Either consumer price inflation or asset inflation typically leads to a crash. Crashes reduce interest rates but not in the way intended.)

B. The eventual target for interest rates should be zero. Stock dividends should also eventually be zero.

   (Reminder: This means nothing is scarce and nobody has to wait for anything.)

C. We should not worry about discouraging savers with low interest rates (or high taxes on saving). As noted above, we do not want saving. Or if we do want saving, low interest rates, not high rates, will produce more of it. (This is an example of a Keynesian paradox within a paradox.)

D. Crashes are caused by credit problems related to inflation or debt bubbles. Credit is controlled by the US Federal Reserve and other central banks. Nevertheless, crashes are not caused by central banks.

E. Because it is difficult for national central banks to separate themselves from politics, it would be better to have one world central bank which will be free from politics.

V. Keynesian Economic Bailout Paradoxes

A. Keynes was right: the private sector is driven mostly by "animal spirits." Crises are psychological in origin. They just come when they come, with no particular rhyme or reason.

B. Keynesian economists George Akerlof and Robert Shiller help us better define these nonrational "animal spirits." They include, among other elements, confidence, clashing views on fairness, and corruption.[8] Viewed in this light, bailouts are a multipurpose tool. They not only restore public confidence. They also reassure the public that the economy is being run in a fair way and that money is not corrupting public decisions.

C. It is also reassuring to know that the government officials in charge of bailouts and stimulus are free from fluctuating confidence, clashing views on fairness, corruption, or animal spirits in general.

D. If the largest commercial and investment banks are allowed to fail, there will be no one left to lend.

E. Profits, even profits from highly speculative leveraged investments, should accrue to private investors, but losses should be covered by government and ultimately taxpayers. There are times when it is the patriotic duty of small taxpayers to pay off the debts of rich investors.

F. Because bailouts simply transfer money from one group in society to another (e.g. taxpayers to rich investors), they are not economically damaging. (This argument is offered by distinguished Keynesian Robert Solow, retired professor of economics at MIT and Nobel Prize winner. As he says, "[These] are not ethically satisfying transfers, but it is not clear how they do long-term damage to the economy.")[9]

G. Rewarding past speculative excesses will reduce such excesses in the future.

H. Rewarding failure will increase the likelihood of future success.

I. To make bailouts work, it is best to rely on seasoned hands, the people who got the companies in trouble in the first place.

J. If the problem is that some companies are considered "too big to fail," merge failing companies into bigger ones, thereby making the survivors bigger and bigger.

VI. Other Keynesian Government Economic Leadership Paradoxes

A. Wall Street is always a short-term speculator. Fortunately, as noted, government does not worry about the next election but rather takes "long views." This makes government a more effective investor than the private sector. (Do not worry that Keynes called politicians "utter boobies."[10] That was just a private joke.)

B. Speaking of the advantage of "long views," we must still remember that any attempt to save is taking an over-long view. In this case, we must remind ourselves that "In the long run we are all dead."

C. When a company fails, it is supposed to die. When a government agency (such as the US Federal Reserve) fails, we should give it ever more power and ever more freedom from Congressional oversight.

D. Although Wall Street is a corrupt place, bringing government in to run it will not corrupt government.

E. Although Wall Street is a mess, it is the best place from which to draw knowledgeable and experienced people to run government economic and financial policy.

F. We do not have to worry about people shuttling back and forth between jobs in Washington and in Washington-run industries such as finance, medicine, and drugs. Political-financial oligarchies only pose a threat to banana republics, not developed economies.

G. The best thing about government regulation is that we never have to worry about who will regulate the regulators.

H. The banking industry is already one of the most heavily regulated industries, so more regulation will fix it.

I. If banking goes back to being "boring," as Keynesian economist Paul Krugman recommends,[11] all will be well. Yes, times change. Old style "boring" banking at the mega bank level may now be redundant—no longer needed. But not to worry. Government will find a way to help it survive anyway.

As noted above, this is a very partial list of Keynesian paradoxes and partial paradoxes.* What do all these paradoxes mean? Is there any common theme to them? What is really wrong here? These last questions bring us to the central paradox of Keynesianism.

* In Note CCC, we list a few more of them, including some of the more technical.

22

What Is Really Wrong Here: The Central Paradox of Keynesianism

THE CENTRAL PARADOX of Keynesianism is that it attempts to "fix" the price and profit system—by subverting it. No free price or profit relationship is left untouched.

Does this sound exaggerated? Consider the following direct or indirect government price controls that comprise the Keynesian Policy Prescription:

A. Price controls

1. Interest Rate Controls

As we have previously noted, interest rates are some of the most critical prices. All prices are interrelated to a degree, but interest rates especially influence other prices. In the Keynesian system, followed by all world governments, interest rates are supposed to go in only one direction, down. If they rise, it is supposed to be for short periods only.

2. Subsidies

Some specific interest rates, such as home mortgages in the US, are manipulated through subsidies as well as price controls. The trouble with subsidies is that they increase demand without increasing supply, which leads to rising prices. This is why housing subsidies designed to help low income homebuyers backfired in the 2000s; they made homes less and less affordable for the first-time buyer. Subsidies in the healthcare area have had the same effect of increasing demand (without increasing supply) and thus driving prices up.

3. Indirect (or Direct) Currency Controls

There is no such thing as a global free market in currencies. Some governments control the world price of their currency completely; some control less. Like interest rates, these crucial world prices are not supposed to rise.

4. Asset Price Floors

Unlike interest rates and currencies, asset prices are not supposed to fall. If they fall or seem in danger of falling, additional money may be printed and interest rates lowered to support them. If that is not enough, direct subsidies may also be used.

So-called toxic mortgages held by US and global banks during the Crash of 2008 illustrate how specific classes of assets may be singled out for subsidy support. As we initially discussed in chapter 14, the Bush administration proposed to "get banks lending again" by buying their bad mortgages in the fall of 2008. The program was sold to a reluctant Congress. But how to buy them? There were no prices! That was the problem. It was not primarily a bank solvency or liquidity crisis. It was a pricing crisis. The mortgages lived in a neverland of the government's making unrelated to any real prices. Worse, the government was insisting that they had to be "marked to market" even though there were no market prices.

The Bush administration gave up. The Obama administration then developed its own "creative" solution. It decided to lend large amounts of government money on giveaway terms to Wall Street firms in the hope that they would buy the mortgages. This was supposed to establish a price. But would it establish a real price? Of course not. It would establish yet another subsidized price.

The sad truth is that US economic policy makers, Keynesians all, might not know a genuine price if it stared them in the face. They are accustomed to dealing with manipulated prices, and their imagination knows no bounds in devising new ways to manipulate prices further. The need to devise new methods of manipulation is always urgent, because each prior manipulation keeps presenting unanticipated (and unwanted) outcomes.

5. Wage Floors

Wages are yet another key price that Keynesian policy makers will not leave alone. Keynes said that both falling and rising wages are dangerous. Falling wages diminish workers' ability to buy. Rising wages hurt business confidence. In practice, however, it is falling wages that must be prevented. If wages must be adjusted, it should be economy wide, not company by company.

This is complete nonsense. For an economy to work, wages (like other prices) must adjust themselves company by company and industry by industry, not economy wide. The adjustment must be ongoing. Wages should be free to rise or fall. In this way, profits, jobs, and workers' incomes are protected.

Have contemporary Keynesians relearned any of this? No. Just look at how both President Bush and Obama handled the meltdown of General Motors and Chrysler. Immediate wage cuts were one of a number of sensible remedies that should have been considered. But they were not even discussed. They were off the table. Massive job losses suited both union and government better than even small wage cuts.

Consider President Obama's "Cardcheck" legislation. This would not only eliminate the secret ballot when workers vote on whether to join a union. Buried in the bill and little discussed is another provision that would require mandatory arbitration of wage disputes between companies and unions. This means that if companies do not reach agreement with a union, the wage decision will be taken out of the company's hands. In effect, companies will no longer have control over their own costs.

6. Executive Compensation Controls

Wages should not fall, but executive compensation should. This reflects Keynes's view that market solutions for wages and executive compensation are "unfair." Robert Shiller, a distinguished Keynesian economist, agrees that "compensation practices in the US need to be made fairer."[1] Unfortunately, neither Keynes nor Schiller tells us how compensation will be decided—or by whom. It cannot be decided for an entire nation in one fell swoop. The whole point of the price system is that it sorts out specific cost/price relationships that then determine profit levels. It is an absurdity to think that we can get any of the benefits of the price/profit system if compensation is uniform or if it is decided in Washington.

This is clear enough in the abstract. Even so, Washington cannot stop itself from jumping into executive compensation issues. Following the Crash of 2008, there was a hue and cry in Congress and the White House about bonuses paid to employees of bailed-out companies, frantic legislation to cap them, and further legislation to control executive compensation in general.

In the early 1990s, Congress decided (for no apparent reason) to cap the tax deductibility of all public company chief executive compensation. This little discussed piece of legislation led to the abandonment of large-scale CEO cash compensation in favor of stock option grants. The emphasis on stock option grants led in turn to large scale corporate borrowing in order to boost stock and option prices, and ultimately, through a series of circuitous steps, contributed to the stock market bubble that followed.[2]

If governments really want to reduce lavish financial rewards, why do they set up winner-take-all lotteries? Why an immense payoff for one winner, not a series of small payoffs for a much larger number of winners? Why not at least set an example of "fairness" and "equality" in lotteries? The answer, of course, is that more equal lottery rewards do not sell tickets, (and thereby generate the sought after revenue).

7. Direct Price Controls

Governments still use these, too. In 2008, the World Bank listed 21 countries that price controlled food. In the US, medical services are price controlled in Medicare, Medicaid, and the Veterans Administration system. Sometimes the price controls are intended to keep prices from rising. Sometimes they are intended to keep prices from falling. In the latter case, the price control is usually described as a "quality control," as when only doctors are allowed to perform services that a nurse or other healthcare professional could provide just as well.

8. Trade Barriers

Today governments prefer, whenever possible, to control their trade balances by manipulating currencies. This is what *The Economist* calls "subtle protectionism," although it is not very subtle.[3] There is still, however, plenty of old-fashioned protectionism in the form of tariffs and nontariff barriers, and those increased with the Crash of 2008, especially in Russia.

In general, prices are the signals that make markets work. They tell us the truth about what is scarce, what is in surplus, what is happening. When governments, encouraged by Keynes, relentlessly dismantle and circumvent market pricing, it is because they find the truth to be unpalatable. But no economy can thrive very long on lies, half-truths, evasions, or even well-intentioned fictions.

Moreover, it is not just the price system that Keynesianism subverts. It is the profit system as well. Consider a few more elements of the Keynesian policy prescription and how they affect traditional profit disciplines:

B. Interference with the profit system

1. The stick of recessions and bankruptcy is dismissed with a wave of the hand.

We have covered this ground sufficiently before in chapters 10 and 15. A brief summary runs as follows. The profit system is really a profit and loss system. The stick of loss and bankruptcy is arguably more important than the carrot of profit in motivating the players and regulating the system. But Keynesianism rejects loss and bankruptcy as an unnecessary anachronism. Recessions are, if possible, avoided, and if not, papered over with bailouts and artificial stimulus. As a result, the errors of the past are never liquidated and new errors are piled atop the old.

Some Keynesians still tell us that economies are not self-correcting, that once falling, they will fall forever if not rescued. Most Keynesians now admit this is wrong. A more common argument is that an economic contraction is too painful, involves too much lost production, takes too long. But a recession is actually a period of recovery and, if aborted, the patient will never fully recover.

2. A persistent policy of inflation creates illusionary profits, confuses the players, and rewards the speculators.

Business owners and managers may know that government is steadily inflating, filling the economy with newly created money. But since the new money mostly enters as debt, no one knows at any one time where it is, where it is going, or how much of it there is. Are today's profits real or an inflationary illusion? It is hard for even the most sophisticated to know. Meanwhile the speculators can use the cheap new money to make bets and with luck win vast fortunes, while ordinary mortals and plodders just seem to fall further behind.

3. The word "profit" is excised from macroeconomic textbooks.

Keynes thought that unemployment was the central macroeconomic problem. He told us that employment rises with demand. But this is a half-truth. Employment actually rises with profits (real profits, not inflationary bubble "profits"), as the chronicler of business cycles, Wesley Mitchell, showed almost a century ago.

4. "Accounting" profits replace real profits.

In early 2009, the world was told that American bank profits were recovering, and that this was a positive post-crash sign. But modern banks are artificial government constructs, as are their profits. So long as they remain artificial constructs, only loosely related to real market prices, cash flows, and profits, they will remain a mortal threat to economic stability.*

---

* This is further discussed in chapter 16, section 1B.

5. Monopolies (which government is supposed to uproot) are instead fostered and protected.

We have previously discussed this topic in chapter 14. There are many government-supported monopolies in the US, ranging from the small (financial rating) to the large (animal slaughter) to the vast and all pervasive (mortgages and drugs). As regulated industries increasingly become "government-sponsored" industries, the potential for using government to create and enforce a monopoly increases.

6. Taxes encourage borrowing and speculation, penalize normal profit seeking.

It is widely acknowledged that corporate profits taxes are not really paid by corporations. They are indirectly paid by workers, consumers, and shareholders. Why then tax corporate profits directly, when profits are the best leading indicator for employment?

Profits paid to shareholders are taxed twice, once inside the corporation and again when paid as a dividend. Because interest payments are tax deductible and dividends not, this encourages corporations to borrow rather than to finance themselves by selling stock. During the 1990s, companies responded to the tax structure by borrowing heavily in order to retire their stock. This contributed to the stock market bubble and to the overall debt bubble of the 1990s and 2000s.

We also need to keep in mind that most US small businesses are not set up as corporations and therefore do not pay profits taxes on a corporate tax return. Instead they pay profits taxes on individual tax returns. If we must raise taxes on higher incomes, it would not be difficult to make small business profits deductible so long as they are retained in the business. By doing so, we would create many more jobs, because it is small business which does the most hiring.

———•◆•———

This then is the central Keynesian paradox. The price/profit system is to be saved by poking it, pushing it, pulling it apart, one price and profit relationship at a time, only, in the end, to leave it in a complete shambles. Naturally some of the pulling apart does more damage than the rest. The assault on market interest rates and currency levels are particularly destructive, because these prices are so crucial for the economy as a whole. But all of it is destructive in some way.

There are many ironies here. For one, it was only a few decades ago that Communism collapsed. At that time, Marx (it was thought) was finished; capitalism (it was thought) had triumphed. The great majority of people around the world concluded that markets had at least some virtues.

That in turn became part of the problem. As Lawrence Summers, former Treasury Secretary, Harvard president, and President Obama's top economic advisor said, "[The old idea was to] oppose and suppress markets. . . . [The new idea is to] use markets [to achieve progressive aims].[4] This sounded constructive. Markets were good, but could be made much better. It was just what Keynes said—there was nothing wrong with markets that a little tinkering could not fix.

So the tinkerers went back to work, full of renewed enthusiasm. US Federal Reserve chairmen Alan Greenspan and Ben Bernanke and other central bankers took the lead. Masses of new global money were printed up. Bubbles formed, then popped. By 2007–2008, the tinkerers found that markets did not need a little work. They needed a complete overhaul.

President Obama says that "I strongly believe in a free market system."[5] There is no reason to doubt his word. He probably also agrees with Australian Prime Minister Kevin Rudd that the market needs to be purged of "free market fundamentalism" and "excessive greed."[6] Neither Obama nor Rudd presumably have the slightest inkling that they are jamming long, fat sticks into the spokes of the market wheel, then loudly exclaiming that the wheel is not moving and in urgent need of government repair.

It is what Keynes would have called a "muddle." But we do not need Keynes's powerful intuitive brain to lead us out of it. We just need to stop trying to save the price/profit system by subverting it in every way imaginable.

Part Six

Envoi

23

Saying Goodbye to Keynes

CONSERVATIVE COLUMNIST DAVID BROOKS captured the mood in the United States at the beginning of the Obama presidency by stating:

> To come up . . . with a stale, Government is the problem, you can't trust the federal government is . . . not where the country is, it's not where the future of the country is.[1]

The trouble with this statement is that government is the problem, although it is not really government, but rather the Keynesian doctrine that guides every government in the world. Government could actually become the solution. Improbable as it might seem, it could return to its essential role of protecting the public from force and fraud, establish sound laws governing the operation of markets, and embrace a vision of true sustainability rather than gaming everything for the next election. It could also, through judicious changes in the tax law, build a much larger, stronger nonprofit, charitable sector to help those who cannot help themselves and truly need assistance from others.ᴰᴰᴰ

Instead, governments bet the future of their countries on untested and poorly defined Keynesian experiments. What kind of stimulus is needed? The answer seems to be: whatever Congress cobbles together. How much stimulus is needed? Keynesian economist Robert Schiller answers, "It must be done on a big enough scale." How long will it be needed? "For a long time in the future." Keynesian Christina Romer, Chairman of President Obama's Council of Economic Advisors, adds, "Beware of cutting back on stimulus too soon." How will we know it is working? Ask us later.[2] Given the size of the sums bet on these experiments, the answers need to be better than this.

Let us also keep in mind that a demand for better answers is not a partisan exercise. As we have seen, most Republicans are broadly Keynesians, as are most Democrats, as are most parties throughout the world. This is what "everyone" has been taught. We are all thus caught up together in a circular argument (that Keynesianism is right because most people assume it is right). If we want to save our children from more failed experiments, we will need to embrace change, real change, not the "change" promised by President Obama and other political leaders that just takes us back to the 1930s.

In his second book, Keynes told how British Prime Minister Lloyd George "bamboozled" US President Woodrow Wilson during the peace conference following World War I. Then, wishing to reverse some decisions, he found that "it was harder to de-bamboozle this old Presbyterian [Wilson] than it had been to bamboozle him."[3] This describes our predicament today. Keynes has bamboozled us and it is very difficult to de-bamboozle ourselves.

In the same book in which he described Lloyd George and Wilson, Keynes said that ideas are a subsidiary factor in human history.[4] At the end of *The General Theory*, he reversed himself and said that ideas rule the world. Unfortunately, Keynes's ideas do, for the moment, rule the world. But intellectual bubbles, like other bubbles, do not last forever.

In a little bookshop in Beijing, tucked away on the ninth floor of an office and residential building, one can find the complete works of Mao, all laid out in spanking new editions with colorful wrappers. A small band of true believers repair to the shop. Sales are even up a bit with the Crash of 2008.[5] Perhaps this store, appropriately named "Utopia," also treasures and propagates the works of Karl Marx.

One day in the future, there may be such a store devoted to Keynes. His words will no longer carry much weight in the wider world, but in this place his complete works will be beautifully presented and his name discussed in hushed and reverential tones.

Let us hope that we do not have to wait too long for Keynes to join Mao and Marx and other faded and false utopians. To turn away from false utopias does not mean giving up on entirely attainable ends and ideals. We can have a stable economy, one built on truthful prices and profits. That economy can be sustainable both financially and environmentally, and it can, with work and persistence, finally put human poverty behind us.

Endnotes

A: Phillip Wicksteed

The feasibility of a commonsense economics is not of course a new topic. In his 1910 two-volume work, *The Common Sense of Political Economy*, Phillip Wicksteed complained that economics had degenerated into "a mere armory of consecrated paradoxes that cannot be understood because they are not true, [but] that everyone uses as weapons."[1] And this was before Keynes added his own arsenal of paradoxes. Wicksteed was a prominent economist in his day. He was esteemed by Henry Hazlitt and also by Lionel Robbins, Keynesian critic and then ally, who arranged for a reprint of *The Common Sense of Political Economy* in the 1940s. As noted in the text, Keynes reviewed *The Common Sense of Political Economy* and thought it too long.

B: The General Problem of What Social Thinkers Really Said

It is easy to distort the ideas of leading social thinkers. For example, a public television documentary, The Commanding Heights, tried to contrast the positions of Keynes and Friedrich Hayek, Keynes's great critic, on depressions. Keynes, the script says, thought that depressions, if not treated, will lead to a loss of freedom. Hayek is alleged to have said that we must accept depressions as the price of freedom, since any government intervention to fix the depression will compromise freedom. This is very misleading. It omits Hayek's argument that government intervention creates the depression in the first place.

WHERE KEYNES WENT WRONG

C: Commonsense, Reality, and Keynes's Model

Elsewhere in *The General Theory*, Keynes tells us that he has worked out his ideas within the context of what we would now call an economic model, a simplified and abstracted version of the economy. In his model, the size and skill of the labor force, science and technology, the degree of competition, consumer preferences, and many others vital factors are assumed to be frozen in place with no possibility of change. In other words, it is not only not a commonsense world. It is not even a real world.

D: Did Roosevelt Follow Keynes?

The degree to which Keynes influenced Roosevelt cannot be determined. The two met for an hour at the White House in 1934, but by then New Deal policies characterized as Keynesian were already in place. Had Roosevelt read Keynes? Raymond Moley, a member of the president's "Brain Trust," said that "I never knew him to read a serious book."[2]

Accounts of the Roosevelt-Keynes meeting differ. Felix Frankfurter reported to Keynes that the president said he had "a grand talk and liked him immensely." But Frankfurter was a friend of Keynes, as Roosevelt knew, and other accounts indicate that Roosevelt did not take to Keynes.[3] Keynes's open letter to the president, published the previous December in the *London* and *New York Times*, had been written in a somewhat condescending tone, which may not have helped, although Walter Lippmann, the most prominent American journalist and friend of the astonishly "networked" Keynes, said that the open letter had persuaded the US government to cap long-term interest rates by buying in bonds.

E: Keynes on the History of Interest Rates

Keynes thinks that interest rates almost always tended to be too high, with the notable exception of when Spanish conquistadors flooded the "old world" with gold and silver seized from the Aztecs and Incas. This flood of what was then money reduced interest rates. The resulting low rates, per Keynes, then made possible the beginning of what became the industrial revolution.

F: Governments "Printing" Money

Governments do not actually print new money in our electronic age, but it is still customary to refer to printing money. This book would normally have put quotation marks around the word "printing," to indicate that it is not to be taken literally, but in this context the quotation marks might create confusion about whether this is a word Keynes himself used. The mechanics of "printing" money are covered in Note SS.

G: What Keynes Meant When Referring to Interest Rates

Keynes wanted to bring down both short- and long-term interest rates. He felt that long rates would fall on their own if it was made sufficiently clear that short rates would not rise.[4] But, one way or another, if necessary by "direct attack,"[5] he had no doubt that governments could "make the long-term rate of interest what they choose."[6]

H: What Keynes Meant by a "Low" Interest Rate

The goal of zero interest rates was for the next generation. So, from time to time, Keynes would suggest what he meant by a low rate of interest at that moment. In 1945, he recommended a maximum of 3% for long interest rates, 1% for the rate paid to depositors by banks, and other rates in between.[7] In 1934, he said that a 3½% long rate "is far above" what would be compatible with "full employment."[8] In general, his aim was always to nudge rates down, never to raise them.

I: Another Policy Option for Controlling an Overheated Inflation-Ridden Economy

Keynes also mentioned the possibility of raising the exchange rate of the country's currency, because that will make exportable products more expensive, and thus lead to fewer export sales, which is another way to dampen the economy. If tariffs are simultaneously lowered, that will make imports cheaper, further discouraging domestic production.[9] On the other hand, the currency exchange rate cannot be raised by raising interest rates, because the latter must always be kept down.

J: On Income and Payroll Taxes

How high might taxes on the rich be taken? On this point, Keynes seems to have had different ideas at different times. In one conversation, he seems to have said 25%, but that does not appear to be his usual view.[10] At times, he seems to have advocated confiscatory rates.

About payroll taxes, which hit the poor especially hard, Keynes was ambivalent. It appealed to him that benefit payments funded by these taxes could be made off-budget. That would keep the reported government deficit down, which had political advantages. On the other hand, he agreed that "a poll tax on the employed and an employment tax on the employer [were] both very bad kinds of taxes [because they make employment more expensive and thus contribute to unemployment."[11]

K: Keynes's "Paradoxical" View of the Relationship between Saving and Investment

Although Keynes said that it was "absurd" to think that investment would always match savings, he also said, rather confusingly, that savings and investment were "just different aspects of the same thing"[12] and are therefore "equal."[13] By this, he presumably did not mean "equal" at the same time. He thought that consumption and investment together (overall demand) would determine employment, employment would determine national income, and income would determine the ability and desire to save (the obverse of the so-called propensity to consume described on page 64 of *The General Theory*.)

Consequently if investment lagged savings, the result would be lower income and, in time, lower savings. In this way, investment and savings, left to their own devices without government intervention, would tend to converge, but with an unfortunate tendency most of the time to lower rather than raise income. The contention that saving is a function of investment (rather than vice versa) is of course a direct challenge to commonsense, because all of us observe in real life that saving must precede investment.

L: Individual Virtue or Public Vice?

As we noted in chapter 1, the formal name for the situation that Keynes describes in chapter 3 is the fallacy of composition. Because it is rational for each one of us to try to save more during economic adversity, we assume it is rational for all of us to do so. But, per Keynes, if we all try to save at the same moment, especially during an economic downturn, the result will be an even greater mismatch between saving and investment, an even weaker economy, an even lower employment and national income level. This in turn will lead, in the end, to less rather than more savings, which, paradoxically, will help.

M: Jeremy Bentham

Bentham notoriously emphasized material goods and advantages over cultural ones.[14] Keynes completely rejected Benthamism as a young man and continued to reject it throughout his life. What Keynes wanted above all was to spend money on arts and culture, which he considered the essence of the good life, and he practiced what he preached by funding a theater in Cambridge and many other arts projects as well as by supporting individual artists. By doing so, he may also have sought to redeem his money-making in the eyes of his youthful friends, most of whom wrote or painted.

N: Genuine Epicureanism

Epicurus's competitors among ancient philosophers unfairly and inaccurately charged him with mindless hedonism, the opposite of what he believed in, as the quoted passage attests.

O: Keynes on the State as a Balancing Force

Even Keynes's careful biographer, Robert Skidelsky, says at one point that Keynes wanted to "avoid [both] booms and slumps."[15] But Keynes specifically said in *The General Theory* that we should not avoid the boom.[16] To think otherwise is a "serious error."[17] In the early 1920s, he partly endorsed the idea of the state as a balancing force during both extremes of the cycle. He wrote then that the state should "counteract" private actions that would tend to raise or lower consumer prices.[18] But over time, he came to see higher consumer prices as less of a threat, and put his emphasis on keeping a boom going.

P: Keynes on Marx (and Vice Versa)

Michael Straight, a Cambridge economics student, reported Keynes saying that "Marxism was even lower than social credit as an economic concept. It was complicated hocus-pocus."[19]

Marx would almost certainly have said the same thing about Keynes. In a sense, he did. On page 827–29 of *Capital*, he skewered what later became the Keynesian policy approach. Here is what Marx wrote (keep in mind that if Marx could criticize Keynes in advance, then perhaps Keynes's "New Economics" is not so new):

> The only part of the so-called national wealth that actually enters into the collective possessions of modern people is—their national debt. Hence, as a necessary consequence, the modern doctrine that a nation becomes the richer the more deeply it is in debt. Public credit becomes the *credo* of capital. And with the rise of national debt-making, want of faith in the national debt takes the place of blasphemy against the Holy Ghost, which may not be forgiven.

> As with the stroke of an enchanter's wand . . . [the public debt] endows barren money with the power of breeding and thus turns it into capital, without the necessity of its exposing itself to the troubles and risks inseparable from its employment in industry or even in usury. The state creditors actually give nothing away, for the sum lent is transformed into public bonds, easily negotiable, which go on functioning in their hands just as so much hard cash would. . . .

> As the national debt finds its support in the public revenue, which must cover the yearly payment for interest, &c., the modern system of taxation was the necessary complement of the system of national loans. The loans enable the government to meet extraordinary expenses, without the taxpayers feeling it immediately, but they necessitate, as a consequence, increased taxes. On the other hand, the raising of taxation caused by the accumulation of debts contracted one after another, compels the government always to have recourse to new loans for extraordinary expense. Modern fiscality . . . thus contains within itself the germ of automatic progression. Overtaxation is not an incident, but rather a principle.[20]

Q: The Green Cheese Factory

This refers to a very old saying (John Heywood's *Proverbs*, 1546) still very prevalent in the 1930s. It goes along the lines of: The moon is made of green cheese, and if you believe that, you will believe anything.

R: Characteristics of a Financial Crash and Ensuing Slump

A financial crash typically begins with one or more banks or other financial institutions on the verge of bankruptcy. If nothing is done, everyone will try to withdraw their funds from the threatened institution. If it is a bank, this is called "a run on the bank." To meet the demand for cash, the bank in turn will start calling in loans. Since the proceeds of these loans may have been deposited in other banks, these banks too may have to start calling in loans. Meanwhile word of all this spreads, people wonder which banks are still sound, but as a precaution begin withdrawing money from all banks.

As many banks (or other lenders) stop lending, numerous businesses are adversely affected. Perhaps these businesses have loans that they expected to renew routinely, but can no longer renew. If other funds cannot be found, otherwise sound businesses may become insolvent too. Other businesses may need loans to carry them through the months or even years it may take to make a product, sell it, and finally get paid for it. If these loans are unavailable, production may grind to a halt.

Customers of both the banks and the businesses are by now thoroughly frightened and stop buying. As buying plummets, the price of consumer and other goods begins to fall. Missing customers and falling prices mean that business revenues collapse. Businesses that cannot get their costs down fast enough go bankrupt.

Even businesses that do not go bankrupt find their debts have increased. Assume that they borrowed $40,000 before the crash and used it to buy four widgets. Now widget prices are down 50%, so $40,000 buys eight widgets. This means that the value of the company's loan, expressed in widgets, has doubled.

Assuming that the company makes zidgets, which also sell for 50% less, twice as many zidgets must be sold in order to generate the money to pay off the old loan. As the cost of the old loan keeps increasing, the business will find it harder and harder to repay it, at the very moment when everything else is harder as well.

A financial crash, especially one that deepens into a severe business slump, can best be described as a vicious circle, then a downward spiral that, as Keynes said, feeds on itself.

S: Who Holds the National Debt?

As a later American Keynesian, Stuart Chase, put it:

> If the national debt is all internal, as ours is, the nation can hardly go bankrupt. The American people are on both sides of the balance sheet.[21]

Today this is no longer true.

T: Why Should Government Borrow Money When It Can Simply Print it?

Keynes himself did not address the important question of why he wanted government to borrow in order to fund its deficit spending. Why not just print the money instead? As it is, the government often issues a bond as its method of borrowing, only to have the government's central bank buy the bond back with a fictitious check. Why not then handle all government borrowing this way, or just print the new money, which would be the simpler and more direct way to do it?

We will recall that Keynes did not object to his economic planners resorting to a bit of subterfuge. It might be more disturbing for the public to see money actually being printed, as opposed to bonds being stealthily retired as part of an impenetrably secretive central bank process. On the other hand, there is no evidence that Keynes wanted central banks to buy up all government debt and retire it stealthily, thereby eliminating any need to repay it.

Keynes's contemporary and eventual disciple William Beveridge wrote the celebrated 1942 "Beveridge Report." This dry government document laid the foundation for the post-war British "welfare state" and sold a remarkable 500,000 copies. With respect to the relative merits of financing a government deficit by issuing bonds or by printing new money, Beveridge expressed the opinion that there was not any "substan[tial] difference" between the two. It was only a "difference of degree" and certainly not "an issue of principle."[22]

U: "Normal" Deflation

A steep price decline is a symptom of depression. Deflation in general, however, is a perfectly natural and normal phenomenon, not just a symptom of depression. As Keynes himself noted, profit-making firms are always striving to become more productive, which means being able to make products better and more cheaply. They may hope to make products more cheaply without reducing prices, thereby boosting profits.

Over time, however, the need to keep the best workforce means that some of the savings from making products more cheaply goes to workers. And, if there is normal competition, lower costs also lead to lower consumer prices as well. Indeed, over time, all the cost savings typically go to workers and customers. Consequently, a successful market economy is one where prices fall 2–3% a year, year in and year out, even when there is no sign of economic trouble.

From the Keynesian perspective, even this natural and gentle fall in prices is dangerous. It is hard on debtors. And a gentle fall can too easily turn into a steep fall. Government must therefore create enough inflation to wipe out even a gentle fall in prices.

V: Additional Reasons for Keynes's Opposition to Gold in the 1920s

Following World War I, Britain did not own a lot of gold. In his *Treatise on Money*, Keynes recorded that, as of 1919, the French had considerably more than the British, the Americans more than four times as much. Even countries such as Argentina and Japan were not far behind. By 1929, Britain's gold position was even weaker.[23]

Moreover, at the end of World War I, Britain owed very large sums to the United States, payable in gold, but was in turn owed large sums by Germany and other European states, which were clearly going to be paid, if at all, in paper.[24] Keynes's preferred policy was to make all debts paper debts, and then to help pay the old debts by inflating them away, that is, by printing more money or otherwise increasing the money supply. As new money appeared, the amount owed on the old debts would steadily shrink in relation to the amount of money circulating in the economy. This is an old government technique, practiced through the ages: repay debt, but do so in money that is worth less. It was a practice that the classic gold standard was intended to stop.

W: SDRs

Keynes was disappointed that the International Monetary Fund was not allowed to create new money when it was first established. In 1969, however, an "overdraft" facility was set up that allowed countries to utilize Special Drawing Rights (SDRs) to supplement their foreign exchange reserves. SDRs are unrelated to IMF loans and are available in proportion to a country's capital contribution, although rich countries can reallocate their SDRs to poorer ones.

The IMF says that SDRs are not currency, especially not newly created currency, but it is hard to see them as anything else. Importantly, at its April 2009 meeting, the G-20 (twenty nations with the largest economies) decided to increase the SDR pool by $250 billion. This both reaffirmed the SDR concept, and made it more likely that the IMF will in future create more global "liquidity," i.e. more new money.

X: Whatever Keynes Felt About a Global Economy, He Liked the Idea of Maintaining Local Cultures

During World War II, Keynes wrote that:

> [In] the post-war world . . . we should encourage small political and cultural units. It would be a fine thing to have thirty or forty capital cities in Europe, each the center of a self-governing country entirely free from national minorities (who would be dealt with by migrations where necessary). . . . But it would be ruinous to have thirty or forty entirely independent economic and currency unions.[25]

Did Keynes really endorse forced migration of populations? Was this the kind of national or international planning he had in mind? Perhaps it was just the written equivalent of a slip of the tongue, like his occasional startlingly anti-Semitic remarks.[26] The problem, here as elsewhere, was that both his mind and his fancy were so fertile that they were always conceiving new ideas, many in contradiction to one another, and it was difficult to say where he really stood.

Y: Keynes's Theory of Interest

The more one delves into Keynes's "theory" of interest rates, the odder it becomes. He says that interest rates are determined in large part by the "liquidity preference" of lenders. (Liquidity preference may here be translated as "cash preference.")[27] This means that rates will depend on lenders' willingness to lend, not a startling idea, but not a complete one either, since the borrower has as much to say about it. Keynes did add that the amount of cash in the economy also matters.[28]

The truth is that the price of anything depends on supply, demand, and the amount of money in the economy. In the simplest economy imaginable, for example that of two shipwrecked sailors on an uninhabited South Sea island with three salvaged knives and $3, we can expect each knife to be priced at $1. If one knife is lost, the price of the remaining two might rise to $1.50. If three additional dollars are found in a bottle on the beach, the amount of money doubles, so the remaining two knives might be worth $3 each.

The pricing of loans (interest rates) is not so different from that of knives. The supply of money available to borrow is one factor, the demand for money to borrow another, and the total amount of money in the economy yet another. Since loans are all made in money, the first and third factors will influence each other, but we can still think of them as separate factors. As we shall see later, an increase in the total amount of money in the economy may initially increase the amount of money available to borrow, but if the extra money leads to inflation, the opposite may happen.

When we speak of supply and demand for anything, this is shorthand for a host of underlying fundamental factors. What are the fundamental factors that most directly shape the supply and demand for loans and thus the price for those loans as expressed by interest rates? One is profit potential. If a business investment might earn 7% a year, the business owner certainly will not pay 7% or higher in interest to finance it. The higher the potential business profit, the higher the interest rate can be.

But what about on the lender's side? What factors operate there? A critical one is time preference. Keynes's account of time preference is garbled, and is anyway incidental to his theory.[29] The best treatment of this subject is by economist Ludwig von Mises.

The essence of the time preference concept is not hard to follow. A lender knows that he or she can spend money today or lend it and, with good fortune, have more to spend tomorrow. A child generally will not want to defer gratification, even for a large reward in the end. An adult may be willing, and this willingness may grow weaker or stronger for many reasons. The borrower too will have personal time preferences.

In this sense, interest rates may be regarded as the price of time, and it is easy to see how important this makes them, because time is such an important part of so many economic transactions.

The Swedish economist Knut Wicksell (1851–1926) explored the idea that there might be a "natural" interest rate which would tend to keep an economy free from either inflation or extreme deflation, that is, keep other price changes within an economy on a smooth path. Austrian economist Ludwig von Mises then corrected and built on Wicksell's insight. (Keynes was familiar with this work, but both rejected and misrepresented the idea of a natural rate of interest in *The General Theory*, 243). It was understandable that he would reject it, because he actually favored a policy of inflation, the very thing which a natural rate of interest is intended to prevent.

Keynes took particular delight in turning the conventional wisdom on its head. An example is his claim that higher interest rates reduce saving, the opposite of what might be expected. Why? Won't potential savers be encouraged by earning more money? Yes, said Keynes, but high rates discourage businesses from borrowing. This reduces business investment, which in turn reduces national income, which will eventually reduce saving. So viewed correctly, investment leads to saving, not saving to investment.[30]

This is a nice paradox, but a false one. If the rise in interest rates is accompanied by an increase in investment opportunity, perhaps even caused by it, then businesses will not cut back on investment. It is, in fact, usually the case that interest rates rise as economic growth accelerates. Conclusion: saving leads to investment, just as everyone assumes.

Economic writer Henry Hazlitt has noted that the tendency of interest rates to rise during a boom and fall during a slump is itself a refutation of Keynes's liquidity preference based theory of interest.[31] If Keynes were right that interest rates are largely determined by lenders' liquidity (cash) preference, they should do the reverse: fall during an economic boom and rise during a slump. This follows because individuals want to get in on a boom, not hold cash, but conversely hold tight to any cash during a slump, thereby making it harder for businesses to borrow.

It must be acknowledged that interest rates may rise at the beginning of a slump. At that point, businesses and individuals with inadequate savings may desperately try to borrow in order to pay their bills. If rates do rise, it will not last long. As the slump deepens, rates fall, because economic activity slows and business expansion stops, each of which reduces loan demand.

Keynes knew very well that interest rates during a slump fall, and should have known that this contradicted his theory. He should also have realized that his idea of an interest rate approaching zero is possible for the very short term, but not for longer periods, because it implies that a consumption good deferred is just as desirable as a consumption good consumed right away, that waiting has no value and should not be rewarded. At best, Keynes's theory of interest seems confused and half-baked, hardly a firm foundation on which to base his aggressive recommendation for government to force down interest rates.

Z: The Younger Keynes on Inflation

In his second book, *The Economic Consequences of The Peace*, written immediately after World War I, Keynes warned about the evils of inflation:

> Lenin is said to have declared that the best way to destroy the Capitalist System was to debauch the currency. By a continuing progress of inflation, governments can confiscate, secretly and unobserved, an important part of the wealth of their citizens. By this method they not only confiscate, but they confiscate *arbitrarily*; and while the process impoverishes many, it actually enriches some. . . . As the inflation proceeds . . . the process of wealth-getting degenerates into a gamble and a lottery. Lenin was certainly right. There is no subtler, no surer means of overturning the existing basis of society than to debauch the currency. The process engages all the hidden forces of economic law on the side of destruction, and does it in a manner which not one man in a million is able to diagnose.[32]

Keynes's reference to Lenin in the passage above is ironic for several reasons. It is ironic to turn to a Communist for an accurate diagnosis of what ails capitalism. But it is even more ironic because Lenin completely failed to see that inflation was a threat to any economic system, not just a capitalist one, and was therefore completely taken by surprise when his own Communist regime became wracked by hyper-inflation in 1920. This communist inflation raged so uncontrollably that, as Keynes said at the time:

> In Moscow . . . if you buy a pound of cheese in a grocer's shop, the grocer runs off with the roubles as fast as his legs will carry him to the Central Market to replenish his stocks by changing them into cheese again, lest they lose their value before he gets there.[33]

By the late 1980s, the dying Soviet government under Gorbachev was again running its currency printing presses at a red-hot rate, flooding the country with money. People did not initially understand what was happening. Prices of consumer goods were rigidly controlled, there was little to buy anyway, and what could be bought required an endless wait in line.

By 1992, however, rigid price controls had been lifted. It then quickly became apparent that all the new Soviet money had rendered the old Soviet money nearly worthless. Many Russians had scrimped and saved over a lifetime. Suddenly it was all gone. Most people thought this was the fault of "liberalization." They did not realize that the value of their money had actually disappeared during the Communist regime, and that the hidden inflation of the 1980s had itself contributed to the collapse of the Soviet Union.

In 1922, Keynes was asked by the German government for advice about how to control its own hyper-inflation. In less than two years, prices had already jumped by over twenty times. Europe had not seen anything like this for over a century, and many Britons bought marks on the assumption that the inflation could not possibly continue. Unfortunately, they could not have been more wrong.[34]

Keynes recommended that the government stop spending so much, balance its budget, and above all stop printing so much money. This was ignored, and prices jumped another 3,000 times over the next year. At one point, prices were doubling every 3.7 days. Finally the new head of the Reichbank, Dr. Hjalmar Schacht, adopted Keynes's hard money policy and the inflation came to an abrupt end. But by then millions of middle class Germans had been wiped out and embittered, thus setting the stage for the Nazi era which shortly followed.[35]

The German episode of the early 1920s is usually cited as the classic example of hyper-inflation. But others have been worse: Communist Yugoslavia in January 1994 (prices doubling every day and a half) and especially Zimbabwe in October 2008 (prices doubling every day).[36]

There have even been hyper-inflations (although not this virulent) in America. Leaving aside the Great Inflation of the 1970s, inflation rose at a peak monthly rate of 40% during the Civil War and 47% during the Revolutionary War. What all three American inflations had in common was that government printed large quantities of paper money, physically printing it in earlier years, electronically "printing" it in the 1970s.[37]

Writing in his younger years, Keynes pointed out that inflation operates very much like a tax, but a hidden tax which may be collected effortlessly. He illustrated his point with some math. A simplified version would go along the following lines: Assume that an economy consists of one dollar and some goods and services. If government decides to tax at 25%, it gets 25¢, which will put one-fourth of the fruits of the economy at its disposal. But that is the hard way. Why not print 33⅓¢ and spend it? Since there is now $1.333 floating around the economy, 33⅓¢ will still buy the same one-fourth of all goods and services. If government also owes money, the inflation will be doubly welcome, because the government's debt can be paid back in money which, in real (inflation adjusted) terms, is worth less.

The younger anti-inflationary Keynes concluded that

> [The] progressive deterioration in the value of money through history is not an accident, and has had behind it two great driving forces—the impecuniosity [money hunger] of governments and the superior political influence of the debtor class.
>
> A government can live for a long time ... by printing paper money. .... It is the form of taxation which the public finds hardest to evade and even the weakest government can enforce. [38]

As these passages suggest, no more eloquent foe of the elder Keynes's policies can be found than the younger Keynes himself.

AA: Not Everyone Thinks that the Consumer Price Index Understates Inflation

For an argument that the CPI overstates inflation, see Broda, C., and Weinstein, D., *Prices, Poverty, and Inequality*.[39] The authors do not address why it is that previous government methods of calculating inflation, if applied today, would produce a higher CPI. Their book is primarily concerned with the question of whether Americans with the lowest income are making progress. With respect to this point, it is important to note that the people in the lowest income decile are constantly changing, partly because of immigration.

BB: Do Earlier Bubbles Refute Mises?

Critics of Mises's theory of the business cycle sometimes object that economic bubbles pre-dated the modern banking system. This being so, government efforts to reduce interest rates artificially by printing money and injecting it into the economy via the banks cannot be the root cause of the business cycle.

The pre-eminent example of a bubble predating the modern banking system is the Mississippi Scheme organized in the early 1700s by John Law and supported by the French government. Although it may have begun as a legitimate business venture, it quickly metamorphosed into an attempt to pour new money into the economy and, in effect, to debase the currency. This and other early bubbles support rather than contradict Mises's view that the business cycle results from artificial efforts to inflate the money supply. They remind us, however, that the methods used to debase the currency historically take many forms. As noted in chapter 1, government efforts to control interest rates and other prices can be dated back to the ancient Babylonians.

CC: New Money and Interest Rates Levels

The impact on interest rates of new money injected into an economy is always complex. We have seen that new money can lead to inflation or expectations of inflation and thence to higher interest rates, or, alternatively, to disguised inflation and a bubble, but even this is an over-simplification. Consider, for example, the decision of the US Federal Reserve in 2009 to buy long-dated US treasury bonds with money created "out of thin air." This was a sharp departure, since the Fed had not bought long bonds in this way since shortly after World War II.

The initial impact of the Fed's announcement was dramatic. Long-term treasury yields fell. The bond market evidently concluded that the Fed would not let long rates rise, so it might be profitable to buy such bonds. But then long yields began to rise. Why? Perhaps because foreign governments, holding more US treasuries than they wanted, saw this as an ideal moment to start selling them. Foreign governments presumably did not intend to sell so many US bonds that yields rose. This would depress price and thus threaten the value of their substantial remaining holdings. But with the Fed buying such bonds, why not take advantage of this window of opportunity to sell? From a foreign government perspective, the Fed could be seen as a "sucker" willing to take overpriced and unwanted merchandise off their hands at full price.

Looked at in this way, the Fed's action might not achieve what the Fed wanted. Instead of holding long treasury yields down, buying these bonds might instead trigger enough foreign selling to raise rates. If so, who would "blink" first? The Fed, which wanted to manipulate the market with as few purchases as possible? Or the foreign government sellers with their vast holdings of unwanted US bonds? It was impossible to say, but the advantage seemed to lie with the foreign governments. Why would they stop "dumping" their bonds on the Fed, so long as the Fed was willing to buy them at full price with "make believe" money?

DD: More Money Alone Does Not Make Us Richer

This fallacy is easy to catch when you think about the economy as a whole, less easy to catch in a specific case such as the US government's healthcare policy. The government quite deliberately subsidizes health care either by paying for it or by providing additional money to pay for it. This increases demand, but nothing is done to increase supply, in fact supply is restricted with myriad regulations about who can do what. With more demand and less supply, the additional money just leads to higher prices, which then typically leads to rationing. This problem is also touched on in chapter 22.

EE: Origins of the 1929 Crash and the Great Depression

The bubble of the 1920s was to a remarkable degree the work of one man, Benjamin Strong, president of the Federal Reserve Bank of New York. Strong dominated US monetary policy and led the world financial system with his close ally, Montagu Norman, head of the Bank of England. Strong and Norman worried that the US rejection of the League of Nations Treaty following World War I had left a leadership vacuum in global politics. Both agreed that the US, acting with Britain, could at least take responsibility for stabilizing the global economy.

At that time, the entire world (but especially Britain) owed vast sums to the United States. How would these loans be paid? In theory, other countries could export to the US and thus earn the dollars with which to repay their debts. But high US tariffs made this difficult. Strong and Norman together worked out policies designed to address this problem.

Strong in particular had been experimenting with methods that the newly created Federal Reserve could use to lower interest rates. Keynes noted (in an admiring obituary notice) that

> Open-market policy [the technical term for the primary method of "printing" money and injecting it into the economy through the banks as lendable funds] . . . was largely his creation.[40]

Strong further developed the idea that if US interest rates were driven down by "open-market policy," the US would boom. If it boomed, it would be able to buy more goods from abroad. At the same time, some of the new money created by the government could be sent abroad as new loans. The new loans would not only help refinance the old loans. They would also encourage foreign governments to buy American goods. (In some instances, a requirement to spend part of the funds in the US was incorporated into the loan itself.)

This system was somewhat analogous to the understanding that developed between China and the US in the 1990s. The US would buy very large quantities of goods from China, but China would lend the purchase price back to the US, in effect financing the sale. In a similar way, the US in the 1920s was financing the sale of US goods in Europe, and also refinancing the World War I loans in order to maintain the fiction that they would eventually be paid.

Herbert Hoover, first as Commerce Secretary under President Coolidge, then as president himself, supported the policy of cheap loans abroad because he thought that even bad loans would boost exports and thus also boost employment.[41] Later, when the bubble of cheap money and cheap loans (both domestic and international) burst, Hoover made the resulting depression much worse than it would have been by trying to hold wages up as prices plummeted. (We will discuss this further when we get to Keynes's recommended policies for depression.) The shrewd Calvin Coolidge, who reportedly expected a Crash and declined to run for another presidential term in 1928, reportedly said about Hoover: "That man has offered me unsolicited advice for six years, all of it bad."[42]

Keynes did not anticipate the Crash and lost a great deal of money in it. Even after the Crash, he described the performance of the US Federal Reserve in 1923–1928 as a

triumph.

What neither Strong nor Keynes recognized was that the cheap money policy was steadily creating inflation, albeit (as in the 1990s and first years of this century) a disguised inflation. The new money kept prices from falling, as it otherwise would have, and in any case much of it went into stock speculation.

In 1927, Strong and Norman decided to lower rates further. The former wrote to the Deputy-Governor of the Bank of France that

I will give a little coup de whiskey to the stock market.[43]

This last boost to speculation proved to be a tragic error. But Strong did not live to see the results. By 1928, he was dead at age 51.

FF: Economist Ludwig von Mises on High Tax Rates

Mises took an especially dim view of heavy taxation in the upper brackets. He argued that "The essence of the much glorified 'progressive' economic policies of the last decades was to expropriate ever-increasing parts of the higher incomes and to employ the funds thus raised for financing public waste and for subsidizing the members of the most powerful pressure groups."[44]

GG: Why a Higher Interest Rate May Also Be "Stimulative"

So far in our discussion, we have assumed that low interest rates will "stimulate" investment and economic growth while high rates will do the reverse. But we must keep in mind that the relationship of different interest rates matters a great deal as well. A 1% Fed Funds Rate would normally be much more "stimulative" than a 4% rate, but it might not be depending on the level of other rates.

A bank makes it money from a "spread," the difference between the rate at which it borrows and lends. Although it prefers a 1% borrowing rate to a 4% borrowing rate, if it can borrow at 1% and lend at 3%, that is not as good as being able to borrow at 4% and lend at 7%. In this case, the 4% Fed Funds Rate may be more "stimulative" than the 1% rate, because it will encourage more bank lending.

Banks are not the only "spread" investors. Hedge funds and others do the same. When hedge funds borrow at short rates and simultaneously lend at longer rates, often using different currencies, it is called a "carry trade."

HH: Unintended Consequences of Government Student Loans

As in medicine, so also in higher education, subsidies increase demand. If demand increases, but supply does not, the effect is simply to raise prices. The most effective way to help people afford education or anything else is to increase the supply, not the demand. To increase demand without worrying about supply is completely counterproductive. Of course supply of the best-known US universities cannot be increased; they enjoy a unique position and reputation. But other educational opportunities can be increased, thereby increasing supply and putting an overall limit on prices.

II: Say's Law

The idea that a society which produces will not lack the income with which to spend, with which to buy the products produced—may seem puzzling at first. It is natural to ask: What if buyers do not have the money to buy the goods produced? What then? Fortunately the very act of production releases the money needed to buy the goods. To see why this is so, look at the following profit and loss statement for a business:

ACME PRODUCTS COMPANY

Sales (Income)	$10,000,000

EXPENSES

purchases	$2,000,000
employees	$6,000,000
other costs	$1,000,000
Total	$9,000,000
Profit	$1,000,000

Each expense item represents money that is going out into the economy before the Acme product appears. Every dollar of it can be spent.

These dollars will probably not be spent on Acme products, but they will be spent on something.

Does this mean that Acme will always find a buyer for its products? Of course not. Acme will only find buyers if its products are of good quality, no more expensive than similar products, and represent something that people want. But regardless of whether people buy Acme products, there will always be money to buy them, because total economic production in an economy always generates the money necessary to buy all the products produced. The problem is not how to generate the buyers or the buying power. The problem is how to get the production going in the first place.

Wait a minute, the observant reader will say. The expenses that Acme paid out into the economy only represented 90% of its sales. What about the 10% that Acme made as profit?

The answer is that this 10% profit flows out into the economy too, although it flows out later than the expenses, and only if the Acme products are bought. Assuming that there is a profit, the owners of Acme may spend it on personal consumer goods. If not, they will save it. If they save it within the company, the company will spend it on expanding the business, and this money too will flow out into the economy where it can be used to buy something else. If the owners invest the profit outside the company, it will be spent starting or expanding another business.

The idea that (for an economy as a whole) production provides the income with which to buy its products, or, as it is often put, supply creates its own demand, is perfectly sensible when thought through. Neither Keynes nor anyone else has been able to refute it, for the simple reason that it is correct. (For a more complete explanation of why Say was right and Keynes wrong, the works of the economist W. E. Hutt are a useful resource.)

JJ: Saving and Investment (Which Comes First?)

Keynes also makes the paradoxical claim that the level of investment determines the level of savings, the opposite of the commonsense observation that saving must precede investment. This is part of Keynes's more encompassing paradoxical claim that spending in general determines the level of saving, and that spending, not saving, makes us wealthy.

It is true that consumer and business spending determine income. But it does not follow that we grow rich by spending. The so-called classical economists dismissed by Keynes were quite correct that the circular flows of the economy begin with hard work, production, and saving. These in turn lead to spending which flows back to the producers as income. To start one's analysis quite arbitrarily and misleadingly in the middle of the flow, and then to present this as an important new insight or discovery is merely to play semantical games.

In thinking about this, we must also keep in mind that Keynes saw private savings as only one element of society's "savings." He also considered newly printed money injected into the economy through the banking system as "savings."

KK: Large Unused Savings and Deep Deflations

It is misleading to think, as Keynes does, of large unused savings causing deep deflation. This is an example of tautological reasoning. The two variables, far from representing cause and effect, are really just different ways of describing the same thing. If money is hoarded rather than invested, the money supply in the economy drops. Because there is less money circulating, prices drop. As prices drop, either wages must drop, or profits will disappear. If profits disappear, bankruptcies and unemployment will result. There will be more discussion of this in later chapters.

LL: Keynes's Confusions about Hoarding

Keynes is so eager to find examples of uninvested savings that are lying idle and (thus interrupting the financial flows of the economy) that he falls into a surprising number of factual or logical errors. For example, he says that individuals or companies in effect build up cash hoards so they can repair buildings or replace plants.[45] But, as Henry Hazlitt has pointed out, these are almost never true cash hoards. Either they are an accounting convention (depreciation allowance) with no effect on cash holdings or they are reserves, and if reserves are usually invested.

Even more puzzling is Keynes's assertion that buying shares of an existing company on the stock market does not put savings to work.[46] The idea seems to be that one is just buying an old investment, not a new one. This makes no sense. As Keynes himself says, buying shares is a two-sided transaction. There must be a seller. If I buy the seller's shares, the cash passes to him or her. The seller in turn will either spend the money or buy other shares. Eventually the new cash will find its way either into consumer or business spending.

In the same way, it is sometimes argued that buyers of gold bullion are hoarders, because they earn no investment return on the bullion. But if there is a buyer of gold, there must be a seller, so the buyer's cash remains active in the economy, although now in the seller's hands. Anyway, why does the buyer want to own gold in the first place? Usually the buyer is motivated either by fear of a government-engineered inflation, fear of a devaluation of government-issued paper money, or fear of a stealth devaluation of paper money through inflation.

MM: How Government Encourages Stock Market Gambling

Injecting money and low cost credit into the economy is the primary way that governments create bubbles and fuel stock market speculation. But there are many other ways that governments encourage speculation. For example, if we can tax deduct the cost of a mortgage loan, why not take more mortgage than you need and put the extra borrowed money into stocks, especially into a tax-favored retirement plan? You aren't supposed to do this directly, but who can stop you from doing it indirectly by making a smaller home down payment? If you invest in a taxable account, you will of course want to avoid solid companies with reliable dividends, because government taxes dividends at a higher rate than capital gains (after already taxing the dividends previously at the company level).

Double taxation of dividends is also one of the reasons that companies in the 1990s borrowed money to buy in their stock, which propelled the stock market bubble of that era. Another reason that companies in the US did this is because Congress had just made executive cash compensation of more than $1 million nondeductible by public corporations. This led to mass issuance of stock options to executives, which in turn made it compellingly attractive to borrow to buy stock in, boost the price, and thereby inflate the stock options. This is also touched on in chapter 22.

NN: Definition of Speculation

Although Keynes said he was writing *The General Theory* for specialists, he used a layman's definition of speculation. In the technical language of economics, a speculator is a useful citizen who helps producers insure against unavoidable uncertainty. For example, speculators on grain prices may buy a farmer's crop before it is planted, thereby protecting the farmer from worst case outcomes, and perhaps allowing the farmer to plant more. By contrast, gamblers take completely avoidable risks, such as at a casino, and thus serve no economic purpose at all. Keynes knows this, but his account does not distinguish between the two very different activities.

OO: Obligations of the US Government in 2007

(*Expressed in $ billions; the first digit or two digits are trillions*)	2000	2007	annual growth rates
Nominal GDP	$9,817	$13,841	5.0%
Public dept outstanding	5,662	9,229	7.2
Federal employee and veteran benefits	2,758	4,769	8.1
Expected expenditures for Social Security	3,845	6,763	8.4
Expected expenditures for Medicare	9,193	34,085	20.6
Ginnie Mae guarantees	603	428	−4.8
FHLB liabilities	622	1,218	10.1
Fannie and Freddie MBS and liabilities	3,345	6,537	10.0
FDIC insured deposits	3,055	4,293	5.0
Totals	**$29,083**	**$67,321**	**12.7%**

Source: *Grant's Interest Rate Observer*, July 25, 2008, 2.
Note: Many of these items soared after 2007.

PP: A New "Populist" Alliance?

The merger of Wall Street and Washington, emblematic of a larger merger of big business and Washington, has opponents from completely different sides of the political spectrum.

Populists on the left are critical because they think that Washington is catering to the rich, and will be corrupted by big business's money. Distinguished economist Joseph Stiglitz is a leader in this camp. He said that "[The designers of the bailout are] in the pockets of the banks or they're incompetent. It's a real redistribution and a tax on all American savers. This is a strategy of trying to recreate the bubble."[47]

There are also critics from what is often regarded as the political right, especially libertarians, saying much the same thing. They would not usually agree with Stiglitz, but in this case share his conviction that government is corrupting itself, in addition to doing great harm to the economy.

Perhaps at some point there will be an alliance of "populists" from both left and right trying to stop the corrupting flow of money back and forth between Washington and special interests.

QQ: Do Union Wage Gains Hurt Other Workers?

Looking at the question from an economy-wide perspective, most of the gains of unionized workers do not come at the expense of employers, but rather at the expense of nonunionized workers. In the first place, higher wages in the unionized industry mean there are fewer jobs there, so more workers compete for other nonunionized jobs and thereby reduce the wages paid for those jobs. In the second place, the products of the unionized industry generally cost more; to the degree that other industries have to buy them, those industries have less to pay workers. In addition, if workers buy the unionized product (e.g. autos), they will pay more, and thus have less money to spend on other things. If the unionized work is in government, everyone has to pay the higher price through additional taxes or through the hidden tax of inflation associated with deficit spending and printing money.

RR: Economics: The Art of Drawing Working Hypotheses From What is Always Inconclusive Evidence

Was the return of sound money in 1879 merely coincident with the end of the Depression, or does it explain the end? In economics, one must always make do with inconclusive evidence. But sound money as the cure in this instance seems a strong hypothesis.

SS: The Creation of New Money by Banks

An example will help us understand how this works. Assume that I deposit $1,000 in my bank. The bank lends out $900 to some other party. It holds back the other $100 in case some depositor demands cash. After my money has been lent out, the $1,000 has grown to

$1,900. Why? Because I still have my $1,000 and the borrower now has $900 as well for a total of $1,900. If the borrower deposits the $900 in another bank, perhaps $810 of that will also be lent and $90 held back as a reserve. Assuming a 10% reserve, my original $1,000 may, over the course of time, grow to $10,000 in total money moving around the economy.

It must be emphasized that none of this lending has increased wealth. $9,000 of newly created money has been borrowed and must be repaid. So, although there is now $10,000, there is still only $1,000 of wealth.

This does not end the story, however. Government can encourage banks to create more or less money by varying the reserve requirement. It can also increase the bank's reserves directly through what is knows as "open market operations."

In open market operations, the Fed may buy a government bond from a bank, not by actually paying for the bond, but by crediting the bank's account at the Fed. This creates more new money "out of thin air." In addition, because the bank has new reserves, it can lend up to ten times the amount of new reserves. Each new dollar of bank reserves has the potential to become $10 in new loan money for the economy at large. In this way, money newly printed by the government multiplies itself through the banking system. (For more on the Fed, see Hunter Lewis's *Are the Rich Necessary?* Revised Edition, Axios Press. Mt. Jackson, VA, October 2009).

TT: The 100% Bank Reserve Concept

With 100% reserves, the amount of money in the economy would no longer fluctuate unpredictably. Bank runs could no longer happen, so Bagehot's lender of last resort would not be needed. Finance would no longer be the weak link in the economy.

The supply of money being fixed, prices would tend to drift down gently as productivity improves, that is, as we learn to make goods more cheaply. This would especially help the poor, because they could buy more with the same income. Interest rates would tend to be lower, since loans would be repaid in money that would generally have a greater purchasing power. If price declines were the norm, contracts might also require repayment of less than 100% of face value.

Opponents of a fixed money supply argue that it would restrict the expansion of production. But if production expanded without expanding the money supply, it would just result in lower prices. Lower prices are not a threat to the economy, provided that they are expected, and do not come too rapidly. Even proponents of an "elastic" or expanding money supply do not explain why the present system of expanding money randomly and erratically through bank loans can possibly make any sense.

For a more complete exposition of the 100% bank reserve concept see various books and papers by economist Murray Rothbard. Economist George Reisman also discusses it in his book *Capitalism*.

UU: Federal Reserve Bank Reserve Requirements

The last reduction in required bank reserves was in December 1992: from a sliding scale with a maximum of 12% to a sliding scale with a maximum of 10% on transaction deposits. Non-transaction account requirements were reduced to zero in 1990.

VV: Obama's Deficit Projections

President Obama crafted his first budget so that projected deficits fall sharply before the 2012 election year, then rise again thereafter.[48] The Obama budget also showed a projected budget deficit of $600 billion in 2018, the year that the United States is expected to run out of social security funding. The Nonpartisan Congressional Budget Office says that Obama has also underestimated the 2018 deficit by $400 billion. If so, it would be $1 trillion even before the additional social security spending hits.[49]

WW: Further Observations on the Keynesian Multiplier

Even if the multiplier does not self-destruct by becoming infinite, it produces peculiar results. Henry Hazlitt shows how, by Keynesian math, his own personal spending ought to multiply by 100,000.[50] He also shows how Keynes keeps confusing nominal (before inflation) and real (after inflation) values.[51]

It is also incorrect, as George Reisman has pointed out, that the money would travel from one worker to another as it is multiplied. The spending of the first set of workers would actually be expected to increase the profits of businesses.[52] Reisman also notes in his book *Capitalism* that

Keynes's "multiplier" doctrine contradicts his own "marginal efficiency of capital" (read profits) doctrine.[53] This is awkward for Keynes for two different reasons. In the first place, he does not want to acknowledge the role of profits in creating employment. In the second place, profits are savings, and the multiplier formula assumes that savings are not spent. If savings are spent, the multiplier becomes infinite, as we have seen. If savings in the form of profits are not spent, there will be no multiplication. The best way to deal with all this is to put a quantified and forecastable multiplier where it belongs: in the dustbin.

XX: Do Employed Workers Gain From Severe Deflation?

To make an exact calculation for any severe deflationary period, we would need to have consumer as well as producer prices, average hourly wages, and especially number of hours worked. Even then, the result would only be an average, and the dispersions around the average would be large.

YY: Bernanke and Gold

The price of gold was $480 an ounce when Bernanke was nominated to the Fed.[54] It then doubled in price, fell back during the Crash of 2008 as purchasers using credit had to sell, then rebounded sharply in 2009. The same thing had happened during and after the Crash of 1929. Gold fell, but recovered after the initial phase of asset liquidation.

ZZ: Did Keynes Say Something New?

Carl Horowitz of the National Legal and Policy Center, a critic of Keynes, calls him a "highly flawed though highly original thinker."[55] But there are reasons to doubt that Keynes was highly original.

It is very difficult to say something completely new in economics or any other "social" subject. What seems new is usually a new treatment of an old theme or perhaps a rediscovery of it. It does seem fair to say that Keynes's *General Theory* as a whole is a revival of earlier Mercantilist doctrines. Keynesianism is, broadly speaking, Mercantilism.

In addition, some Keynesians felt that Michal Kalecki had anticipated at least part of what Keynes said. Joan Robinson, Keynes's protégé, agreed with this. Henry Hazlitt also notes the claims of L. Albert Hahn, a German who wrote *Geld und Kredit (Money and Credit)* in 1924. Hahn does seem to anticipate Keynes in many ways, although he eventually repudiated his own early works as well as Keynes's in his 1949 book, *The Economics of Illusion*.

AAA: Mixing Up Real and Nominal Series

Examples are to be found on pages 117, 64 and 90 of *The General Theory*. For a complete discussion see Henry Hazlitt, *The Failure of The New Economics*, pages 64, 85, 107, 145 among others.

BBB: The Rabbit Hole

Lewis Carroll (Charles Dodgson, 1832–1898) was a mathematician and logician. His book, *Alice in Wonderland*, which introduced the "rabbit hole," is about logic as well as fantasy.

CCC: More Keynesian Paradoxes and Partial Paradoxes (Supplement to Chapter 21)

Keynesian Spending and Saving Paradoxes

1. Unemployment has nothing to do with employer profits, wage levels, and other prices. To solve it, we just need more spending.

2. Just as new money printed by government represents a form of savings "just as genuine" as traditional savings, so too are bubble business profits just as genuine as traditional profits.

3. Taxing away the saving and investment of a lifetime accumulated in an estate will create even more investment.

More Money Printing Paradoxes

4. If driving interest rates down creates a bubble, government should not intervene. If bubble turns to bust, then government should intervene.

    (Reminder: This way, we can encourage everyone to keep creating more bubbles.)

5. Bubbles are not inherently bad. The problem is how to perpetuate them. *New York Times* reporter Thomas Friedman reflected this point of view when he wrote that "America needs an energy technology bubble just like the information technology bubble."[56]

    (Reminder: Bubbles waste resources, produce bad debt and end in crashes.)

6. If printing money and driving interest rates down cause inflation, there are worse things than inflation. Deflation (falling consumer prices) is always poison for an economy.

   (Reminder: The more productive we are, the more costs and prices should fall. The more prices fall, the more we can buy. This is called economic progress.

   Some of the most prosperous periods of US history have been during gentle deflations. The best examples were in the second half of the 19th century, but we did well during the Eisenhower deflation of August 1954–August 1955 as well.

   We also need to keep in mind that inflation creates dislocations. These dislocations can easily lead to extreme deflation, just what inflationists most want to avoid.)

7. Inflation helps the poor.

   (Reminder: The poor benefit the most from gently falling prices. Most studies show that inflation makes the rich richer relative to others—and the poor poorer. Not surprising: the rich understand inflation and how to exploit it.)

8. Inflation fears are exaggerated. True inflation can only occur when everyone is employed.

   (Reminder: After the 1970s, Keynesians abandoned this idea in its most extreme form, but it still flourishes among US Federal Reserve economists and others.)

9. If inflation does get serious, government, the creator of the inflation, will not only stop inflating. It will even stop spending!

10. Printing new money helps us solve economic problems. US Federal Reserve Chairman Ben Bernanke expressed this point of view when he said that his actions during the 2008 Crash and its aftermath were designed "to solve this problem."[57]

    (Reminder: Pouring new money into the economy does not make us more productive or richer. Pouring water into milk does not make more milk. Money printing does not fix problems.)

11. New money injected into an economy can be taken right out again if necessary to avoid inflation. This is true even if the injection is on a massive scale, as it was following the Crash of 2008.

(Reminder: This has never been done before. Politics makes it much easier to inject lendable funds than to withdraw them. Even if politics permits, the withdrawal may cause a collapse.)

12. Gold is a "barbarous relic."

(Reminder: The advantage of precious metals is that, unlike paper money, they cannot be multiplied ad infinitum by governments.)

13. We need to produce more and more money as the economy grows. Gold is a straitjacket which does not permit this.

(Reminder: If we produce more and more goods without producing more money, the result is that the goods cost less.)

14. Central banks have largely succeeded in moderating inflation, moderating the business cycle and stabilizing the economy. This success may have inadvertently (and paradoxically) encouraged Wall Streeters to take on more and more risk, leading to the Crashes of 1929 and 2008. This paradox is advanced by Donald Kohn, vice chairman of the US Federal Reserve.[58] Although Kohn's idea broadly reflects Keynesian thinking, it more directly reflects the ideas of Hyman Minsky, another Keynesian economist who described this kind of scenario in his *Can "It" Happen Again?," Essays on Instability and Finance*,[59] and in his 1986 book, *Stabilizing An Unstable Economy*.[60]

(Reminder: Although the 1920s, 1990s, and 2000s were not marked by consumer price inflations, they were marked by asset inflation [bubbles]. The absence of high levels of consumer price inflation did not mean that all was well. Quite the contrary.

Nor is the Fed's record on consumer price inflation one to boast about. As noted earlier, since the formation of the US Federal Reserve, the dollar has lost over 95% of its consumer purchasing power. The US economy has also been less stable, with more and deeper downturns, under Federal Reserve management. The Federal Reserve is responsible for the Crash of 2008, but not because of any prior "success." It is responsible because, in conjunction with other central banks, it printed too much money. This excessive new money in turn led to the bubbles and then the Crash. In effect, as noted in chapter 14, the Fed poured the nearly free drinks that enabled Wall Street to get drunk.)

Keynesian Bailout Paradoxes

15. Governments should borrow from foreigners to bail out bank bondholders. (In some cases, bank bondholders may be the same foreigners.)

16. Once bad debts are transferred from private to public hands, they no longer threaten the economy with deflation.

    (Reminder: There are only two ways to get rid of bad debt: liquidation [deflation] and inflation. There are no other ways.)

17. If some companies are failing, infuse funds into the entire industry, lest failing companies be singled out and consumers learn the truth about them.

18. Rely on government's "long views" to choose the right bailout candidates. Government will not be influenced by campaign contribution potential or key voter blocks.

19. If bailout candidates have too much production capacity, do not reduce the capacity. Instead stimulate the economy to grow so that the capacity will be needed.

    (Reminder: There is not just a question of too much or too little capacity. There is also a question of having the right kind of capacity, the kind of capacity the economy actually needs. But government will know whether it is the right kind of capacity.)

20. Government guarantees can make almost any problem disappear, from potential bank runs to worries about whether an auto company will deliver a promised motor tune-up.

21. Piling new debt atop old, bad debt in a bailout gives the economy time to adjust.

    (Reminder: It also makes the adjustment much harder.)

Other Keynesian Paradoxes

22. Government should rely on economic experts. It is appropriate for these experts to engage in a bit of deception from time to time, since the public cannot be expected to grasp the underlying issues. (Secretary of the Treasury Henry Paulson provided a somewhat crude illustration of this principle when he ordered the head of the Bank of America to proceed with the absorption of the big broker Merrill Lynch in December 2008 and not to reveal Merrill Lynch's gaping 4th quarter loss despite a legal obligation to do so.[61] Other illustrations of the Keynesian

principle of deception: [A] the outlandish economic growth projections in President Obama's first budget, and [B] the Federal Reserve's decision to insert an obscure provision in President Bush's October 2008 bank rescue bill [TARP] that vastly increased the Agency's powers.)

23. Speaking of deception, government experts (and politicians) should be under no obligation to speak plainly. It is perfectly sensible to call massive money printing "quantitative easing"; using this kind of money to buy government debt "monetization"; government spending "investment"; government transfer payments to non-income tax-payers "tax cuts"; new taxes "budget savings"; spending increases (at a slower rate) "cuts," non-market prices "mark-to-market," and so on.

24. The best thing about experts is that they do not wear a political party logo on their back. They are always coolly apolitical and just worry about doing the right thing. We also need not worry about the rule of experts gradually supplanting democratic government.

    (Reminder: It is happening in Europe.)

25. Private vested interests without the slightest concern for the public welfare have controlled the economy too long. We should not let laissez-faire cant prevent us from bringing the government in, not just as a source of law and rule, but as a day-to-day regulator or even manager. We do not have to worry that the private vested interests will use this opportunity to take over the government.

26. Alternatively, private vested interests have already taken over the government. This is a likely explanation for why the crisis arose in the first place. If so, the private vested interests can be purged from government and not return.

27. If government takes over an industry such as student loans or medical insurance, that will be cheaper. Government run enterprises are generally operated more efficiently and cheaply than profit-making ones.

28. If government enters an industry in which private companies still operate, it will do very well as both player and umpire.

DDD: Expanding the Nonprofit Sector

See Hunter Lewis, *Are the Rich Necessary?*, last chapter, for a discussion of how to build up the charitable sector.

Citations

Part One: Introduction

Chapter 1: Commonsense Economics

1. Caroline Baum, Interview, *Bloomberg News*, March 2, 2009.

2. *Harvard Magazine* (November–December, 2008): 60.

3. Marc Faber, *Gloom, Boom, and Doom Report* (March 2009): 4.

4. Peter Bernstein, *Economics and Portfolio Strategy* (July 15, 2008):

5. *Marc Farber, Gloom, Boom, and Doom Report* (September 2008): 20. Housing bubble quotations compiled by Fred Sheehan.

6. CNN interview, cited in *Weekly Standard* (February, 2, 2009): 15; and interview with Cal Thomas, *Washington Times* (January 12, 2009), n. p.

7. G. Mankiw, "Sunday Money," *New York Times* (November 30, 2008): 4.

8. Jacques Rueff, in Henry Hazlitt, ed., *The Critics of Keynesian Economics* (New York: D. Van Nostrand, 1960), 239.

9. M. Continetli, "The Stimulus Trap," *Weekly Standard* (January 19, 2009): 21.

10. John Maynard Keynes, *The General Theory of Employment, Interest, and Money* (Amherst, NY: Prometheus Books, 1997), 83.

11. John Maynard Keynes, "Newton, the Man," in *Collected Writings*, vol. 10, *Essays in Biography* (London: Macmillan; New York: St. Martin's Press, 1972), 365.

12. Henry Hazlitt, *The Failure of The "New Economics"* (New Rochelle, NY: Arlington House, 1978), 6–7.

13. John H. Williams, in Hazlitt, *Critics of Keynesian Economics*, 285.

14. Robert Skidelsky, *John Maynard Keynes*, vol. 2, *The Economist as Savior 1920–1937* (London: Macmillan, 2000), 344.

Part Two: What Keynes Really Said

Chapter 2: Drive Interest Rates Down

1. Keynes, *General Theory*, 351.

2. John Maynard Keynes, Memo related to Macmillan Committee Report, in *Collected Writings*, vol. 20, *Activities 1929–31: Rethinking Employment and Unemployment Policies* (London: Macmillan; New York: St. Martin's Press, 1981), 273.

3. Keynes, *General Theory*, 242.

4. Ibid., 351.

5. Ibid., 174, 351.

6. Ibid., 208, 309.

7. John Maynard Keynes, *Collected Writings*, vol. 6, *A Treatise on Money: The Applied Theory of Money* (London: Macmillan; New York: St. Martin's Press, 1971), 339.

8. Keynes, *General Theory*, 309.

9. Ibid., 167–68, 197–99, 268, 298.

10. John Maynard Keynes, *The Collected Writings*, vol. 5, *A Treatise on Money: The Pure Theory of Money* (London: Macmillan; New York: St. Martin's Press, 1971), chap. 2 discusses mechanics.

11. Keynes, *General Theory*, 167–68, 267–68.

12. Ibid., 82–83.

13. Ibid., 328.

14. Ibid., 220.

15. Ibid., 376.

16. Ibid.

17. Ibid., 221, 376.

18. Keynes, BBC Broadcast, in *Collected Writings* (vol. 20), 325.

19. John Maynard Keynes, *Collected Writings*, vol. 28, *Social, Political, and Literary Writings* (London: Macmillan; New York: St. Martin's Press, 1982), 391–93, 398. In this case Keynes at least considers the possibility of deliberately raising interest rates to help cool inflation.

20. Keynes, *General Theory*, 322n, 326.

21. Ibid., 322.

22. Keynes, *Collected Writings* (vol. 6), 176.

23. Keynes, *General Theory*, 320.

24. Ibid., 322.

25. Ibid., 321.

26. John Maynard Keynes, *London Times* (January 12–14, 1937), in *Collected Writings*, vol. 21, *Activities 1931–39: World Crisis and Policies in Britain and America* (London: Macmillan; New York: St. Martin's Press, 1982), 38; also cited in Robert Skidelsky, *John Maynard Keynes*, vol. 3, *Fighting for Britain 1937–1946* (London: Macmillan, 2000), 22.

27. John Maynard Keynes, *Collected Writings*, vol. 22, *Activities 1939–45: Internal War Finance* (London: Macmillan; New York: St. Martin's Press, 1978), 281.

28. Keynes, *General Theory*, 303.

29. Ibid., 300.

30. Ibid., 303.

31. Joan Robinson, *An Introduction to The Theory of Employment* (London: Macmillan, 1937), 96; also cited in Skidelsky, *John Maynard Keynes* (vol. 2), 603.

32. Keynes, *General Theory*, 249–50.

33. Ibid., 321.

34. Keynes, *London Times* (January 12–14, 1937), in *Collected Writings* (vol. 21), 390.

35. Byrd Jones, "The Role of Keynesians in Wartime Policy and Postwar Planning," *American Economic Review*: 127–28, cited

in Skidelsky, *John Maynard Keynes* (vol. 3), 121; see also 43, 88–90, 503.

36. Keynes, *General Theory*, 372.

37. Ibid.

38. Ibid., 164, 243, 308–9.

39. Ibid., 164.

40. Skidelsky, *John Maynard Keynes* (vol. 3), 227, 247, 255, 302–3.

41. Keynes, *Collected Writings* (vol. 6), 193.

42. Keynes, *General Theory*, 340.

43. Ibid., 334.

44. Ibid., 335, 341.

45. Ibid., 353.

46. Ibid.

47. Ibid., 371.

48. Ibid.

Chapter 3: Spend More, Save Less, and Grow Wealthy

1. Ibid., 104.

2. John Maynard Keynes, "Economic Possibilities for Our Grand-children," in *Essays in Persuasion* (New York: W. W. Norton, 1963), 370.

3. John Maynard Keynes, *The Economic Consequences of the Peace* (New York: Harcourt, Brace & Howe, 1920), 19.

4. Ibid., 19–20.

5. Amy Kass, *Giving Well, Doing Good: Readings for Thoughtful Philanthropists* (South Bend, IN: Indiana University Press, 2008), cited in *Weekly Standard* (May 26, 2008): 47.

6. *Essays in Persuasion*, 84–85.

7. Keynes, *General Theory*, 32.

8. Ibid., 26.

9. Ibid., 309.

10. Ibid., 210.

11. Ibid., 347.

12. Ibid., 111.

13. Ibid., 105, 217–18.

14. Ibid., 220.

15. Ibid., 129.

16. Ibid.

17. Ibid.

18. Keynes, letter to Poet T. S. Eliot, in *Essays in Persuasion*, 384; also cited in Skidelsky, *John Maynard Keynes* (vol. 3), 279.

19. Keynes, *General Theory*, 372–73.

20. Ibid., 373.

Chapter 4: The Immoralist (A Digression)

1. The author must apologize for the lack of a citation. The incident was recounted in a book read long ago and a search for a citation proved unavailing.

2. Keynes, "My Early Beliefs," in *Collected Writings* (vol. 10), 446.

3. Keynes, *Essays in Persuasion*, 298.

4. Ibid.

5. Skidelsky, letter to Cyril Connolly," in *John Maynard Keynes* (vol. 3), 169.

6. Skidelsky, *John Maynard Keynes* (vol. 2), 475.

7. Ibid., 423.

8. Keynes, *Essays in Persuasion*, 125.

9. Keynes, *Collected Writings* (vol. 10), 446–47, second note.

10. Skidelsky, *John Maynard Keynes* (vol. 3), 18.

11. Skidelsky, *John Maynard Keynes* (vol. 3), 493.

12. Michael Holroyd, *Lytton Strachey: The New Biography* (New York: W. W. Norton, 2005), 105.

13. Keynes, "My Early Beliefs," in *Collected Writings* (vol. 10), 441.

14. Levy, the Bloomsbury Group, in Milo Keynes, ed., *Essays on John Maynard Keynes* (New York: Cambridge, 1975), 69; also in Paul Johnson, *Modern Times: The World from the Twenties to the Eighties* (New York: Harper & Row, 1983), 30.

15. Robert Skidelsky, *John Maynard Keynes*, vol. 1, *Hopes Betrayed 1883–1920* (London: Macmillan, 2000), 158–59.

16. Keynes, "My Early Beliefs," in *Collected Writings* (vol. 10), 445.

17. Ibid.

18. Keynes, *Essays in Persuasion*, 319.

19. Ibid., 321.

20. Ibid.

21. Ibid.

22. Ibid., 366.

23. Ibid., 372.

24. Matt. 19:28; and Keynes, *Essays in Persuasion*, 372.

25. Matt. 19:24.

26. Keynes, *Essays in Persuasion*, 368.

27. Ibid., 367.

28. Wilhelm Röpke, *A Humane Economy: The Social Framework of the Free Market* (South Bend, IN: Gateway, 1960), 109.

29. Skidelsky, *John Maynard Keynes* (vol. 2), 233.

30. Keynes, *Essays in Persuasion*, 300.

31. Ibid., 324.

32. Ibid., 319.

33. Ibid., 338.

34. Skidelsky, *John Maynard Keynes* (vol. 2), xx.

35. Charles Dickens, *David Copperfield* (London).

36. Wilhelm Röpke, *Economics of the Free Society* (Chicago: Henry Regnery, 1963), 223.

37. Skidelsky, *John Maynard Keynes* (vol. 2), 62.

38. Epicurus, letter to Menoeceus, John Gaskin, ed., *The Epicurean Philosophers* (London: Everyman, 1945), 45; also in Axios Institute, ed., *Epicureans and Stoics* (Mt. Jackson, VA: Axios Press, 2008), 26.

39. Friedrich Hayek, in Hazlitt, *Critics of Keynesian Economics*.

40. Keynes, *Essays in Persuasion*, 136.

41. Keynes, *Collected Writings* (vol. 5), xxii.

42. John Maynard Keynes, *The Collected Writings*, vol. 4, *Tract on Monetary Reform* (London: Macmillan, and New York: St. Martin's Press, 1971), 155.

43. Skidelsky, *John Maynard Keynes* (vol. 2), 224.

44. John Maynard Keynes, *Collected Writings*, vol. 14, *The General Theory and After: Defence and Development* (London: Macmillan; New York: St. Martin's Press, 1973), 296.

45. Skidelsky, *John Maynard Keynes* (vol. 3), 264.

46. Keynes, *Essays in Persuasion*, 321.

Chapter 5: What to Do about Wall Street

1. Keynes, letter to Poet T. S. Eliot, in *Essays in Persuasion*, 384; also cited in Skidelsky, *John Maynard Keynes* (vol. 3), 279.

2. Keynes, *General Theory*, 242.

3. Ibid., 150.

4. Ibid., 152.

5. Ibid., 153.

6. Ibid., 150.

7. Ibid.

8. Ibid., 50, 161–62.

9. Ibid., 162.

10. Skidelsky, *John Maynard Keynes* (vol. 2), 316.

11. Keynes, *General Theory*, 154.

12. Ibid., 319.

13. Ibid., 159.

14. Ibid.

15. Ibid., 157.

16. Ibid., 316.

17. Ibid., 155, 157.

18. Ibid., 156.

19. Ibid., 157.

20. Ibid., 158.

21. Ibid., 159.

22. Ibid., 374.

23. Keynes, *Essays in Persuasion*, 94–95.

24. Keynes, *General Theory*, 317.

25. Keynes, *New Statesman and Nation* (1933), in *Collected Writings* (vol. 21), 239.

26. Keynes, *General Theory*, 320.

Chapter 6: Look to the State for Economic Leadership

1. Skidelsky, *John Maynard Keynes* (vol. 3), 273.

2. Walter Lippmann, *Interpretations: 1931–1932* (New York: Macmillan, 1932), 38; Walter Lippmann, *The Method of Freedom* (New York: Macmillan Company, 1934), 58–59.

3. Keynes, *General Theory*, 220.

4. Ibid., 322.

5. Keynes, "Boom Control," *London Times*, in *Collected Writings* (vol. 21), 384–94; also in Skidelsky, *John Maynard Keynes* (vol. 2), 629; and (vol. 3), 20–21.

6. Keynes, *General Theory*, 164; and *Collected Writings* (vol. 21), 145.

7. Keynes, letter, June 6, 1932, in *Collected Writings* (vol. 21), 109.

8. Keynes, *General Theory*, 378.

9. *London Times* (January 14, 1937), cited by Étienne Mantoux in Hazlitt, *Critics of Keynesian Economics*, 121.

10. Keynes, interview, *New Statesman and Nation* (January 28, 1939), in *Collected Writings* (vol. 21), 492.

11. Keynes, *General Theory*, 379.

12. Skidelsky, *John Maynard Keynes* (vol. 3), 235–36, 285.

13. Ibid., 321.

14. Keynes, BBC Broadcast (March 14, 1932), in *Collected Writings* (vol. 21), 86.

15. Keynes, *Essays in Persuasion*, 318.

16. Keynes, *General Theory*, 378.

17. Skidelsky, *John Maynard Keynes* (vol. 2), 266.

18. Keynes, BBC Broadcast (March 14, 1932), in *Collected Writings* (vol. 21), 84.

19. Ibid., 85.

20. Skidelsky, *John Maynard Keynes* (vol. 3), 230.

21. Keynes, *Essays in Persuasion*, 299, 310.

22. Keynes, *Collected Writings* (vol. 28), 333–34.

23. Keynes, BBC Broadcast (March 14, 1932), in *Collected Writings* (vol. 21), 86, 92.

24. Keynes, *Essays in Persuasion*, 337.

25. Skidelsky, *John Maynard Keynes* (vol. 2), 224.

26. Keynes, CBS Radio Broadcast (April 12, 1931), in *Collected Writings* (vol. 20), 515.

27. John Maynard Keynes, *Economic Journal* (December, 1914), in *Collected Writings,* vol. 11, *Economic Articles and Correspondence—Academic* (London: Macmillan; New York: St. Martin's Press, 1983), 320.

28. "The Commanding Heights," Yergin et al, a television documentary, PBS.

29. Skidelsky, *John Maynard Keynes* (vol. 2), 228.

30. Skidelsky, *John Maynard Keynes* (vol. 3), 285.

31. Keynes, *General Theory*, 235.

Chapter 7: In an Economic Crisis, Print, Lend, Borrow, and Spend

1. Ibid., 321.

2. Keynes, BBC Broadcast (February 26, 1930), in *Collected Writings* (vol. 20), 319.

3. Keynes, *General Theory*, 327.

4. Ibid., 322.

5. Ibid., 320–22.

6. Keynes, *Essays in Persuasion*, 136.

7. Keynes, BBC Broadcast (February 26, 1930), in *Collected Writings* (vol. 20), 325.

8. Keynes, speech, Munich Germany, January 8, 1932, in *Collected Writings* (vol. 21), 40, 41, 45.

9. Ibid.

10. For a discussion of Bagehot versus Hankey, see *Grant's Interest Rate Observer* (May 30, 2008); and James Grant, *Mr. Market Miscalculates* (Mt. Jackson, VA: Axios Press, 2008), 28.

11. Keynes, *Collected Writings* (vol. 21), 59–60.

12. Keynes, *Collected Writings* (vol. 20), 348; (vol. 21), 395.

13. *London Times* (January 14, 1937); also in Hazlitt, *Critics of Keynesian Economics*, 121.

14. Keynes, *Collected Writings* (vol. 21), 334.

15. Ibid.

16. Keynes, article in *Nation and Athenaeum* (May 10, 1930), in *Collected Writings* (vol. 20), 349.

17. Keynes, *Collected Writings* (vol. 21), 337.

18. Ibid., 60.

19. Keynes, *Essays in Persuasion*, 153–54.

20. Keynes, *General Theory*, 127.

21. Keynes, *Collected Writings* (vol. 21), 326.

22. Keynes, *General Theory*, 127.

Chapter 8: Markets Do Not Self-Correct

1. Ibid., 267.

2. Ibid.

3. Ibid., 249.

4. John Maynard Keynes, *Collected Writings*, vol. 13, *The General Theory and After: Preparation* (London: Macmillan; New York: St. Martin's Press, 1973), 199.

5. Keynes, BBC Broadcast (January 11, 1933), in *Collected Writings* (vol. 21), 145.

6. Ibid.

7. Keynes, addendum to Macmillan Report, drafted by Keynes, 1930, in *Collected Writings* (vol. 20), 289.

8. Keynes, *General Theory*, 253.

9. Lippmann, *Interpretations*, 103–5.

10. Keynes, *General Theory*, 264.

11. Keynes, open letter to President Roosevelt, *New York Times* and *London Times*, in *Collected Writings* (vol. 21), 323.

12. Keynes, *General Theory*, 267, 269.

13. Keynes, *Essays in Persuasion*, 261, 333.

14. Keynes, *General Theory*, 268.

15. Ibid., 9.

16. Keynes, lecture in Germany, January 8, 1932, in *Collected Writings* (vol. 21), 45.

Chapter 9: Yes, No, and Again Yes to Economic Globalization

1. Keynes, *Collected Writings* (vol. 4), 138.

2. Keynes, *Economic Consequences*, 10–12.

3. Keynes, *Essays in Persuasion*, 200; Keynes, *Collected Writings* (vol. 6), 258.

4. *Essays in Persuasion*, 200.

5. Johnson, *Modern Times*, 164.

6. Keynes, *Essays in Persuasion*, 288; Keynes, *Collected Writings* (vol. 21), 41.

7. Keynes, article in *Daily Mail*, in *Collected Writings* (vol. 21), 273.

8. For a generally positive comment, see Keynes, *Collected Writings* (vol. 6), 298; for a negative comment, see Skidelsky, *John Maynard Keynes* (vol. 3), 208.

9. Keynes, *Collected Writings* (vol. 4), 159; (vol. 6), 268, 303.

10. Quoted in Robert Bartley, *The Seven Fat Years* (New York: Free Press, 1992), 206.

11. Keynes, *New Statesman and Nation* (July 8 and July 15, 1933), in *Collected Writings* (vol. 21), 233.

12. Cited in William Beveridge, *Tariffs: The Case Examined* (London, 1931), 242; also in Hazlitt, *Failure of the "New Economics,"* 338.

13. Keynes, *Nation and Athenaeum* (November 24, 1923), in *General Theory*, 334.

14. Keynes, *Collected Writings* (vol. 20), 488.

15. Hazlitt, *Critics of Keynesian Economics*, 124.

16. Keynes, *General Theory*, 335.

17. Ibid., 338.

18. Keynes, *Collected Writings* (vol. 13), 199; also see Skidelsky, *John Maynard Keynes* (vol. 3), 191.

Part Three: Why Keynes Was Wrong

Chapter 10: *"Drive Down Interest Rates" (and Reap a Whirlwind of Inflation, Bubbles, and Busts)*

1. Keynes, *General Theory*, 351.

2. Lester Brown, press release (November 6, 2001).

3. Keynes, *General Theory*, 242.

4. Ibid., 351.

5. Ibid., 174, 309, 351.

6. Ibid., 167–68, 197–99, 268, 298.

7. Hazlitt, *Critics of Keynesian Economics*, 49, 94, 412.

8. Ludwig von Mises, *Human Action: A Treatise on Economics* (San Francisco: Fox & Wilkes, 1966), 562, 565, 570, 572, 574, 576.

9. Keynes, *General Theory*, 82–83.

10. *The Commercial and Financial Chronicle* (November 21, 1957), quoted in James Grant, *The Trouble with Prosperity: The Loss of Fear, the Rise of Speculation, and the Risk to American Savings* (New York: Random House, 1996), 37–38; also in Hunter Lewis, *How Much Money Does An Economy Need?* (Mt. Jackson, VA: Axios Press, 2007), 19.

11. Keynes, *General Theory*, 328.

12. Hunter Lewis, *Are the Rich Necessary?: Great Economic Arguments and How They Reflect Our Personal Values* (Mt. Jackson, VA: Axios Press, 2007), chap. 8–10.

13. Keynes, *General Theory*, 220, 376.

14. Ibid., 376.

15. Ibid., 221, 376.

16. Mises, *Human Action*, 529; also in Mark Thornton, ed., *The*

Quotable Mises (Auburn, AL: Ludwig von Mises Institute, 2005), 124.

17. Hazlitt, *Failure of the "New Economics,"* 318.

18. D. Dollar and A. Karry, "World Bank Study," cited in *Forbes* (August 6, 2001): 77.

19. Fred Sheehan, quoting Greenspan, in *Gloom, Boom, and Doom Report* (October, 2005): 16.

20. Keynes, *General Theory*, 326.

21. Ibid., 322.

22. Paul Krugman, *Peddling Prosperity* (New York: W. W. Norton, 1994), 32; also cited in Lewis, *Are the Rich Necessary?*, 77.

23. Ned Davis Research, "Institutional Hotline," (June 10, 2008), 1.

24. Hazlitt, *Failure of the "New Economics,"* 329, 331.

25. Keynes, *Collected Writings* (vol. 6), 176.

26. Keynes, *General Theory*, 320.

27. Ibid., 322.

28. Ibid., 321.

29. Keynes, *London Times* (January 12–14, 1937), in *Collected Writings* (vol. 21), 389; also in Skidelsky, *John Maynard Keynes* (vol. 3), 33.

30. Keynes, *General Theory*, 303.

31. Ibid., 300.

32. Ibid., 303.

33. Ibid., 321.

34. Keynes, *London Times* (January 12–14, 1937), in *Collected Writings* (vol. 21), 390.

35. Keynes, *General Theory*, 372.

36. Ibid., 372.

37. Ibid., 164, 243, 308–9.

38. Ibid., 164.

39. Skidelsky, *John Maynard Keynes* (vol. 3), 227, 247, 255, 302–3.

40. Keynes, *Collected Writings* (vol. 6), 193.

41. Keynes, *General Theory*, 39, 41.

Chapter 11: *Spend More, Save Less, and Grow Poorer*

1. Ibid., 104.

2. Keynes, "Economic Possibilities for Our Grandchildren," in *Essays in Persuasion*, 370.

3. John Maynard Keynes, *Collected Writings*, vol. 12, *Economic Articles and Correspondence—Investment and Editorial* (London: Macmillan; New York: St. Martin's Press, 1983), 1.

4. *Money Magazine* (April 2005): 172.

5. *Weekly Standard* (March 27, 2006): 20.

6. *Weekly Standard* (December 1, 2008): 24.

7. Keynes, *Economic Consequences*, 19.

8. Ibid., 19–20.

9. Keynes, *Essays in Persuasion*, 318.

10. Keynes, *General Theory*, 32.

11. Ibid., 309.

12. Ibid., 210.

13. John Stuart Mill, "Of the Influence of Consumption on Production," in *Essays on Some Unsettled Questions of Political Economy* (London, 1844; actually written 1829–1830); also cited in Hazlitt, *Failure of the "New Economics,"* 366.

14. Mill, *Essays*, cited in Hazlitt, *Failure of the "New Economics,"* 367.

15. Ibid.

16. Ibid.

17. Keynes, *General Theory*, 347.

18. *Forbes* (February 16, 2009): 15; also Alan Greenspan, Op Ed, *Wall Street Journal* (March 11, 2009); also Paul Krugman, *New York Times* (March 2, 2009): A–23.

19. Keynes, *General Theory*, 83.

20. Ibid., 111.

21. Keynes, *Collected Writings* (vol. 6), 132.

22. Keynes, *General Theory*, 105, 217–18.

23. Ibid., 220.

24. Ibid., 129.

25. Ibid.

26. Ibid.

27. Keynes, letter to Poet T. S. Eliot, in *Essays in Persuasion*, 384; also cited in Skidelsky, *John Maynard Keynes* (vol. 3), 279.

28. Keynes, *General Theory*, 372–73.

29. Ibid., 373.

30. Hazlitt, *Failure of the "New Economics,"* 375.

31. Keynes, *General Theory*, 373.

32. *Forbes* (February 23, 2002): 226.

Chapter 12: What (Not) to Do about Wall Street

1. Keynes, *General Theory*, 150.

2. Ibid., 152.

3. Ibid., 153.

4. Ibid., 150.

5. Ibid.

6. Ibid., 50, 161–62.

7. Ibid., 162.

8. Skidelsky, *John Maynard Keynes* (vol. 2), 316.

9. Keynes, *General Theory*, 154.

10. Ibid., 319.

11. Hazlitt, *Failure of the "New Economics,"* 175.

12. Keynes, *General Theory*, 159.

13. Ibid.

14. Ibid., 157.

15. Ibid., 316.

16. Ibid., 155, 157.

17. Ibid., 156.

18. Ibid., 157.

19. Ibid., 158.

20. Ibid., 159.

21. Ibid., 374.

22. Keynes, *Essays in Persuasion*, 94–95.

23. "Special Report on Finance," *Economist* (January 24, 2009): 6.

24. *Barrons* (September 22, 2008).

25. Keynes, *General Theory*, 170.

26. Ibid., 127.

27. Keynes, *Collected Writings* (vol. 11), 9–15.

28. Ibid.

29. Ibid., 107.

30. Keynes, *General Theory*, 317.

31. Keynes, *New Statesman and Nation* (1933), in *Collected Writings* (vol. 21), 239.

32. Keynes, *General Theory*, 320.

33. Ibid., 378.

34. *Weekly Standard* (January 19, 2009): 20.

Chapter 13: (Do Not) Look to the State for Economic Leadership

1. Skidelsky, *John Maynard Keynes* (vol. 3), 273.

2. William Beveridge, cited in Hazlitt, *Critics of Keynesian Economics*, 226.

3. T. Blankley, *Washington Times* (March 16, 2009): 32.

4. Lippmann, *Interpretations*, 38; Lippmann, *Method of Freedom*, 58–59.

5. Keynes, *General Theory*, 220.

6. Ibid., 322.

7. Keynes, "Boom Control," *London Times*, in *Collected Writings* (vol. 21), 384–94; also in Skidelsky, *John Maynard Keynes* (vol. 2), 629; and (vol. 3), 20–21.

8. Keynes, *General Theory*, 164; also Keynes, *Collected Writings* (vol. 6), 145.

9. Keynes, letter, June 6, 1932, in *Collected Writings* (vol. 21), 109.

10. Keynes, *General Theory*, 378.

11. *London Times* (January 14, 1937), cited by Étienne Mantoux, in Hazlitt, *Critics of Keynesian Economics*, 121.

12. Keynes, interview, *New Statesman and Nation* (January 28, 1939), in *Collected Writings* (vol. 21), 492.

13. Keynes, *General Theory*, 379.

14. Adam Smith, *The Wealth of Nations*, 2 vols. (London, 1776, 1784), bk. IV, chap. 2; also in R. E. Baxter, Ray Rees, and Graham Bannock, *The Penguin Dictionary of Economics* (London: Penguin Books, 1972), 247.

15. Skidelsky, *John Maynard Keynes* (vol. 3), 235–36 and 285.

16. Ibid., 321.

17. Keynes, BBC Broadcast (March 14, 1932), in *Collected Writings* (vol. 21), 86.

18. Keynes, *Essays in Persuasion*, 318.

19. Keynes, *General Theory*, 378.

20. Keynes, BBC Broadcast (March 14, 1932), in *Collected Writings* (vol. 21), 84.

21. Ibid., 85.

22. Skidelsky, *John Maynard Keynes* (vol. 3), 230; Hazlitt, *Failure of the "New Economics,"* 277.

23. Keynes, *Essays in Persuasion*, 299, 310.

24. Keynes, BBC Broadcast, in *Collected Writings* (vol. 28), 333–34.

25. Keynes, BBC Broadcast (March 14, 1932), in *Collected Writings* (vol. 28), 86, 92.

26. Keynes, *Essays in Persuasion*, 337.

27. Skidelsky, *John Maynard Keynes* (vol. 2), 224.

28. Ibid., 228.

29. Keynes, *Collected Writings* (vol. 20), 515.

30. "Reviews of Samuelson," November 7, 2008, http://www.bloomberg.com; *Weekly Standard* (January 5–12, 2009): 35.

31. *Federal Register* and *Grant's Interest Rate Observer* (June 27, 2008): 11.

32. Skidelsky, *John Maynard Keynes* (vol. 3), 285.

33. Keynes, *General Theory*, 235.

Chapter 14: Government for Sale (A Digression)

1. Goodwin, NPR interview, n.d.

2. *Economist* (March 21, 2009): 57–58.

3. Center for Responsive Politics, http://www.opensecrets.org.

4. http://www.townhall.com (March 25, 2009).

5. *New York Review of Books* (April 9, 2009): 20.

6. *Fortune* (September 25, 2006); http://www.cnnmoney.com.

7. Dick Morris and Eileen McGann, http://www.townhall.com (March 11, 2009).

8. *Grant's Interest Rate Observer* (May 30, 2008): 3.

9. David Reilly, *Bloomberg News* (April 25, 2009).

10. *Atlantic* (March 2009): 55, re: the work of economist Andrew Oswald.

11. *Washington Times* (October 6, 2008): 34.

12. Senate Banking Committee (July 11, 2008).

13. *Grant's Interest Rate Observer* (April 6, 2007): 10.

14. *Grant's Interest Rate Observer* (November 28, 2008): 2.

15. *Forbes* (August 11, 2008): 19.

16. http://www.archierichards.com (October 1, 2008).

17. *Washington Times* (September 29, 2008): 34.

18. David R. Sands, *Washington Times* (September 29, 2008): 34; (February 9, 2009).

19. *Washington Post*, as reported in *Grant's Interest Rate Observer* (October 17, 2008): 1.

20. *Washington Times* (February 6, 2009): 10.

21. "Treasury Department" reported in *Washington Times* (January 26, 2009): 7.

22. *New Yorker* (May 18, 2009): 50.

23. Michael Lewis, http://www.bloomberg.com (March 20, 2009).

24. C. Baum, http://www.bloomberg.com (March 26, 2009).

25. *Bloomberg News* (May 13, 2009).

26. *Bloomberg News* (October 1, 2008).

27. F. Sheehan, March 28, 2007, in M. Faber, *Gloom, Boom, and Doom Report* (September 2008): 19, 22.

28. *New York Times* (June 13, 2008): 1.

29. Lawrence Lindsey, *Weekly Standard* (December 1, 2008): 22.

30. *Bloomberg News* (May 15, 2009).

31. David Boaz, http://www.realclearpolitics.com (January 29, 2009).

32. Gary Null, et al., *Death by Medicine* (Mt. Jackson, VA: Praktikos Books, forthcoming 2010).

33. *Economist* (May 9, 2009): 14.

34. *Economist* (May 2, 2009): 64–65.

35. Ann Woolner, *Bloomberg News* (May 6, 2009).

36. Lawrence Kudlow, *Washington Times* (May 4, 2009): 31.

Chapter 15: In an Economic Crisis, Printing, Lending, Borrowing, and Spending Just Sow the Seeds of the Next Crisis

1. Keynes, *General Theory*, 321.

2. Keynes, BBC Broadcast (February 26, 1930), in *Collected Writings* (vol. 20), 319.

3. Keynes, *General Theory*, 327.

4. Ibid., 322.

5. Ibid., 320–22.

6. US Government Sources, in *Grant's Interest Rate Observer* (April 3, 2009): 4.

7. Röpke, *Free Society*, 219; also in Lewis, *Are the Rich Necessary?*, 76.

8. Friedrich Hayek, quoted in Sanford Ikeda, *Dynamics of the Mixed Economy: Toward a Theory of Interventionism* (London: Routledge, 1997), 183.

9. Röpke, *Free Society*, 248; also quoted in Lewis, *Are the Rich Necessary?*, 51.

10. *Economist* (December 6, 2008): 94.

11. Robert Solow, *New York Review of Books* (May 14, 2009): 6.

12. Keynes, *Essays in Persuasion*, 136.

13. Keynes, BBC Broadcast (February 26, 1930), in *Collected Writings* (vol. 20), 325.

14. Keynes, speech, Munich, Germany, January 8, 1932, in *Collected Writings* (vol. 21), 40, 41, 45.

15. Ibid.

16. Keynes, *New York Evening Post* (October 25, 1929), in *Collected Writings* (vol. 20), 1.

17. Keynes, London lecture, reprinted in *Atlantic Monthly* (May 1932), in *Collected Writings* (vol. 21), 60.

18. Keynes, speech, Munich, Germany (January 8, 1932), in *Collected Writings* (vol. 21), 40, 41, 45.

19. Keynes, *London Times* (January 12–14, 1937), in *Collected Writings* (vol. 21), 385.

20. Ned Davis Research, "Institutional Hotline" (September 22, 2008): 2.

21. Paul Krugman, "What To Do," *New York Review of Books* (December 18, 2008): 8.

22. *Economist* (November 1, 2008): 20.

23. James Grant unearthed and discussed the long forgotten but pivotal Bagehot-Hankey exchange, in *Grant's Interest Rate Observer* (May 30, 2008).

24. Keynes, *Collected Writings* (vol. 21), 59–60.

25. Keynes, *Collected Writings* (vol. 20), 348; (vol. 21), 395.

26. *London Times* (January 14, 1937); also in Hazlitt, *Critics of Keynesian Economics*, 121.

27. *Bloomberg News* (April 14, 2008).

28. *Bloomberg News* (May 20, 2009).

29. *Washington Times* (April 20, 2009): 38.

30. James Grant, *Wall Street Journal* (December 20–21, 2008): W-2.

31. Remarks before the Economic Club of New York (April 8, 2008).

32. Christopher Caldwell, *Weekly Standard* (December 22, 1008): 17.

33. Keynes, *Collected Writings* (vol. 21), 334.

34. Ibid.

35. Keynes, article in *Nation and Athenaeum* (May 10, 1930), in *Collected Writings* (vol. 20), 349.

36. For a review of Romer's work on stimulus, see Edward L. Glavser (a Harvard economist), "Today's Economist," http://www.nytimes.com (December 2, 2008).

37. http://www.chicagomaroon.com (February 3, 2009).

38. Lawrence Kudlow, *Washington Times* (December 1, 2008): 37.

39. *Economist* (November 15, 2008): 62.

40. Yanping and Hamlin, *Bloomberg News* (March 26, 2009).

41. *Economist* (January 31, 2009): 79.

42. *Weekly Standard* (February 16, 2009): 9; *Washington Times* (March 9, 2009): 4.

43. Keynes, speech, Munich, Germany, January 8, 1932, in *Collected Writings* (vol. 21), 40, 41, 45.

44. *Washington Times* (February 16, 2009): 35.

45. Keynes, *General Theory*, 25, 55.

46. Ibid., 280.

47. *Johns Hopkins Newsletter* (January 30, 2009).

48. *Economist* (January 31, 2009): 18.

49. *Cato Institute*, "Cato Blog" editors (March 24, 2009).

50. Nichols and Runninger, *Bloomberg News* (February 25, 2009).

51. *Weekly Standard* (February 23, 2009): 5.

52. *Washington Times* (February 2, 2009): 35.

53. *Weekly Standard* (April 15–20, 2009): 14.

54. Keynes, *Collected Writings* (vol. 20), 13.

55. *Weekly Standard* (November 17, 2008): 32.

56. *Brookings Institution Paper* (January 2008).

57. *Economist* (March 21, 2009): 60.

58. James Mill, *Commerce Defended* (London, 1808), chapter 7; reprinted D. Winch, ed. *Selected Economic Writings of James Mill* (Chicago: University of Chicago Press, 1966), 140; cited in G. Reisman, *Capitalism* (Ottawa, IL: Jameson Books, 1990), 888.

59. AP News, March 25, 2009, http://www.yahoo.com.

60. Keynes, *Collected Writings* (vol. 21), 337.

61. Ibid., 60.

62. Keynes, *Essays in Persuasion*, 153–54.

63. Keynes, *General Theory*, 129.

64. George Reisman, *Capitalism*, 888.

65. Dick Morris and Eileen McGann, http://www.townhall.com (December 11, 2008), 1.

66. Keynes, *General Theory*, 127.

67. Keynes, *Collected Writings* (vol. 21), 326.

68. Keynes, *General Theory*, 127.

69. Hazlitt, *Critics of Keynesian Economics*, 194.

70. Keynes, *General Theory*, 128.

71. Ibid., 115.

72. Ibid., 96.

73. George Reisman, *Capitalism*, 888.

74. Paul Samuelson and William Nordhaus, *Economics* (New York: McGraw Hill, 1989), 167.

75. Skidelsky, Roger Middleton, 1985, in *John Maynard Keynes* (vol. 2), 475.

76. *Forbes* (February 16, 2009): 34.

77. *Bloomberg News* (December 18, 208).

78. Arnold Kling, "Muddled Multipliers," *Cato Institute Blog* (January 2009).

79. Mary O'Grady, March 21, 2009, http://www.wallstreetjournal.com.

80. Keynes, *General Theory*, 127.

81. Ibid.

82. *Bloomberg News* (February 27, 2009).

Chapter 16: Markets Do Self-Correct

1. Keynes, *General Theory*, 267.

2. Ibid.

3. Ibid., 249.

4. Ibid., 265.

5. Franco Modigliani, "Liquidity, Preference, and the Theory of Interests, and Money," *Econometrica* (January 1944): 45–88.

6. Don Patinkin, "Price Flexibility and Full Employment," *American Economic Review (AER)* (1948), revised in AER's "Reading in Monetary Theory," 279; also cited in Hazlitt, *Critics of Keynesian Economics,* 398.

7. Hazlitt, *Failure of the "New Economics,"* 263.

8. Keynes, *Collected Writings* (vol. 13), 199.

9. Hazlitt, *Failure of the "New Economics,"* 258–59.

10. *Forbes* (March 16, 2009): 106.

11. Harold Cole and Lee Ohanian, *Journal of Political Economy* (2004), vol. 112, no. 4; also see *Wall Street Journal* (March 16, 2009).

12. Keynes, BBC Broadcast (January 11, 1933), in *Collected Writings* (vol. 21), 145.

13. Ibid.

14. Keynes, addendum to "Macmillan Report," drafted by Keynes, 1930, in *Collected Writings* (vol. 20), 289.

15. Keynes, *General Theory*, 253.

16. Ibid., 267.

17. Ibid., 304.

18. Hazlitt, *Critics of Keynesian Economics*, 5; Hazlitt, *Failure of the "New Economics,"* 267.

19. Lippmann, *Interpretations*, 103–5.

20. Keynes, *General Theory*, 264.

21. Keynes, open letter to President Roosevelt, *New York Times* and *London Times*, in *Collected Writings* (vol. 21), 323.

22. Keynes, *General Theory*, 232.

23. Ibid., 264, 267.

24. Ibid., 9.

25. Keynes, *Essays in Persuasion*, 341.

26. Ibid., 261, 333.

27. Keynes, *General Theory*, 268.

28. Ibid., 9.

29. Keynes, lecture in Germany, January 8, 1932, in *Collected Writings* (vol. 21), 45.

30. Keynes, *Economic Consequences*, 236.

Chapter 17: Yes to Economic Globalization

1. Keynes, *Collected Writings* (vol. 4), 138.

2. Keynes, *Economic Consequences*, 10–12.

3. Keynes, *Essays in Persuasion*, 200; Keynes, *Collected Writings* (vol. 6), 258.

4. Keynes, *Essays in Persuasion*, 200.

5. Keynes, *Collected Writings* (vol. 4), 132.

6. Keynes, *General Theory*, 348–49.

7. Ibid., 349.

8. Hazlitt, *Failure of the "New Economics,"* 346.

9. Paul Johnson, *Modern Times*, 164.

10. Keynes, *Essays in Persuasion*, 288; Keynes, *Collected Writings* (vol. 20), 41.

11. Keynes, article in *Daily Mail,* in *Collected Writings* (vol. 20), 273.

12. Keynes, *Collected Writings* (vol. 4), 155.

13. For a generally positive comment, see Keynes, *Collected Writings* (vol. 6), 298; for a negative comment, see Skidelsky, *John Maynard Keynes* (vol. 3), 208.

14. Keynes, *Collected Writings* (vol. 4), 159; (vol. 6), 268, 303.

15. Quoted in Bartley, *Seven Fat Years*, 206.

16. Röpke, *Humane Economy*, 242–43.

17. Keynes, *New Statesman and Nation* (July 8 and July 15, 1933), in *Collected Writings* (vol. 21), 233.

18. Cited Beveridge, et al, *The Case Examined* (London, 1931), 242; also in Hazlitt, *Failure of the "New Economics,"* 338.

19. Keynes, *Nation and Athenaeum* (November 24, 1923), in *General Theory*, 334.

20. Keynes, *Collected Writings* (vol. 20), 488.

21. Hazlitt, *Critics of Keynesian Economics*, 124.

22. Keynes, *General Theory*, 335.

23. Ibid., 338.

24. Keynes, *Collected Writings* (vol. 13), 199; also see Skidelsky, *John Maynard Keynes* (vol. 3), 191.

25. Keynes, *New Statesman and Nation* (March 28, 1931), in *Collected Writings* (vol. 20), 502.

26. Keynes, *New Statesman and Nation* (March 16, 1931), in *Collected Writings* (vol. 20), 495.

27. Keynes, *New Statesman and Nation* (April 1931), in *Collected Writings* (vol. 20), 505.

28. Keynes, letter to the *Times* (March 26, 1931), in *Collected Writings* (vol. 20), 508.

29. R. F. Harrod, *The Life of John Maynard Keynes* (New York: Harcourt, Brace, 1951), 469.

30. Keynes, *General Theory*, 348–49.

31. John Maynard Keynes, *Yale Review* (Summer 1933); also quoted in Hazlitt, *Failure of the "New Economics,"* 338.

32. Keynes, *General Theory*, 349.

33. Keynes, *General Theory*, ix.

Part Four: More on Keynes

Chapter 18: How Keynesian Was Keynes?

1. See Röpke, *Free Society*, 225, for one example of this view.

2. Keynes, *Collected Writings* (vol. 14), 150.

3. David McCord Wright, in Hazlitt, *Critics of Keynesian Economics*, 415.

4. John H. Williams, *American Economic Review* (May 1948): 287–88n; also cited in Hazlitt, *Failure of the "New Economics,"* 397.

5. Friedrich A. Hayek, *Economist Centenary Edition* on Keynes (June 11, 1983): 45 (US edition, 39); also cited in Bartley, *Seven Fat Years*, 47.

366 ■ WHERE KEYNES WENT WRONG

Chapter 19: Keynes Speaking

1. Bertrand Russell, *Autobiography*, quoted in Milo Keynes, *Essays on John Maynard Keynes*, and on Wikipedia.

2. Skidelsky, *John Maynard Keynes* (vol. 2), 427.

3. Keynes, *Economic Consequences*, 41.

4. Ibid.

5. "Ten Things You Didn't Know about Keynes," *Evening Standard* (October 21, 2008), quoted on Wikipedia.

6. Holroyd, *Lytton Stratchey*, 104.

7. Skidelsky, *John Maynard Keynes* (vol. 3), 473.

8. Keynes, *Economica*, vol. 11 (November 31, 1931), in *Collected Writings* (vol. 13), 245.

9. Ibid., 252.

10. Keynes, *Hibbert Journal* (October 1910), in *Collected Writings* (vol. 11), 509.

11. Skidelsky, *John Maynard Keynes* (vol. 3), 469.

12. Keynes, Macmillan Committee minutes, in *Collected Writings* (vol. 20), 148.

13. Skidelsky, Dean Acheson, "Present at the Creation," 28–29, quoted in *John Maynard Keynes* (vol. 3), 60.

14. Susan Howson and Donald Moggridge, eds., *The Wartime Diaries of Lionel Robbins and James Meade, 1943–1945* (London: Palgrave Macmillan, 1990), cited in A. Cairncross, ed., *Anglo-American Economic Collaboration in War and Peace, 1942–49* (London: Clarendon, 1982), 71.

15. Howson and Moggridge, Lionel Robbins, June 24, 1944, in *Diaries*; quoted in Skidelsky, *John Maynard Keynes* (vol. 3), 344.

16. Howson and Moggridge, in *Diaries*, vol. 410, June 19, 1941; quoted in Skidelsky, *John Maynard Keynes* (vol. 3), 123.

17. R. A. Gardner, *Sterling-Dollar Diplomacy* (Oxford: Oxford University Press, 1986), 266, note 4.

18. Howson and Moggridge, *Diaries*, 135; also in Skidelsky, *John Maynard Keynes* (vol. 3), 319.

19. Howson and Moggridge, *Diaries*, 135; also in Skidelsky, *John Maynard Keynes* (vol. 3), 127.

20. Armand Van Dormael, *Bretton Woods: Birth of a Monetary System* (London: Macmillan, 1978), 101, re illness; also cited in Skidelsky, *John Maynard Keynes* (vol. 3), 310, which mentions sending the deputy.

21. Skidelsky, *John Maynard Keynes* (vol. 3), 448.

Chapter 20: Keynes Writing

1. Johnson, *Modern Times*, 30.

2. Keynes, *Collected Writings* (vol. 13), 176.

3. Skidelsky, *John Maynard Keynes* (vol. 2), 317.

4. Étienne Mantoux, in Hazlitt, *Critics of Keynesian Economics*, 97.

5. H.W. Spiegel, ed., *The Development of Economic Thought* (Wiley: 1952), 767; also quoted in Hazlitt, *Failure of the "New Economics,"* 2, 89.

6. F. Knight, "Unemployment: And Mr. Keynes's Revolution in Economic Theory," *Canadian Journal of Economics and Political Science–Toronto* (February 1937): 100–123; also in Hazlitt, *Critics of Keynesian Economics*, 67, 92.

7. Joseph Schumpeter, *Essays: On Entrepreneurs, Innovations, Business Cycles, and the Evolution of Capitalism* (New Brunswick: Transaction, 2002), 161.

8. Skidelsky, Hubert Henderson papers, in *John Maynard Keynes* (vol. 2), 589.

9. Skidelsky, Étienne Mantoux, in *John Maynard Keynes* (vol. 2), 101–2.

10. Keynes, *General Theory*, 371.

11. Ibid., 303.

12. Keynes, *Collected Writings* (vol. 20), 496.

13. Keynes, *Collected Writings* (vol. 20), 496; *Canadian Journal of Economics and Political Science–Toronto* (February 1937): 108; also in Hazlitt, *Failure of the "New Economics,"* 16.

14. Keynes, *General Theory*, 137–38.

15. Hazlitt, *Failure of the "New Economics,"* 169–70.

16. Keynes, *Cambridge Review* (November 5, 1903), in *Collected Writings* (vol. 11), 507.

17. Keynes, *General Theory*, 24–25.

18. Ibid., 328.

19. Alvin Hansen, *A Guide to Keynes* (New York: McGraw-Hill, 1953), 27.

20. Keynes, *General Theory*, 96.

21. Keynes, *General Theory*, 106; Benjamin Anderson, in Hazlitt, *Critics of Keynesian Economics*, 203.

22. Keynes, *General Theory*, 102–4.

23. Ibid., 104.

24. Ibid., 329–30.

25. Ibid., 144–45.

26. Hazlitt, *Failure of the "New Economics,"* 166.

27. Ibid., 101.

28. Keynes, *General Theory*, 40.

29. Ibid., 297.

30. Ibid., 305.

31. Keynes, letter to Norman, May 22, 1930, in *Collected Writings* (vol. 20), 350–56; cited in Skidelsky, *John Maynard Keynes* (vol. 2), 351.

32. Wilhelm Röpke, *Against the Tide* (Chicago: William Regnery, 1969), 169.

33. Paul Johnson, *Forbes* (March 16, 2009): 17.

34. Samuel Bailey, *Critical Dissertation on the Nature, Measure and Causes of Value*, quoted by Étienne Mantoux, in Hazlitt, *Critics of Keynesian Economics*, 97.

35. Skidelsky, *John Maynard Keynes* (vol. 3), 147; the words in quotation are Skidelsky's, recounting how Bob Brand said he felt.

36. Keynes, BBC Broadcast, published in the *Listener* (February 26, 1930), in *Collected Writings* (vol. 20), 323.

Part Five: Conclusion

Chapter 21: Upside-Down Economics: What Keynes Would Have You Believe

1. Seneca, *Letters from a Stoic*, XV, translated by Robin Campbell (London: Penguin, 1969), 61; also in Hunter Lewis, *The Beguiling Serpent: A Re-evaluation of Emotions and Values* (Mt. Jackson, VA: Axios Press, 2000), 74.

2. George Akerlof and Robert Shiller, *Animal Spirits* (Princeton University Press, Princeton, 2009); see also Benjamin Friedman for a review of Akerlof and Shiller, *New York Review* (May 28, 2009): 44. In his review, Friedman notes that he made a similar proposal in "Monetary Policy with a Credit Aggregate Target," *Journal of Monetary Economics* (Spring 1983 Supplement).

3. Marc Faber, *Gloom, Boom, and Doom Report* (October 2007): 20.

4. *Economist* (February 14, 2009): 78.

5. Rich Miller, *Bloomberg News* (May 19, 2009).

6. *Weekly Standard* (April 13–20, 2009): 8.

7. *Wall Street Journal* (April 9, 2009): A-2.

8. Akerlof and Shiller, *Animal Spirits*.

9. *New York Review of Books* (May 14, 2009): 6.

10. Skidelsky, Oswald Falk Papers, in *John Maynard Keynes* (vol. 3), 21.

11. Paul Krugman, *New York Times* (April 10, 2009): A-19.

Chapter 22: What Is Really Wrong Here: The Central Paradox of Keynesianism

1. *Bloomberg News* (April 16, 2009).

2. Lewis, *Are the Rich Necessary?*

3. *Economist* (March 21, 2009): 78.

4. "The Commanding Heights," a television documentary, PBS.

5. *Weekly Standard* (April 13–20, 2009): 8.

6. *Economist* (February 14, 2009).

Part Six: Envoi

Chapter 23: Saying Goodbye to Keynes

1. *Yahoo News* (February 25, 2009).

2. Robert Shiller, *Bloomberg News* (April 16, 2009); Heidi Przy-byla, *Bloomberg News* (April 2, 2009), Christina Romer quoted.

3. Keynes, *Economic Consequences*, 55.

4. Ibid., 296.

5. *Economist* (February 7, 2009): 37.

Notes

1. Philip Wicksteed, *The Common Sense of Political Economy*, 2 vols. (London, 1910).

2. Johnson, *Modern Times*, 255.

3. Ibid.

4. Keynes, speech before the annual meeting of the National Mutual Insurance Co., in *Collected Writings* (vol. 21), 375.

5. John Maynard Keynes, *Economic Journal* (September 1932), in *The Collected Writings*, vol. 23, *Activities 1940–43: External War Finance* (London: Macmillan, and New York: St. Martin's Press, 1979), 114.

6. Keynes, *The Times* (January 12–14, 1937): 395, in *Collected Writings* (vol. 21), 375.

7. Skidelsky, lecture to National Debt Enquiry Committee, in *John Maynard Keynes* (vol. 3), 376.

8. Keynes, *Collected Writings* (vol. 21), 315.

9. Keynes, *General Theory*, 220.

10. Skidelsky, *John Maynard Keynes* (vol. 3), 504.

11. Skidelsky, Keynes to Sir R. Hopkins, July 20, 1942, in *John Maynard Keynes* (vol. 3), 268.

12. Keynes, *General Theory*, 64, 74.

13. Ibid., 328.

14. Keynes, "My Early Beliefs," in *Collected Writings* (vol. 9), 466, passim.

15. Skidelsky, *John Maynard Keynes* (vol. 3), 68.

16. Ibid., 322.

17. Ibid., 320.

18. Keynes, *Collected Writings* (vol. 4), 350.

19. Skidelsky, *John Maynard Keynes* (vol. 2), 523.

20. Karl Marx, *Capital* (London: 1887–1894; original German ed. 1867–1894), 827–29; quoted in Jude Wanniski, *The Way The World Works: How Economies Fail—and Succeed* (New York: Basic Books, 1978), 159.

21. Cited in Hazlitt, *Critics of Keynesian Economics*, 342.

22. William Beveridge cited in Hazlitt, *Critics of Keynesian Economics*, 226.

23. Keynes, *Collected Writings* (vol. 6), 266.

24. Keynes, *Collected Writings* (vol. 20), 418–19; also in Johnson, *Modern Times*, 28.

25. Skidelsky, *John Maynard Keynes* (vol. 3), 218.

26. Keynes, *Essays in Persuasion*, 302; Keynes, essay on Einstein, in *Collected Writings* (vol. 10), 382–84.

27. Keynes, *General Theory*, 166–67.

28. Ibid., 167–68.

29. Ibid., 166.

30. Ibid., 110–11.

31. Hazlitt, *Failure of the "New Economics,"* 448.

32. Keynes, *Economic Consequences*, 235–36.

33. Keynes, *Collected Writings* (vol. 4), 161.

34. Keynes, *Collected Writings* (vol. 11), 363.

35. Keynes, *Collected Writings* (vol. 4), 45; Hajo Holborn, *A History of Modern Germany* (New York: Knopf, 1969), 596–98; Johnson, *Modern Times*, 134, 136.

36. Steve Hanke, *Forbes* (December 22, 2008): 106.

37. Ibid.

38. Keynes, *Collected Writings* (vol. 4), 8, 37.

39. AEI Press, Washington, DC, 2009.

40. Keynes, *Collected Writings* (vol. 10), 323.

41. H. G. Warren, *Herbert Hoover and the Great Depression* (Oxford: Oxford University Press, 1959), 27; cited in Johnson, *Modern Times*, 234.

42. Johnson, *Modern Times*, 229.

43. Ibid., 236.

44. Hazlitt, *Critics of Keynesian Economics*, 313.

45. Keynes, *General Theory*, 99–100.

46. Ibid., 212.

47. Quoted by John P. Hussman in *Hussman Letter* (May 18, 2009).

48. *Washington Post* (March 21, 2009); also in *Weekly Standard* (April 13–20, 2009): 8.

49. *Washington Post* (March 21, 2009); also in *Weekly Standard* (April 13–20, 2009): 8.

50. Hazlitt, *Failure of the "New Economics,"* 150–151.

51. Ibid., 145.

52. Reisman, *Capitalism*, 690–91.

53. Ibid., 883.

54. *Forbes* (November 17, 2008): 20.

55. http://www.townhall.com (March 21, 2009).

56. *New York Review of Books* (November 6, 2008): 53.

57. *Economist* (March 21, 2009): 83.

58. *Economist* (December 6, 2008): 38.

59. Hyman Minsky, *Can "It" Happen Again?: Essays on Instability and Finance* (Armonk, NY: M. E. Sharpe, 1982).

60. Hyman Minsky, *Stabilizing an Unstable Economy: A Twentieth Century Fund Report* (New Haven, CT: Yale University Press, 1986).

61. *Bloomberg News* (April 28, 2009).

Index

A

B